The First Book of

Excel 3 for the Mac®

The First Book of

Excel 3 for the Mac®

Christopher Van Buren

SAMS

A Division of Macmillan Computer Publishing

11711 North College, Carmel, Indiana 46032 USA

For my brother, Alexander Van Buren,
whom I greatly respect and admire.

FIRST EDITION
FIRST PRINTING—1991

International Standard Book Number: 0-672-27328-4
Library of Congress Catalog Card Number: 91-61856

Printed in the United States of America

Publisher
Richard K. Swadley

Publishing Manager
Marie Butler-Knight

Managing Editor
Marjorie Hopper

Acquisitions and Development Editor
Mary-Terese Cagnina

Technical Editors
David Knispel and Herbert Feltner

Manuscript Editor
Charles A. Hutchinson

Cover Design
Held & Diedrich Design

Designer
Scott Cook

Illustrator
Don Clemons

Indexer
Johnna VanHoose

Production Team
Claudia Bell, Mike Britton, Joelynn Gifford, Sandy Grieshop, Denny Hager, Debbie Hanna, Betty Kish, Bob LaRoche, David McKenna, Matthew Morrill, Howard Peirce, Cindy L. Phipps, Tad Ringo, Dennis Sheehan, Bruce Steed, Mary Beth Wakefield, Corinne Walls, Jenny Watson

Contents

Introduction

Acknowledgments

I would like to thank my agents Bill Gladstone and Matt Wagner for excellent representation. Also, thanks to Microsoft for their software support. Especially, thanks to Trudy Totty, once again, for listening, making suggestions, and being enthusiastic about my work.

Conventions Used in This Book

As you use this book, you'll notice it included special typographical elements to highlight the most important information.

Text that you should type in is printed in `special computer type like this`.

Many commands are activated by pressing two or more keys in combination, or selecting a menu and then an option. These keypresses or selections are separated by a dash (-) in the text. For example, Alt-F1 means you should hold the Alt key down and then press F1 (you don't type the dash). A command like File-New means you should open the File menu and select the New option from it.

Q Look for the icon for Quick Steps that tell you how to perform important tasks in Excel. Quick Steps are listed on the inside front cover of this book.

Tip: Helpful tips and shortcuts are included in tip boxes throughout this book.

Trademark Acknowledgments

All terms mentioned in this book that are known to be trademarks or service marks are listed below. In addition, terms suspected of being trademarks or service marks have been appropriately capitalized. SAMS cannot attest to the accuracy of this information. Use of a term in this book should not be regarded as affecting the validity of any trademark or service mark.

FreeHand is a registered trademark of Aldus Corporation.

Lotus 1-2-3 is a registered trademark of Lotus Development Corp.

Macintosh, LaserWriter, and MacPaint are registered trademarks of Apple Computer, Inc.

Microsoft is a registered trademark of Microsoft Corp.

Paintbrush is a trademark of Z-Soft Corporation.

Chapter 1

An Introduction to Excel

In This Chapter

1

- *A look at the Excel worksheet*
- *Excel's database features*
- *Excel's charting features*
- *Excel's drawing features*
- *Automating Excel with macros*
- *New features in version 3.0*

This chapter introduces you to Excel's main features. When you purchased Excel, you may have gotten more than you bargained for. Excel offers powerful worksheet features for manipulating numeric information, graphing features for creating many types of charts, database features for simple information management, drawing features for annotating worksheets, and special features for automating and customizing the program. The rest of this chapter explains what each of these features provides and suggests some uses for Excel's powerful capabilities.

What Is Excel?

Excel is a spreadsheet program that offers four main capabilities. The worksheet features are the primary capability of Excel. Worksheet features let you perform numeric tasks, such as calculating an expense report, balancing your checkbook, or determining if a particular investment is a good one. These tasks operate on numeric information. This book uses the term *worksheet* when referring to worksheet features or to worksheets themselves.

Excel also offers database features. You can perform statistical analysis on data contained in your worksheets, sort large batches of data, find records within a large group, and much more.

In addition, Excel offers charting features. Charting is the ability to display numeric information in the form of a graph or chart. Graphs and charts are essential for presenting information in a meaningful and memorable way. Excel's charting features do the work for you by converting numeric data to any number of chart types.

Excel's drawing features let you annotate your graphs and worksheets with simple object-oriented pictures. This capability is excellent for embellishing worksheets and creating presentation graphics.

The Excel Worksheet

The Excel *worksheet* is an electronic version of a columnar pad. It consists of numerous rows and columns. The intersection of a row and a column is called a *cell*, the basic unit of any worksheet. All worksheet information is entered into cells. Besides entering information into cells, you can create formulas that automatically add the columns, add the rows, calculate averages, perform statistical analysis, and more. By moving to the various cells and entering text, numbers, or formulas, you build a worksheet. Some of the worksheets you can build include budgets, income projections, expense projections, travel expenses, checkbook balancing, and loan analysis.

The power of a worksheet comes from the formulas you enter into the cells. Formulas automatically calculate information in the worksheet's cells so that you don't have to calculate manually. With the on-sheet formulas, you can change the worksheet's data at any time, and the formula cells will recalculate new totals based on changes in the data. The worksheet in Figure 1.1 shows an example.

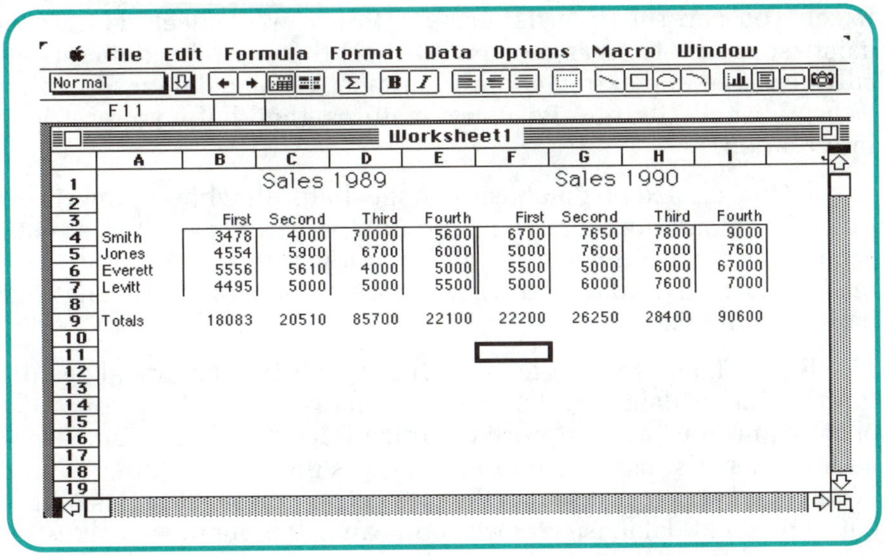

Figure 1.1 A sample worksheet.

Using a formula, each column of numbers in this worksheet is totalled at the bottom. If you change the values in the columns, the formulas will recalculate the results automatically ... and instantly. Using formulas, you can experiment with "what if" scenarios for financial matters. For example, you can compare the amounts of money you would make if you invested your savings over various time periods at various interest rates. Each value you change lets you view an entirely new scenario.

Besides calculating data found in other cells of the worksheet, formulas can access a host of special functions that perform unique operations. One function, for example, computes the average of any group of numbers. Excel offers dozens of special functions.

The Excel Database

A *database* is an electronic version of a file cabinet. It stores data for continual reference and makes that data easily accessible. An electronic database also makes it easy to rearrange data and create reports based on information spread throughout the file. Using Excel, you can set up a database within a worksheet. The Excel database is simply an area of a worksheet that contains data repeatedly accessed and extracted for reference. When a database section is established, it inherits extra features that help you retrieve information.

Using an Excel database can be helpful when numeric or financial calculations also require data storage and retrieval, as with general ledger tasks, payroll, and employee record keeping. You might even find the database a good tool for storing and printing your basic mailing lists.

Excel databases are also useful for getting statistical results from batches of data. The database shown in Figure 1.2 contains a list of contributions to a nonprofit organization. Next to the database is a series of statistical calculations, such as the largest donation, the average donation, and so on. Besides getting these statistics on the entire batch of database records, you can calculate these values for subsets of the database. For example, you can find the largest donation within the past six months.

You can set up a database to hold any information you like. Excel provides the tools necessary for analyzing, storing, retrieving, and sorting that data. In addition, Excel offers an easy-to-use *data form* that helps you add, remove, and find records in the database. The data form that matches the database in Figure 1.2 is shown in Figure 1.3.

Charting with Excel

Charting is the ability to take a table of numbers and represent the data in chart form. Chart types include bar, line, pie, area, scatter, and a host of 3-D charts. Excel's charting capabilities give you total control over each element of a chart. You can adjust the scale, add titles, change the type of chart, stack the chart, change the printer fonts used for the labels, and much more. When the data for a chart changes, the chart adjusts to reflect the changes. Charts are the most powerful way to express numeric data, and Excel's charting capabilities make it easy.

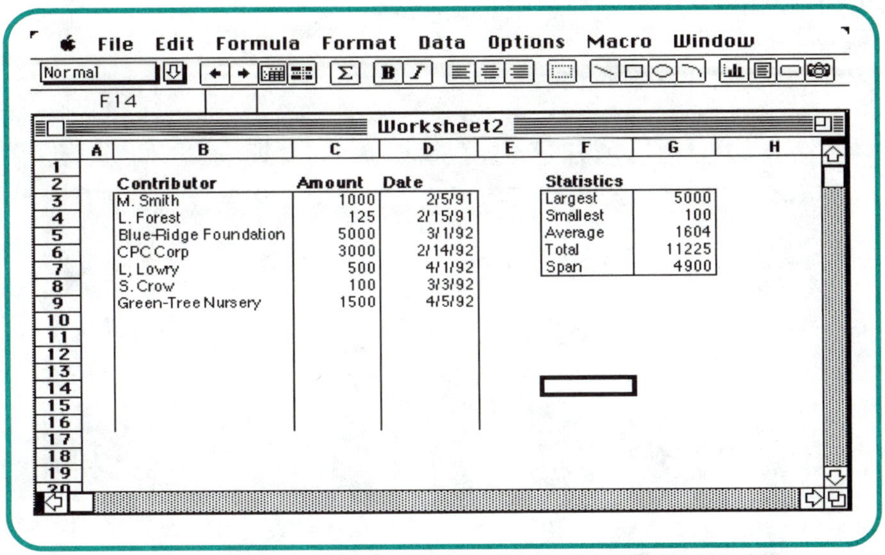

Figure 1.2 A sample database.

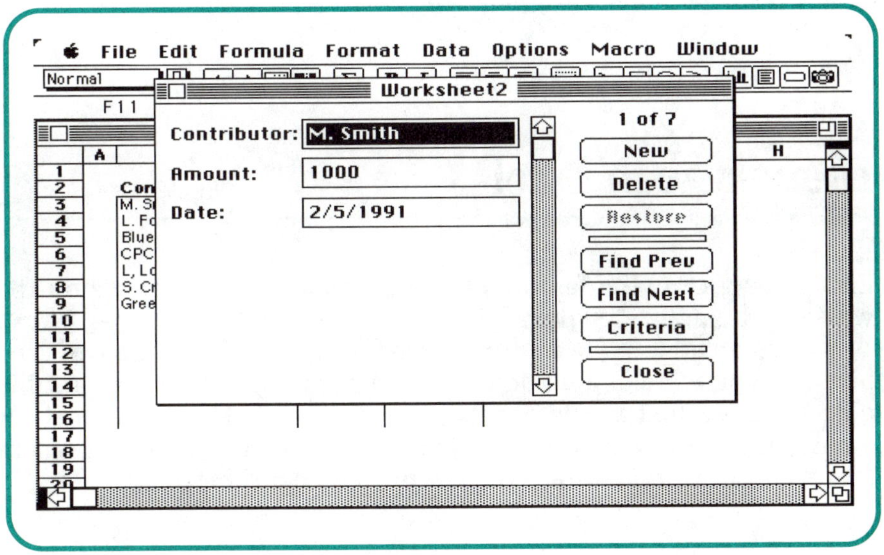

Figure 1.3 Excel's database data form.

The chart in Figure 1.4 is a basic column chart that represents the data in Figure 1.5. Notice that each sales person is represented by an item in the legend. The quarterly sales figures show up as different sets of bars in the chart. This book's section about charts discusses the various chart elements and demonstrates how you can manipulate them.

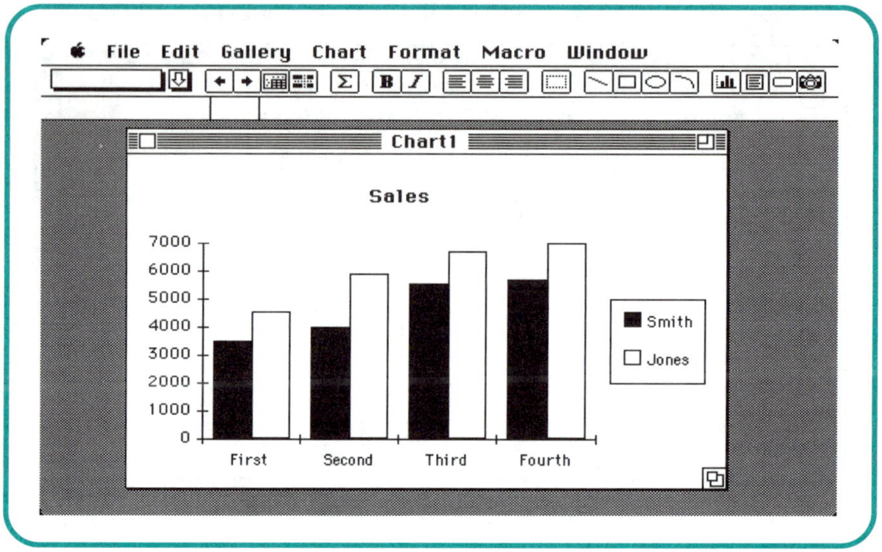

Figure 1.4 A basic column chart.

Drawing with Excel

Excel's new Drawing features let you create simple objects on the worksheet, such as ovals, rectangles, lines, and semicircles (arcs). You also can add text boxes to the worksheet in which you can type text as if you were using a small word processor. Like other graphic objects, these text boxes can be moved around the worksheet for annotating your data. These tools help you spruce up your presentations and printouts. Figure 1.6 shows an example.

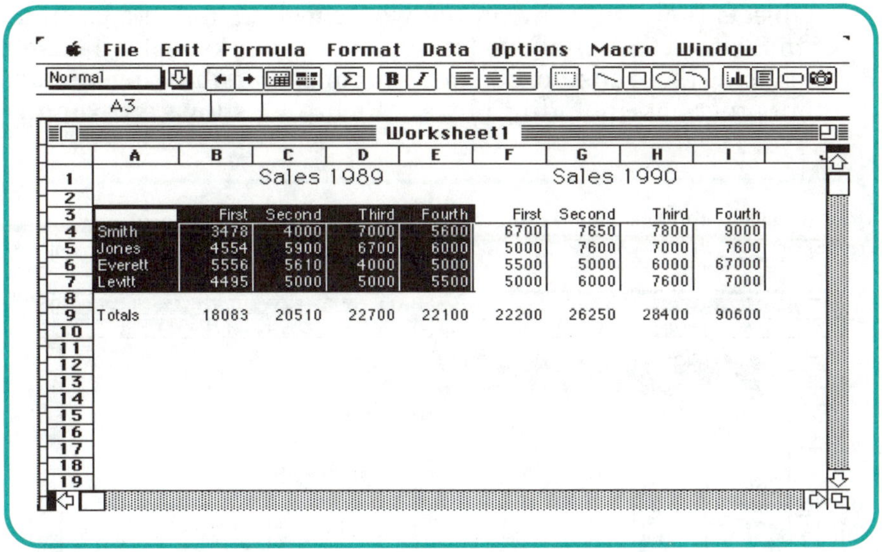

Figure 1.5 Data used to create the chart.

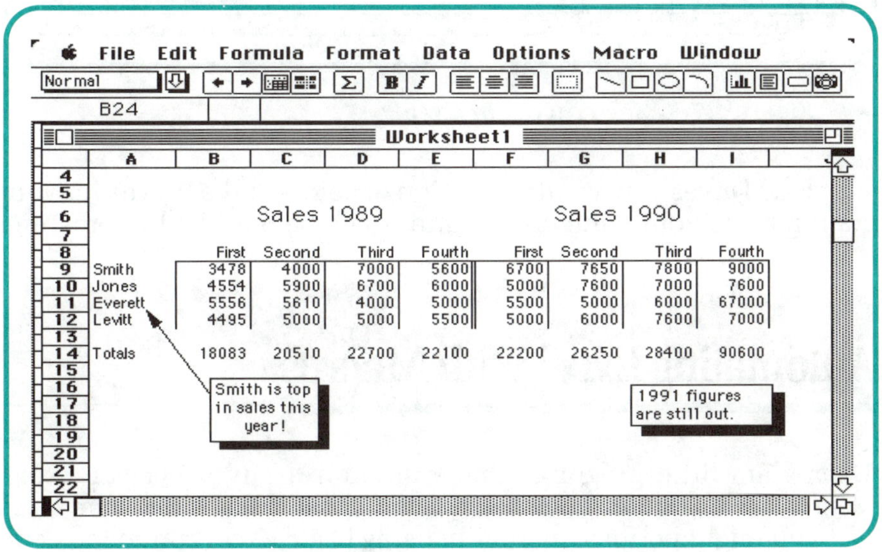

Figure 1.6 Using Excel's new drawing features.

Objects that you draw on the worksheet reside on a graphics *layer* in Excel, which is above (on top of) the worksheet data itself. Besides using these custom objects, you can *import* drawings created by other programs, including clip art. Figure 1.7 shows an example.

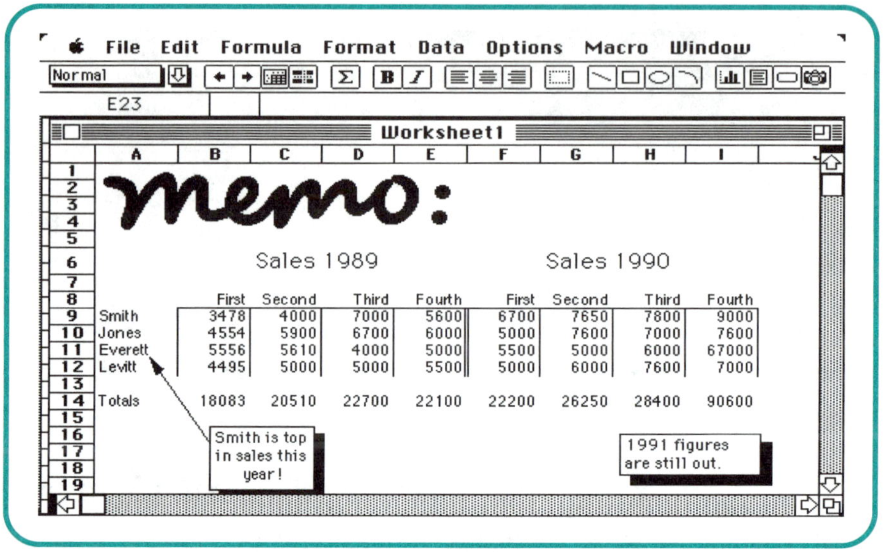

Figure 1.7 Using clip art in Excel.

Excel gives you a wide selection of colors and patterns for your graphics—so your slide presentations can be bold and interesting.

Automating Excel with Macros

Macros are little programs that can control any aspect of Excel. Macros are useful for automating worksheet tasks—the same tasks that you might perform manually using basic Excel commands and options. By building a macro, you can perform complex or repetitious tasks with a simple keystroke. This is especially valuable when you build worksheets that will be used by other operators. Macros can control the information entered, check that the information is correct, and even control where other operators can move within the worksheet.

Macros consist of a series of macro commands. Like any programming language, macro commands must be combined in specific ways. But macros are simple to create and use. You don't have to know anything about programming to build powerful macros. This book shows you the basics of building macros, providing step-by-step instructions for creating and using them. If you are intimidated by the thought of using macros, don't be. This book makes macros just as simple as any other aspect of Excel. In fact, there are many other aspects of Excel that may challenge you more than macros. So, don't hesitate to jump right into the macro chapters of this book after completing the other chapters.

New Features in Excel 3.0

Version 3.0 of Excel provides some important new features that give you more worksheet power and make your work easier. Following is an overview of the new features covered in this book. Besides these new features, version 3.0 has made changes to some existing features—enhancing them or making them easier to use. If you've used an earlier version of Excel, you'll find the new version a major improvement.

Worksheet Tools for "Point & Click" Operations

The new worksheet tools appear at the top of the worksheet in the Toolbar. If you use a mouse with Excel, you can use these tools for simple "point & click" operations that would otherwise take several steps. For example, you can easily sum a column by clicking on the Auto Sum tool. The Toolbar also contains the tools you use for drawing graphics on the worksheet.

Displaying Graphics on the Worksheet

You can now place your graphs and charts onto the worksheet with your numeric information. In earlier versions of Excel, charts were separate worksheets that you had to save and print apart from your worksheet data. Now you can "paste" a chart right into the worksheet with your other data.

New Number Formats

Version 3.0 gives you a few new number formats, including fractional formats for numbers like 3 $^{1}/_{2}$. Previously, fractions had to be displayed as decimal values, such as 3.5.

Wrapping Text within a Cell

Cells can now hold many lines of text. You can *wrap* the text within the cell to create "paragraphs" of information. The word wrap feature is affected by the column widths you choose.

More Formatting Capabilities

Excel now lets you create thousands of colors for your worksheets by using its color palette. The new version has also added several new line styles and patterns for objects and graphs.

Easier Print Margins with Print Preview

The updated Print Preview command lets you adjust margins right on-screen. Using a mouse, you can move the margins visually, rather than by entering numeric settings.

3-D Charts

Charting is improved with several new 3-D chart types. These include 3-D versions of line, bar, column, and pie charts. You also can control the perspective of 3-D charts.

The Solver

Excel 3.0 includes the new Solver utility for advanced business calculations. With the Solver, you can create useful "what if" models for a host of business needs.

What You've Learned

This chapter gave you an overview of Excel's main features: the worksheet, the database, drawing, and charting. Following are some points to remember:

- The Excel worksheet is used to perform mathematical or statistical analysis on numeric data.
- The database is used for information that requires repeated access and statistical analysis.
- Charting is the ability to represent numeric data in chart or graph form. Excel offers many types of charts and graphs for your worksheet data.
- Drawing features let you create graphic objects and place them on the worksheet with your data.
- Macros can be created to automate complex or lengthy tasks that you might otherwise perform by hand.

Chapter 2

Getting Started with Excel

In This Chapter

- *Starting Excel*
- *Examining the Excel worksheet*
- *How Excel uses your keyboard*
- *Moving around the worksheet*
- *Using Excel's menus and options*
- *Getting help*
- *Quitting Excel*

This chapter gets you started with Excel basics. Before you can really begin creating your own worksheets, you need to know some fundamental things about how Excel works. This chapter includes information about starting Excel; using menus and the keyboard; and some special topics, such as getting help in Excel and using pointer movement commands.

Starting Excel

If you have not installed Excel onto your hard disk so that it appears on your desktop as a program icon, then turn to Appendix A now.

This appendix will show you how to install Excel for your system. A basic familiarity with the Macintosh will help you use Excel 3.0.

You can now start Excel as you would start any Macintosh application. Following are the steps.

Starting Excel

1. From the desktop, locate the Microsoft Excel application icon. You may have to open the appropriate folder by double-clicking on it.

   Figure 2.1 shows an example of the open folder.

2. Double-click (two quick clicks) on the icon.

   You will enter Excel with a new, blank worksheet in view. Figure 2.2 shows the screen at this point. □

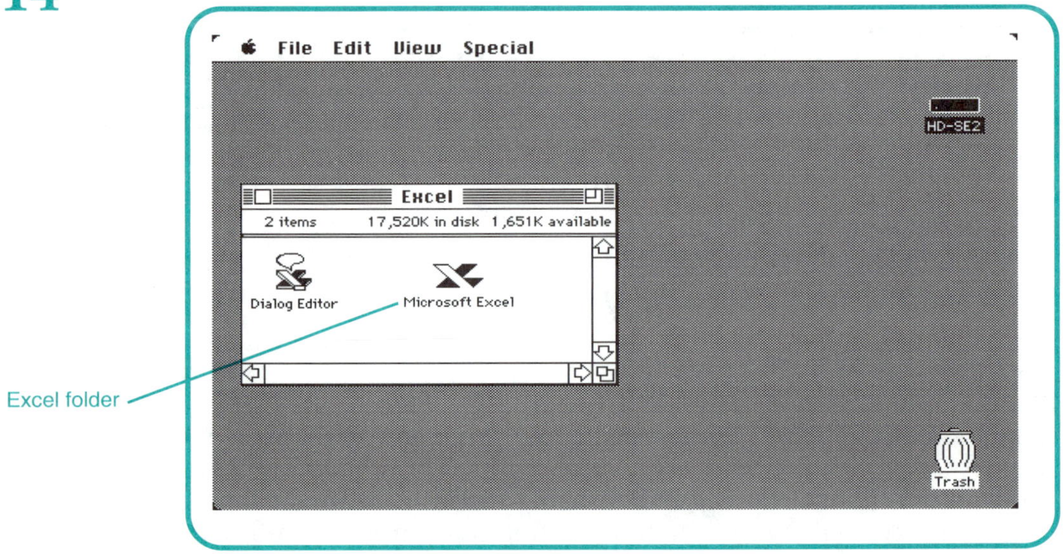

Figure 2.1 The Excel icon.

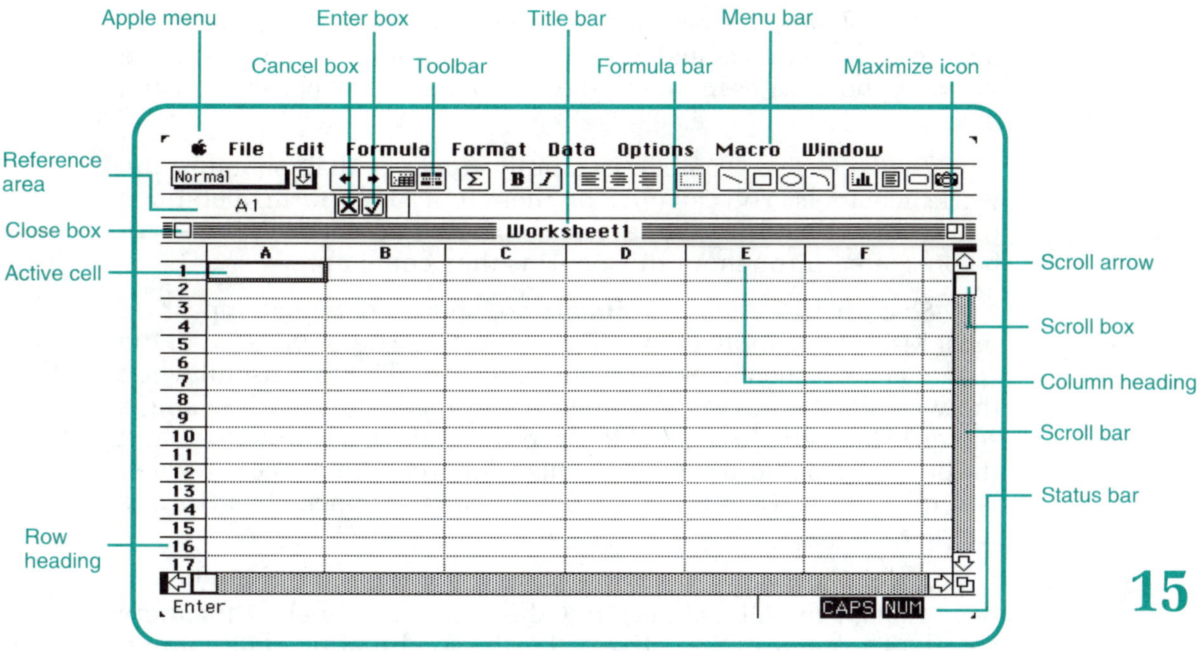

Figure 2.2 The Excel worksheet.

The Excel Worksheet

If the preceding steps worked correctly, you should see the Excel worksheet on the screen. This worksheet looks like Figure 2.2.

Using Figure 2.2 as a guide, descriptions of the elements in Excel follow. The names used for the elements will be used throughout the book.

Title bar—The worksheet title bar contains the name of the current worksheet. In Figure 2.2, the title bar shows the name `Worksheet1`. When you open a new worksheet, Excel gives it the name `Worksheet`, followed by a number that indicates how many sheets you've opened this session. Later, you'll see how you can have more than one worksheet open at a time and how the worksheet names play an important role in recognizing which is which.

Menu bar—The menu bar contains the names of the Excel menus. The menus contain commands and options to manipulate the worksheet. Later in this chapter, you'll get an overview of using menus.

Toolbar—The Toolbar is simply an area that contains the worksheet tools. You can click on these tools to perform operations that would otherwise take several steps. The Toolbar's options will be presented throughout this book as they come up.

Scroll bars—These scroll bars are special bars that appear on most Macintosh applications. They let you see other portions of the "page" or worksheet when you click on them. They are useful when the worksheet contains too much data to be displayed in a single screen. There are three parts to a scroll bar: the bar, the arrows, and the box. Each of these parts performs a slightly different action when you click on it. Details about these elements appear later in this chapter.

Reference area—This area displays the name of the active cell. See "Cells, the cell pointer, and the active cell" below for more details. The name of the active cell is the combination of its column letter and row number. For example, the intersection of column C and row 5 is the cell named C5. This reference is called an address.

Cells, the cell pointer, and the active cell—As you know from Chapter 1, a worksheet is made up of cells, which are the intersections of rows and columns. All data is entered into these cells one by one. By activating various cells (one at a time), you can enter data throughout the worksheet. The active cell is highlighted by the cell pointer. You can tell which cell is active in two ways. It is surrounded by the extra thick border, and its reference name (address) appears in the reference area. Later, you'll see how to activate any cell you want.

Row and column headings—These headings on the worksheet show you where each row and column is located. As you see in Figure 2.2, rows are numbered and columns are lettered. The intersection of a row and column is a cell.

Status bar—This is a bar across the bottom of the screen that displays information about current settings and the currently selected command (if a command is selected). For example, when you press the Num Lock (Shift-Clear), Caps Lock, or Scroll Lock key, indicators appear in the status bar.

Formula bar and cursor—When you enter information into a cell of the worksheet, it first appears in the formula bar. The cursor indicates the point where information will be inserted when you type. If you like what you have typed, you can accept it to be placed in the appropriate worksheet cell.

Enter and cancel boxes—You can click on the enter box to accept data you have typed or the cancel box to reject it.

How Excel Uses Your Keyboard

The next step is to familiarize yourself with the keyboard and how Excel uses various keys for special purposes. As you use Excel, you will find that many commands and actions can be performed using a number of keyboard methods. Many commands have special mouse shortcuts, making keyboard versions less attractive.

Take a look at the keyboard illustrations in Figure 2.3 and find the one that matches yours. Then, review the following information about the various keys and their significance in Excel.

Special Keys

No matter which keyboard you have, there are some keys that deserve special note. Besides the typical alphabet and numerals, keyboards include keys that perform special functions. They are as shown in Table 2.1. When two or more keys are separated by a hyphen in the instructions (such as Ctrl-2), you should press and hold the first key while pressing the second key.

The Numeric Keypad

The numeric keypad serves two purposes. It acts as a 10-key pad for numeric entry and as directional keys for moving around inside Excel. By pressing the Shift+Clear key, you can switch between these two basic purposes. When you first start Excel, the number keys are active on the keypad. Therefore, when you press the 2 key, you will get the numeral 2 and not the Down arrow (↓) action. Details about moving around in the worksheet are covered next.

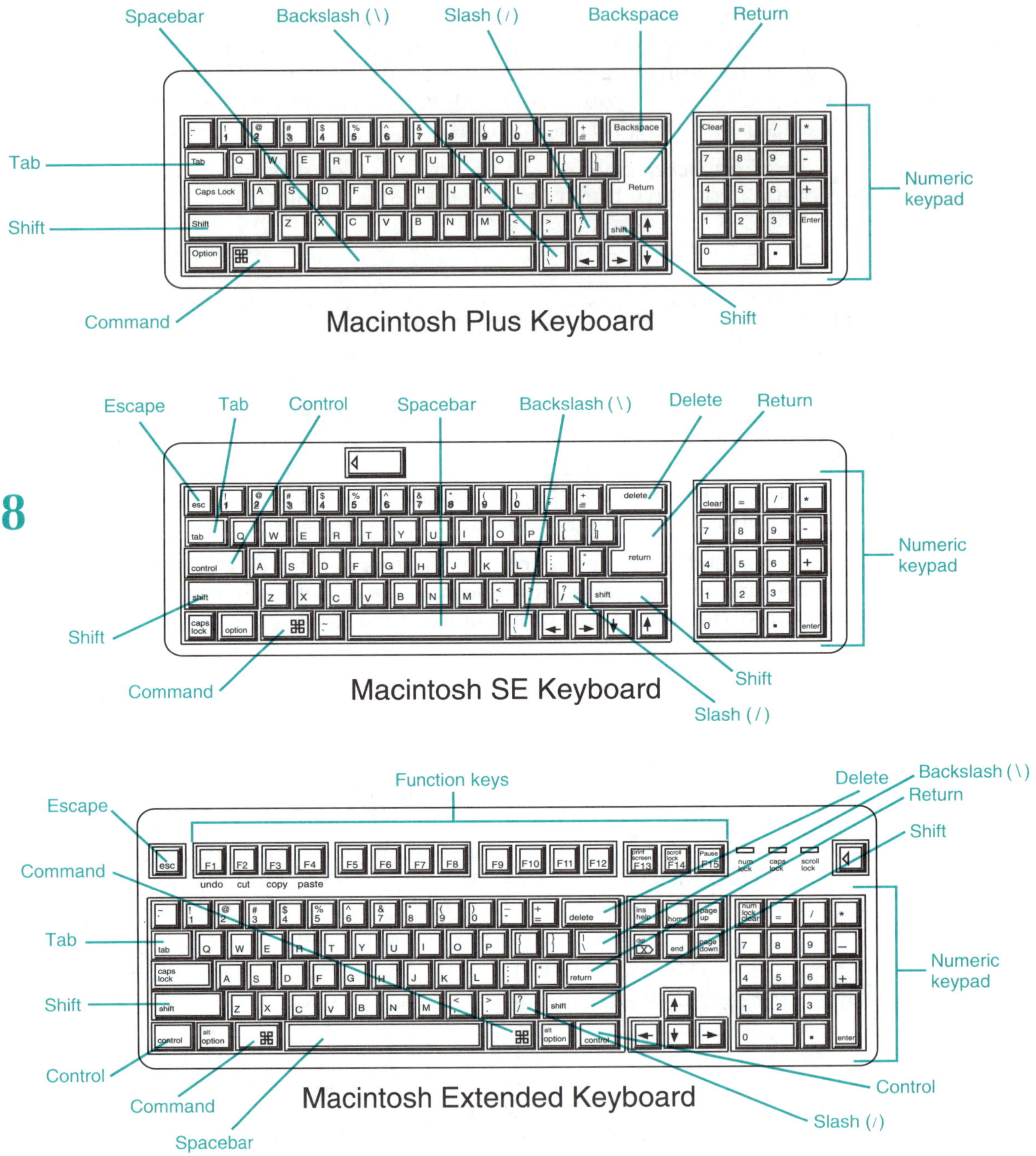

Figure 2.3 Excel's special keys on each of the Macintosh keyboards.

Table 2.1 Special Keys

Key	Function
Return	(Also known as the Enter key.) Accepts an entry or command selection. After typing information, pressing Return places it into the active cell. After highlighting a menu item, pressing Return selects the option.
Shift	Creates uppercase letters when used with the alphabet keys. Shift can also be combined with other special keys to create alternative options. You can view special menu options by holding Shift down while you select the menu.
Command ⌘	Invokes Excel's special commands when pressed along with the function keys or other special keys. For example, Command-X cuts information from the worksheet.
Tab	Moves the cell pointer to the next cell.
Direction arrows ↑↓→←	Move the cell pointer in the direction of the arrow.
Shift+Clear	Changes the numeric keypad into direction keys and vice versa.
Backspace	Blanks the information in a cell. When the cursor is showing in the formula bar, Backspace erases one character to the left of the cursor.
Delete (Del)	Presents options for clearing the information in a cell or selection. When used with the Shift key (that is, Shift-Del), Delete moves information to another location on the worksheet.
Esc	Cancels an action or menu selection.
Scroll Lock	Controls scrolling within a worksheet. With the scroll lock "active," the arrow keys scroll the screen without moving the cell pointer. Pressing the key again deactivates scroll lock.
Pause	Pauses macros.

(continued)

Table 2.1 (continued)

Key	Function
Function keys (F keys)	Perform special functions. By combining these keys with the Control and/or Shift key, still more functions are available.
/	Activates the Excel menus at the top of the screen. After pressing this key, the next keystroke selects a menu.
Option	Performs the same function as the / key (above). You can leave the Option key pressed as you press another key to activate the menu in one smooth action.

Moving Around the Worksheet

Now that you've got some preliminaries out of the way, take a look at an important set of commands in Excel: the commands used to move to various parts of the worksheet. As you read earlier, you use the cell pointer to highlight any cell in the worksheet. The highlighted cell is called the active cell. Most of the commands and options in Excel operate on the active cell. Therefore, you need to know how to activate any cell you want.

To move the cell pointer, simply use the four arrow keys on your keyboard. If you use the numeric keypad arrows, be sure that the Num Lock feature is not active. (The numeric keypad uses the 4, 6, 8, and 2 keys for the Left, Right, Up, and Down arrows respectively.) The pointer will move one cell in the direction of the arrow each time you tap the key. You can hold down the arrow key for rapid repeat. To select a cell using the mouse, simply click on the desired cell in the window. The pointer will move to that cell.

Try moving around the worksheet with the arrow keys or mouse. You might discover that if you go past the edge of the screen, the worksheet continues and the screen "shifts over" and follows the pointer along its merry way. The worksheet is actually much larger than one screen can possibly display at a time, as illustrated in Figure 2.4.

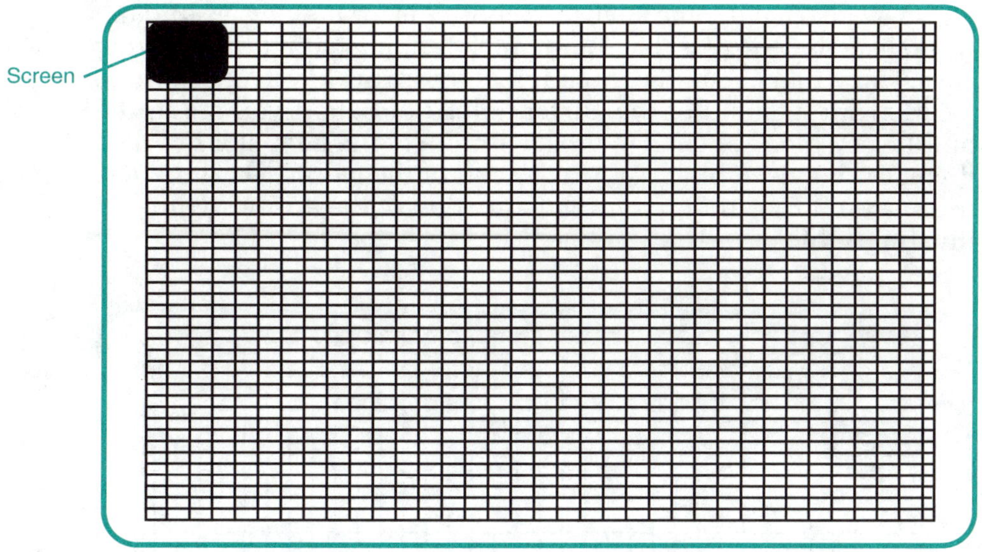

Figure 2.4 The worksheet is much larger than one screen can show at a time.

So, you might be wondering just how big this worksheet is. Well, it's 256 columns wide by 16,384 rows long, for a total of 4,194,304 cells! This is more space than you will ever need. In fact, if you try to fill up all the cells, you'll probably run out of computer memory before you can finish.

With so many cells, you need a shortcut for moving around the worksheet. If you have a mouse, try clicking on the scroll bars to see other portions of the worksheet. Click on the scroll arrows to move slowly in the direction of the arrow. Click next to the arrows in the scroll bar itself to make larger jumps through the worksheet in the direction of the arrow. Or, click on the scroll box and drag it to another location to jump quickly through the worksheet.

▶ **Tip:** Although the worksheet is very large and you can use as much of it as you like, you usually will enter your data into the upper-left cells of the worksheet to conserve space and to reduce the amount of memory required for the data.

You also have some keyboard shortcuts for moving around the worksheet. If you press the Command key along with the four arrow keys, you will move in the direction of the arrow key to one of three locations: to the end of the current block of data if you are in the middle of a block of data; to the beginning of the next block of data if you are between blocks; or to the end of the worksheet if there is no data on the current row in the direction of the arrow. Figure 2.5 illustrates this.

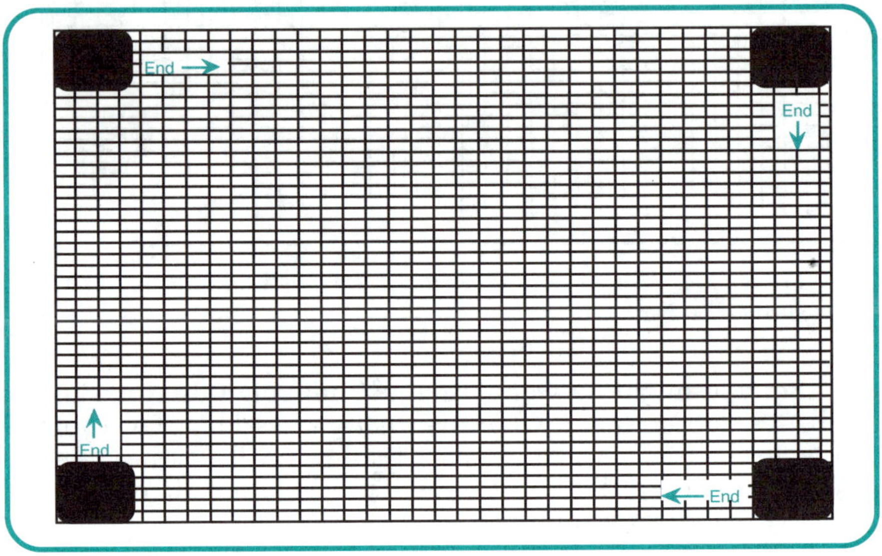

Figure 2.5 Using the Command key with the arrows to move to the far corners of the worksheet.

If you have an extended keyboard, you can move the cell pointer back to cell A1 by pressing Command-Home. Try that now. Cell A1 is always the upper-left corner of the worksheet and is known as the home cell.

Also, examine what End and Command-End do. The End key moves the pointer to the last column in the worksheet that contains data, known as the *high column*. Pressing Command-End moves the pointer to the intersection of the last row and column containing data, known as the *high cell*.

Table 2.2 Worksheet Movement Keys

Key	Moves pointer
↑ ↓ → ←	One cell in the direction of the arrow
Command-↑ Command-↓ Command-→ Command-←	To the four corners of the worksheet or the current block
Command-Home	To cell A1
End	To the high column
Command-End	To the high cell
Tab	One cell to the right
Shift-Tab	One cell to the left

Using Excel's Menus

Most of Excel's features and capabilities are controlled by menu options. Excel groups menu options into eight worksheet menus that you see on-screen (not including the Help menu). The following section provides an overview of the Excel menus. Then, you'll discover how to select options from these menus using either the keyboard or mouse. Details about specific menu options are spread throughout the rest of the book.

Excel offers two ways to view the options in the eight worksheet menus. You can view all options at once, or you can view a subset of the options—just those options you'll need for basic tasks. The shorter version, often used by beginners for simplifying the menus, contains fewer options and is called *short menus*. Excel starts out with *full menus* active.

> ▶ **Tip:** To switch between short and long menus, select the Options-Menus command. Each time you enter the command, Excel will switch between the long and short menus.

File menu—The File menu shown in Figure 2.6 contains options for opening new and existing worksheets, closing the current worksheet, saving worksheets, setting up the print options, printing, and print previewing. You can use these commands to create many different worksheets containing unique data. Each worksheet is a separate file which can be manipulated with the File menu's options.

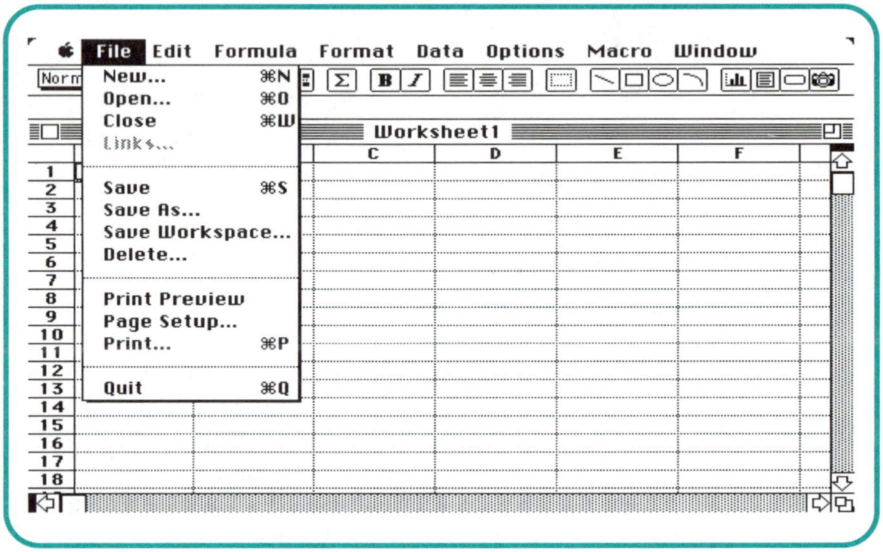

Figure 2.6 The File menu.

> **Tip:** If you close the worksheet using the File-Close command, and if no other worksheets are open, only a few menus remain on-screen. This happens because the other seven menus contain options that apply only when a worksheet is active. When no worksheet is active, only the File, Edit, and Window menu options apply. As soon as you open another worksheet, the other menus will reappear.

Edit menu—Options in the Edit menu, shown in Figure 2.7, let you move information within a worksheet or between worksheets, undo errors, insert or delete data, and copy data. You'll find this a frequently used menu.

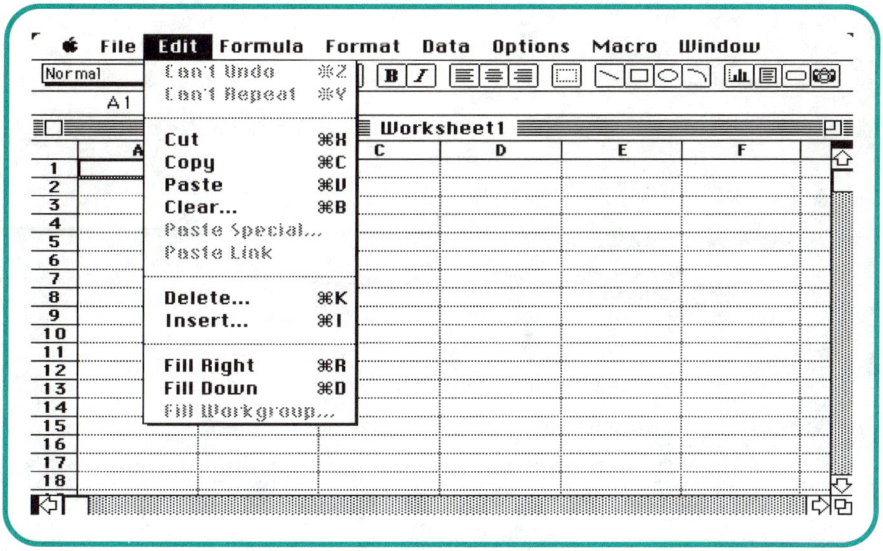

Figure 2.7 The Edit menu.

Formula menu—The Formula menu options are used when you are creating formulas in the worksheet. The options include naming cells, naming ranges and formulas, and finding specific information in cells and formulas. A particularly useful option in this menu is the Note option, which lets you type a special note that applies to a specific cell. This menu is shown in Figure 2.8.

Format menu—Format menu options help make your worksheets more attractive and readable. You can select printer fonts, sizes, and styles for worksheet data; change the appearance of numbers and dates; add borders and boxes around cells; and change the heights of the rows and widths of the columns in the worksheet. The Format menu is shown in Figure 2.9.

Data menu—The commands in the Data menu, shown in Figure 2.10, control Excel's database features. Using these options you can set up a database, search the database for information, and extract information. Other options let you sort worksheet information and set up special data tables for advanced worksheets.

Options menu—This menu contains some special options for printing and displaying the worksheet. This menu is shown in Figure 2.11.

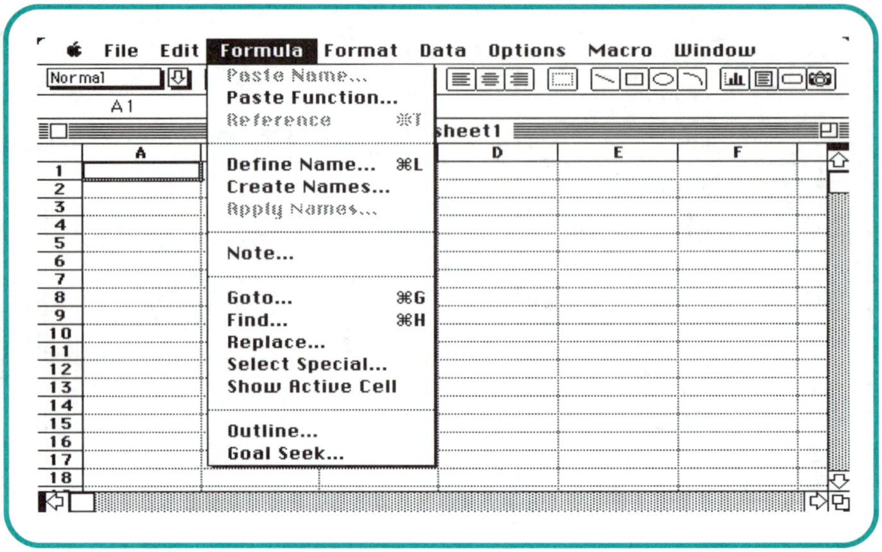

Figure 2.8 The Formula menu.

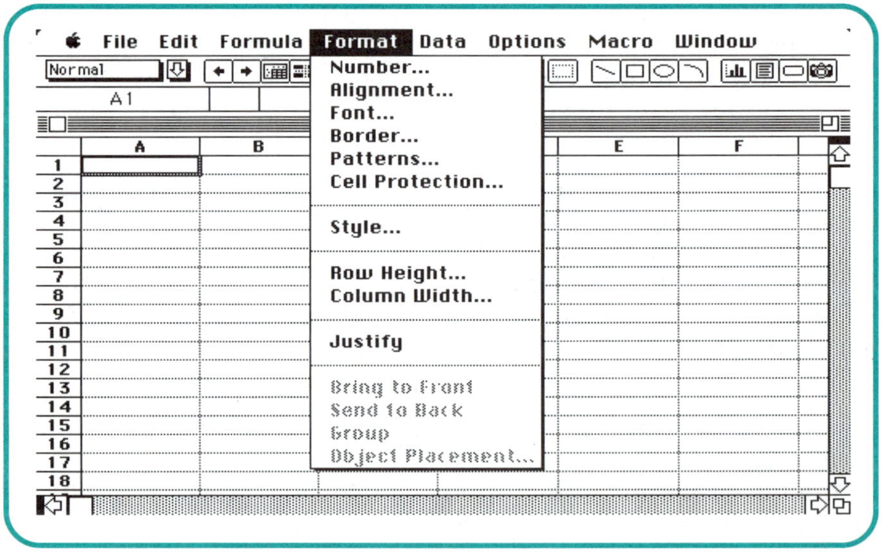

Figure 2.9 The Format menu.

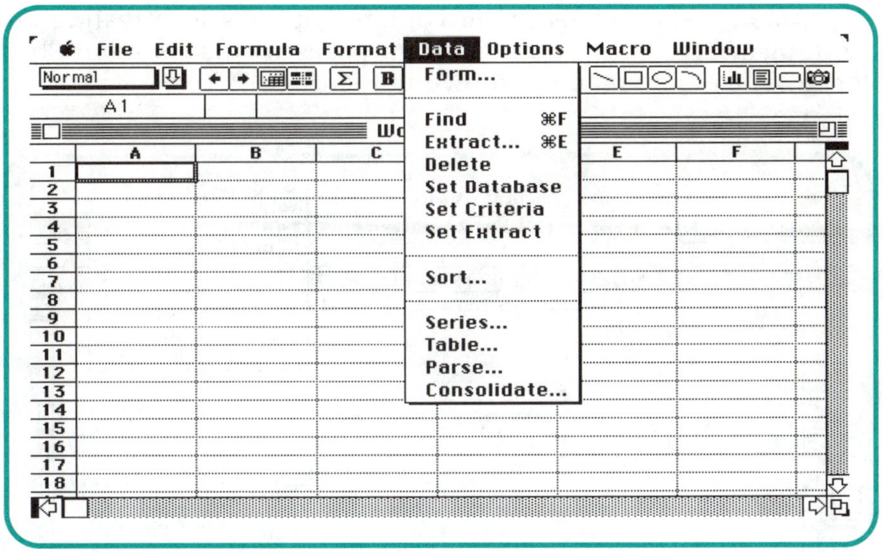

Figure 2.10 The Data menu.

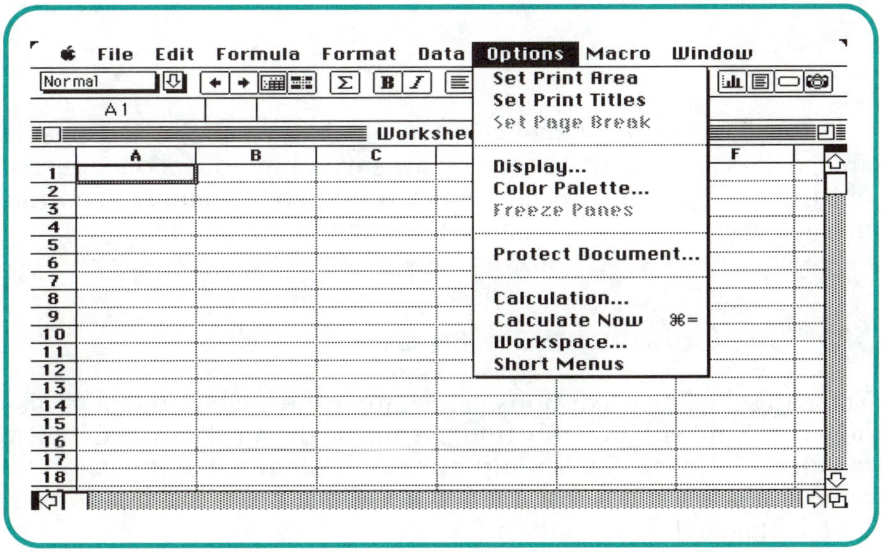

Figure 2.11 The Options menu.

Macro menu—This menu contains options for creating and running macros. Macros and their purposes are discussed in Chapter 12. The Macro menu is shown in Figure 2.12.

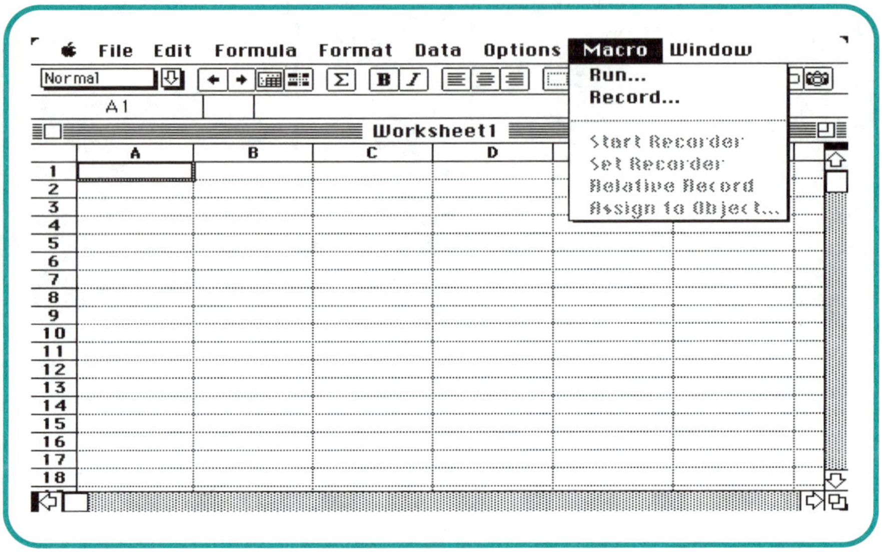

Figure 2.12 The Macro menu.

Window menu—Excel displays each worksheet in a special area, called a window. You can view several windows on-screen at one time and perform special window operations using the options in the Window menu, which is shown in Figure 2.13.

Selecting Options from Menus

You can select menu options using either the keyboard or a mouse; however, you will probably find the mouse the most convenient way to select options. You should already be familiar with using the mouse to select menu commands from Macintosh applications, so here is the keyboard method.

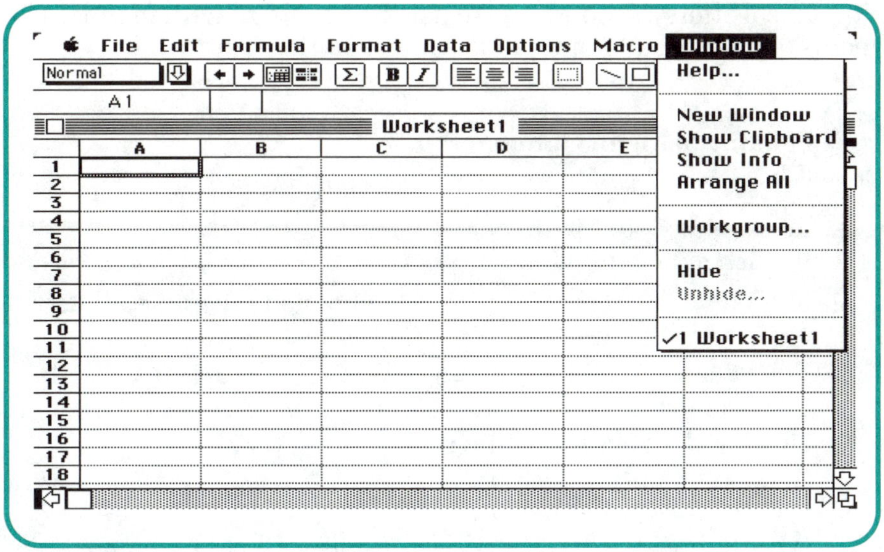

Figure 2.13 The Window menu.

Q Selecting Menus with the Keyboard

1. Press / (slash) and then the underlined letter in the desired menu name. You don't have to release your finger from the / before pressing the letter of the desired menu. — Activates the menu bar. The desired menu appears, or "pulls down."
2. Press the underlined letter in the desired menu option. — Selects the option within the active menu. □

> **Tip:** You can combine Steps 1 and 2 into a single action by pressing the letter of the desired menu before releasing the slash key.

Excel offers a second way to use the keyboard with menus. This technique lets you "point" to the menu option you want.

Q Pointing to Menu Options

1. Press /. — Activates the menu bar.
2. Press → or ← to highlight the desired menu name.
3. Press Return. — The menu displays all its options.
4. You can press → or ← again to view other menus.
5. Use ↑ and ↓ keys to highlight the desired option within the selected menu.
6. Press Return. — Selects the highlighted option. □

> **Tip:** This book will refer to menu options by identifying the menu name and then the option name. For example, if the book says "Select the File-Quit command," activate the File menu and choose the Quit command within it.

Getting Help

You can get help at any time while you're using Excel by simply pressing Command-? or choosing the Help command from the Window menu. Help information can provide important details about the command or option in question. If a menu option or dialog box is active when you press Command-? for Help, then the Help screen will appear containing helpful information about the active menu or dialog box. Excel is intelligent enough to know what you are doing and provides help for that action. Similarly, you can press Command-? whenever Excel presents a message on-screen. Doing so will give you help about that specific message.

Another way to use Help is to press Shift-F1. This changes the pointer into a question mark. You can now select any command or option in the program and, instead of performing the command you select, Excel will present a Help screen about your selection. This is a way of getting help on a specific topic.

The final way to use Help is to simply press Command-? in the normal worksheet mode—or use the Index of topics to locate desired help, as shown in Figure 2.14.

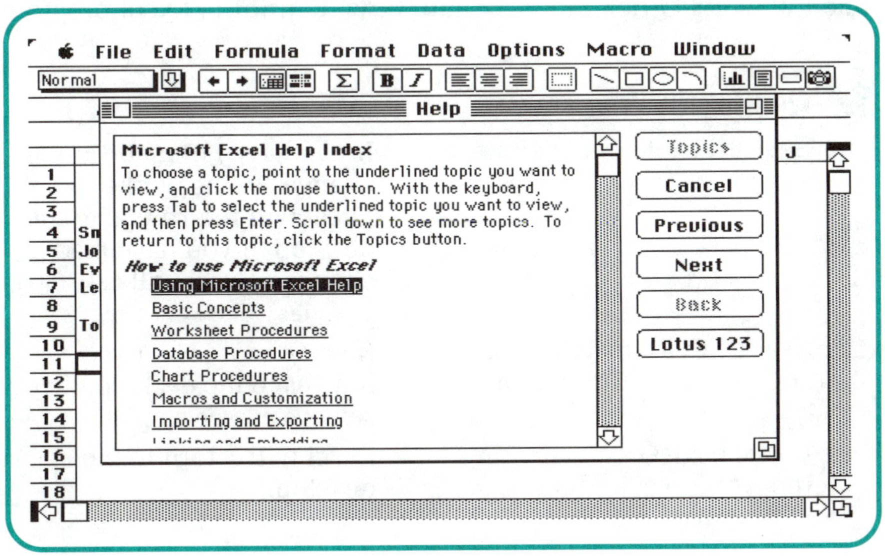

Figure 2.14 The Help menu.

Select the Topics option to see a list of topics for which you can get help. Next, click the mouse on the desired topic, enter the first letter of the desired topic, or use the ↑ and ↓ keys to highlight it, and then press Return to view another set of related topics. Now select an item from this second list and press Return. Finally, you will see the Help screen with useful information. If the information extends past the edge of the Help window, use the PgDn key to move down. Each Help window gives you additional buttons as described below:

Topics	Return to the initial index screen.
Previous	Go back to the previous topic or listing.
Next	Go to the next Help topic or listing.
Lotus 123	Get Lotus help.

Quitting Excel

To quit Excel, use the File-Quit command. Before quitting Excel, be sure to save any data you have created. If you have made changes to existing data, be sure to save the changes. Excel will prompt you to save any worksheets you have changed. Saving worksheets is described in more detail in Chapter 3. At this point, however, you might just want to quit Excel without saving what you have done. The following Quick Steps explain how to quit the Excel program.

Quitting the Program

1. Select the File-Quit command. — If you have not made any changes to the worksheet, Excel will return you to the desktop. If you have made changes, Excel will ask, `Save changes in "Worksheet1"?`
2. Select Yes to save the worksheet or No to throw it out. — If you choose No, Excel returns to the desktop. If you select Yes, see step 3.
3. Enter the desired name for the worksheet and press OK to save it. — Excel will return to the desktop.

What You've Learned

This chapter provided some of the fundamentals for using Excel. You discovered how to install and start the program and what the various Excel screen elements mean. You also learned how to move around inside the worksheet and how to select menu options. Following are some essential points to remember.

- Start Excel by clicking on its program icon.
- The screen displays only a portion of the entire worksheet at one time. Use the various movement commands to view other parts of the worksheet.

- Press the / key to activate the Excel menus, or just click on the desired option.
- Each menu and option in Excel has a letter associated with it. You can type this letter after pressing / (slash) to select the menu or option.
- You can press Esc to back out of any menu before selecting an option.
- Excel offers help at any time. Just use the Window-Help command to display a list of topics.
- To quit Excel, select the File-Quit command.

Chapter 3

Creating Excel Worksheets

In This Chapter

- *Opening a worksheet*
- *Entering data*
- *Using formulas and functions*
- *Using the Auto Sum button*
- *Pointing to cell and range references*
- *Arguments*
- *Excel's most important functions*
- *Changing column widths*
- *Saving a worksheet*
- *Closing a worksheet*

This chapter provides the essential information you'll need to create worksheets. It shows you how to open worksheets, how to enter information into a worksheet, and how to save and close a worksheet. The chapter explains how to enter numbers, text, formulas, and dates. After this chapter, you'll be ready to learn about changing existing data in a worksheet and making the worksheet more attractive.

Opening a New Worksheet

You've already seen that Excel presents a new, blank worksheet when you first enter the program. But you can open another new worksheet at any time. Perhaps you have closed and saved the active worksheet and want to begin a new one. To open a new worksheet, simply select the File-New command from the File menu. The dialog box shown in Figure 3.1 appears.

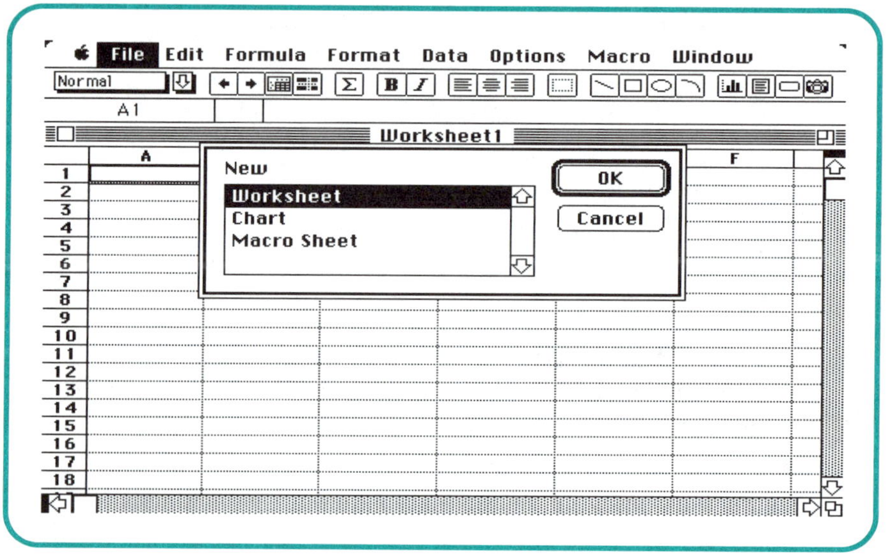

Figure 3.1 Opening a new worksheet.

Excel assumes you want a new worksheet and selects the Worksheet option in the dialog box (as shown in Figure 3.1). Simply press Return to accept this option and open a new worksheet. You can open a new worksheet even if you have other worksheets currently open. Each new worksheet appears in a separate window.

Opening an Existing Worksheet

After you have saved a worksheet (described later), you probably will need to view it or make changes to it later. Or perhaps you want to examine the sample worksheets that come with Excel. You can open an existing worksheet with the File-Open command in the File menu.

The dialog box shown in Figure 3.2 will appear and give you the opportunity to look for existing files in various folders. You can click on the desired file name in the Files list or return to previously open folders by selecting their names from the Folders list that appears above the File list (click on the current folder to view the list).

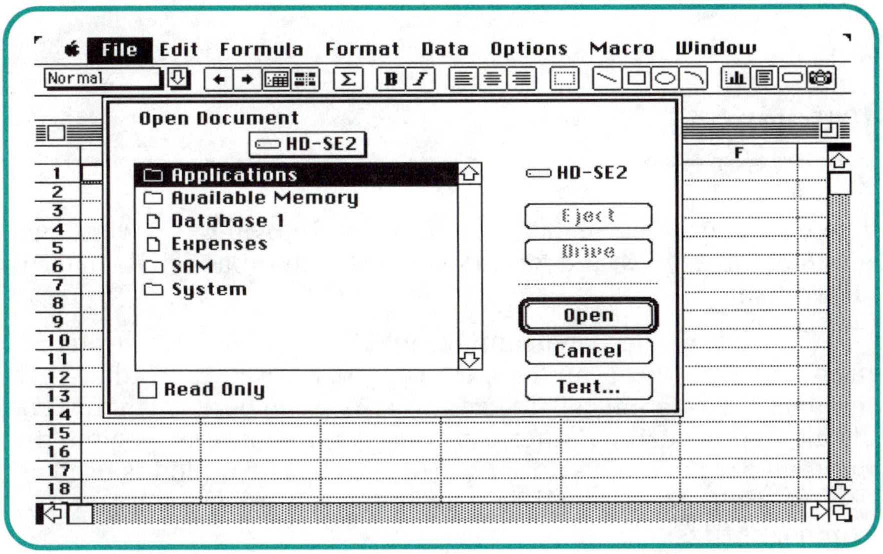

Figure 3.2 The File-Open dialog box.

Opening a Worksheet

1. Select the File-Open command.

   The dialog box shown in Figure 3.2 appears.

2. If the desired file is showing in the Files listing, simply double-click on its name. You can view more files in the list by clicking on the list box arrows.

   The file will come into view.

3. If the desired file is not showing, double-click on the folder in which the file is located. Continue to select folders until the desired file appears in the Files list. To return to previous folders, select the folder from the list just above the list box (click on the current folder name above the list box). □

Entering Data

There are four types of data you can enter into an Excel worksheet: *numbers*, *text*, *dates*, and *formulas*. These four types of data make up all worksheets.

Number entries are useful for making calculations throughout the worksheet. Excel can "read" the number in a cell and add it to the number in a different cell, for example. You can perform many types of calculations using numeric entries. A number must begin with a numeral or one of the symbols: + – . (or $. The period is used as a decimal point for decimal values. Following are some examples of number entries:

1234
$234.23
45%
(35)
–45.89323
5 $^{1}/_{2}$

If your entry contains alphabetic characters or other symbols, Excel will not consider it a number and you will be unable to use it for numeric calculations. Entries that contain alphabetic characters are considered *text* entries. Text entries are useful for adding labels to your worksheets, such as column and row headings or other descriptive information. Text entries can begin with any character, provided they contain at least one non-numeric character (such as a letter). Following are some acceptable text entries:

December
ADB-24
Sixteen
John Smith

Dates are special entries. Excel will recognize the entry as a valid date only if you enter the date in one of the date formats accepted by Excel. If your entries are valid, you can use them to perform *date math*. Date math uses dates in chronological calculations, such as adding a month to a date, calculating a date 30 days from a given date, and so on. Using date math requires a valid date entry, as shown in the following examples:

12/1/91
1-Dec-91
12-1-91

If you enter a date in any of the above formats, Excel considers the entry a valid date and converts it to a numeric value to perform date math calculations. When an entry is valid, the date will be aligned with the right side of the cell, similar to number entries. You can enter a date in any number of other formats, but if you enter the date in a formula that Excel can't convert to a value, Excel will treat the date as a text entry that cannot be calculated with date math features. Non-valid date entries align with the left sides of the cells, just as any other text entry.

> **Tip**: After you enter a date using one of the valid styles, you can change the style. This is described in Chapter 5.

Formulas are special entries that tell Excel how to make calculations based on the values in other cells. Usually, formulas "refer" to other cells containing numeric values. These references are the primary value of worksheets.

Entering Numbers, Text, and Dates

To enter numbers, text, and dates, move the pointer to the desired cell and type the entry. The entry will appear in the formula bar as you type it. If you are making a numeric entry, be sure that the entry contains only numeric characters or Excel may treat it as a text entry. A numeric entry will align with the right edge of the cell.

Press Return or use any pointer movement command to accept the entry. If you press Esc before accepting the entry, Excel will not enter the information into the worksheet. You can also click on the enter box to accept the entry or the cancel box to reject it. When you accept the entry, Excel places it into the cell on the worksheet.

If you make a mistake as you type the information, use the Backspace key to back up and correct the entry. If you have already accepted the entire entry, you can move back to the cell and retype the entire entry. The new entry will replace the old.

> **Tip**: You can also edit your worksheet data by clicking in the formula bar after selecting the desired cell. Use editing procedures to change the data in the formula bar, and then press Return. This is explained in more detail in Chapter 4.

Note that text entries can exceed the width of a cell—or they can "wrap" to fit into a single cell. This is explained in greater detail later in this chapter, and under "Number Formats" in Chapter 5.

Figure 3.3 shows a worksheet with various numeric and text entries. By pressing an arrow key after each entry, you can move to the next cell and accept the previous entry at the same time. Notice that the numeric entries are aligned with the right side of the cell and the text entries are aligned with the left.

> **Tip**: You can change the way Excel aligns numbers, dates, and text using the Format-Alignment command, and you can cause text entries to "wrap" by using the Format-Numbers command. If you don't like the formats shown for dates, but you want to perform date math calculations, you can enter a date in an accepted format and then reformat the date using the Format-Numbers command. Chapter 5 describes both these commands in more detail.

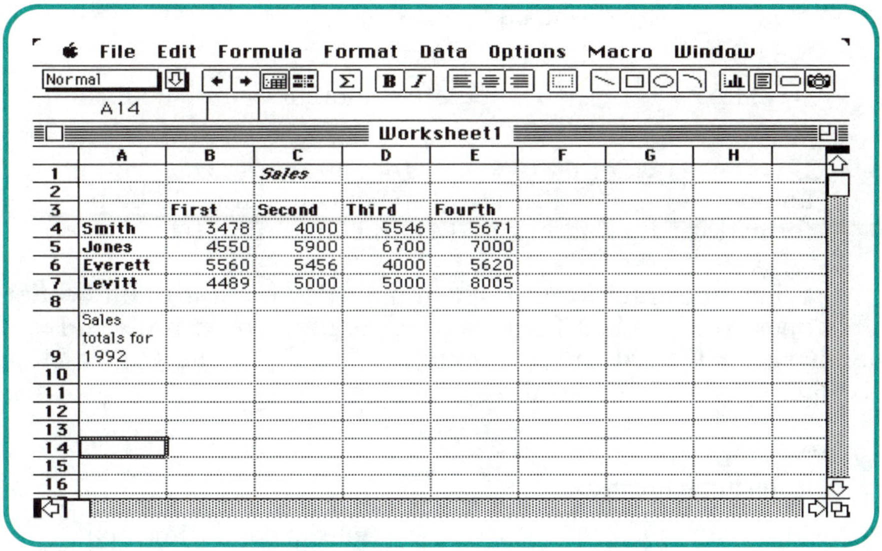

Figure 3.3 Some numeric and text entries in a sample worksheet.

When entering numbers as fractions, such as $5\ ^1/_2$, you can simply type each character: 5, 1, /, and 2. If you don't have an integer preceding the fraction, be sure to begin with a zero, as in $0\ ^1/_5$. This assures that Excel does not think you are entering a date. You also can enter fractional values in decimal form, such as 5.5 for $5\ ^1/_2$.

Entering Formulas

As explained before, formulas calculate the values in other cells of the worksheet. A formula entered into one cell can refer to the contents of other cells by using cell references. (A cell's reference consists of its column letter followed by its row number.) The formula uses references along with mathematical operations to produce calculated results. In general, formulas consist of the following three elements:

- An = (equal) sign at the beginning. (An = sign is necessary to create a formula.)
- One or more values or cell references that will be calculated. Some examples include:

=5	(one constant value)
=5+9	(one cell reference)
=G2+A2+5	(two calculated references and a constant value)

► If you use two or more values (or cell references), you need an operator that defines the type of calculation to be performed, such as addition (+) and subtraction (–).

When you enter formulas, you'll need to use one of the acceptable operators. Table 3.1 shows the operators you can use in Excel for basic mathematical calculations. The following Quick Steps explain how to enter formulas into cells.

Entering a Formula

1. Move the cell pointer to the desired cell. This cell should be any cell other than those to which the formula will refer. For example, you might enter a formula in cell A3 that adds the values of cells A1 and A2.	Selects the desired cell.
2. Type the = sign to begin the formula.	Your entry appears in the formula bar as you type.
3. Follow the = sign with an expression that contains the cell references and an operator.	At this point, your formula might look like `=A1+A2` in the formula bar.
4. Press Return or use one of the pointer movement keys to accept the entry. Press Esc to reject the entry and start over.	The entry appears in the cell. If you used Return to accept the entry, the cell pointer will remain on the cell and the formula will be showing in the formula bar. □

Table 3.1 Operators for Formulas

Operator	Description	Example
+	Addition	=A1+A2
–	Subtraction	=A1–A2
*	Multiplication	=A1*A2
/	Division	=A1/A2
^	Exponentiation	=1^2

Figure 3.4 shows formulas added to an example worksheet. Notice that the pointer is currently located on a cell containing a formula. This displays the contents of the cell in the formula bar at the top of the screen. However, the cell itself displays the *result* of the formula. The beauty of a formula is that you can change the values in the referenced cells, and the formula will automatically recalculate its value based on cell changes.

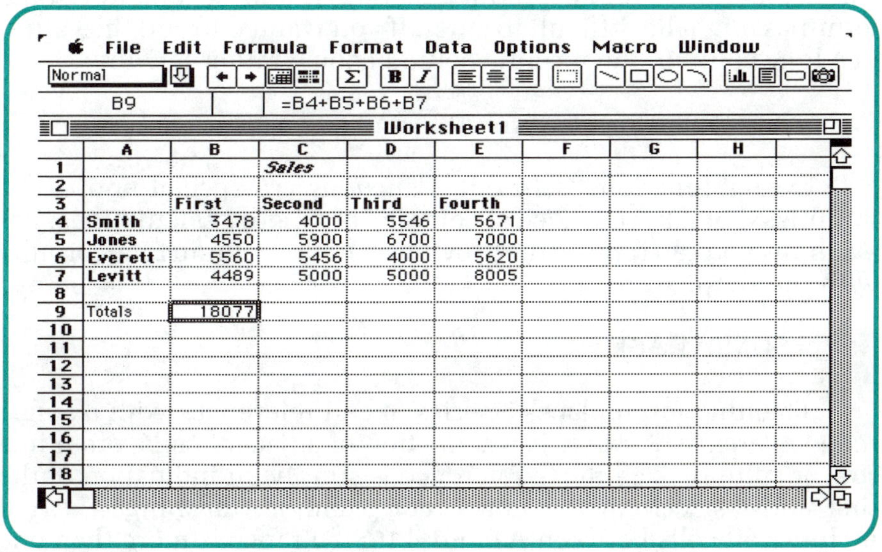

Figure 3.4 Using formulas.

You can stack several expressions together in a single formula if desired. This lets you calculate the values in several cells. An example might read =A1+A2+A3. Figure 3.4 also shows this procedure.

> **Tip**: Your formulas don't have to use cell references only. You can use constant values in formulas between the operators. For example, you can multiply the value in cell A1 by 5 using this formula: =A1*5. You'll get the same result as the formula =A1*A2 and entering 5 in cell A2.

Using Functions (An Introduction)

You might be thinking about some of the calculations you can perform with formulas. You can use them to add the numbers in a column or to calculate product markups, and so on. But some formulas might be difficult to enter. If you wanted to add the values in a long column, the formula could become rather lengthy:

=A1+A2+A3+A4+A5+A6... and so on

Excel's functions help out. *Functions* are special entries for formulas that take the place of complex or lengthy calculations. For example, you can replace the previous lengthy column total formula with the simple function

=SUM(A1:A6)

The function replaces a series of cell references with a single *range reference*. A *range* is a collection of adjacent cells, often in a row or column. The range reference is simply an indication of the first and last cell in the range. For example, the range A1:A10 includes all cells between A1 and A10. If a range is more than one row or column (that is, a block of cells), then the reference should be to the upper-left and lower-right corners. The reference A1:C3 includes a block of nine cells. All functions consist of the following parts:

- The = sign. In the example above, = is entered to make the entry a formula. It is required only when the function appears at the beginning of the entry.
- The function name. Each function has a unique name. The example above uses the function named SUM.
- The function arguments contained in parentheses. In this case, the argument consists of a range reference.

You must enter all functions into cells or formulas using all three parts. If the function is the only thing in a cell (as often is the case), then you should enter it as a formula by including the = sign in front of it. The parentheses are the same for all functions. Parentheses hold the arguments and come directly after the function name.

Arguments

45

The arguments differ greatly from function to function. Arguments are the values on which a function operates. Arguments can be constant values, as in SUM(5,10). They can be cell references, as in SUM(A5,C3,G6). They can be range references, as in SUM(A1:A10). They can be formulas, as in SUM(A1+35). And they can be other functions, as in SUM(A5,SUM(A1:A10)). Other special arguments are also used. A particular function may not allow all argument types. The syntax of the function determines which types of arguments it takes. (By the way, the SUM function happens to accept all these types of arguments, which is why it's used in this chapter as an example.)

One of the helpful features of range references in formulas is that they expand and contract to accommodate changes to the worksheet. Suppose that you enter a formula into cell B10 that adds the range B1:B8 using the function =SUM(B1:B8). Later, you decide to insert a row above row 3. This expands the range to B1:B9 in order to cover the same data. Excel automatically changes the range reference in the formula. Likewise, when you delete, copy, or move information, Excel adjusts the cell or range references. Range arguments are also useful because you may only enter 14 arguments per function.

Excel's Most Important Functions

Excel offers dozens of special functions for many purposes. You will probably not need to learn them all. But there are some functions that you should know a little about. These are the functions you'll use most in your applications. This section discusses the most important Excel functions, providing examples of their use.

Summing Columns and Rows (SUM)

You've already seen how the SUM function works. It's used to add the values in a group of cells. This group can be either a range of cells or a list of references, as in the following examples:

```
=SUM(A1:A10)
=SUM(A1,A2,A6,B4,B9,C32)
```


Notice that the list can include cells that are not adjacent to one another. This is the advantage of using a list. Any of the references in the list can be an expression itself, as in the following example:

```
=SUM(A1,A4,C5+10,R22)
```

The third reference in the list is the expression *C5+10*. If any of the cells in the range or list are blank or contain text, Excel treats them as zeros.

Calculating an Average (AVERAGE)

The AVERAGE function is used to calculate the mean average of a group of numbers. Although you could accomplish this task with basic worksheet formulas, the AVERAGE function makes it easy. Often, the numbers being averaged will fall in a row or a column, but you can also average randomly plotted values. Hence, you can use a range reference or list of references as the argument, as follows:

```
=AVERAGE(A1:A10)
=AVERAGE(A1,C3,B25,G10)
```

The first example is a range of cells. You can use any valid worksheet range, including a block of cells. The second example is a group of cells placed at various spots in the worksheet. As in most functions, you can substitute constant values, calculations, or other functions as the arguments.

Keep in mind that including zero values inadvertently in the argument may destroy the accuracy of an average. When used with a range reference, the AVERAGE function ignores text entries and blank cells. Hence, when you use a range as the argument, it's okay if some of the cells in that range are blank or contain text. If you use the AVERAGE function with a list of cells, the function interprets text *and blank cells* as values of zero. So be careful not to use a reference to a cell that is either blank or text.

Using Worksheet Logic (IF)

The IF function is perhaps the most powerful and useful of all worksheet functions. It provides most of the logic you'll need for evaluating information. The IF function uses *conditions*, or tests regarding the value of a cell. For example, a condition might test if the value of A1 equals 100. The value of A1 is either 100 or not. Hence, the condition answer is either true or false. If the condition proves true, one value is returned. If the condition proves false, another value is returned. A simple logical statement can be the basis of some powerful operations. Logic lets your worksheets perform different actions based on different values.

A condition must use a logical operator to create a test. Excel offers several logical operators, as listed:

>	is greater than
<	is less than
=	is equal to
>=	is greater than or equal to
<=	is less than or equal to
<>	is not equal to

With that, here's an example of the IF function at work. This function might be placed in cell A4:

```
=IF(A1=100,"Must be less than 100",A1*2)
```

This function says, if the value of A1 is equal to 100, then place the message "Must be less than 100" in cell A4; otherwise, calculate the value of A1*2. The function requires that you enter the arguments in this order: first the condition followed by a comma, and then the *value if true* followed by a comma, and finally the *value if false*.

The value if true and the value if false can be any constant value, text string, cell reference, or formula. Notice that this example uses a text string for the value if true and a formula for the value if false. If you use text as one of these values, it must be surrounded by quotation marks as shown in the example. Figure 3.5 shows what the previous example might look like on the screen.

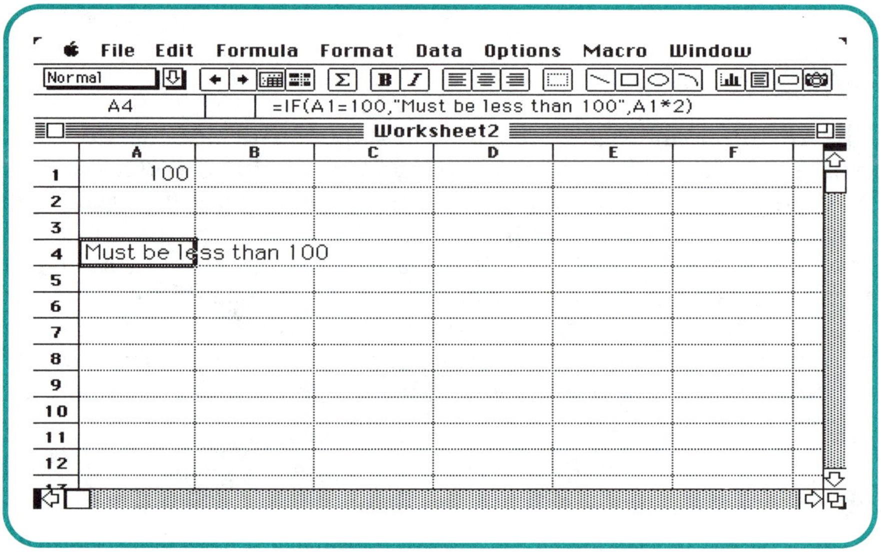

Figure 3.5 Example of the IF function.

You can enter different values into cell A1. If you enter 100, the message appears in cell A4. If you enter anything else, cell A4 contains the value of that number times two.

In the previous example, you might substitute => for = in the condition. The function would read

=IF(A1=>100,"Must be less than 100", A1*2)

This way, any value equal to or greater than 100 will produce the message.

Pointing to Cell and Range References

Any time you use a cell reference in a formula or function, you can enter the reference in one of two ways. You can type the reference or point to it. Typing the reference has already been covered. Just type all information in the formula, including the cell references. If you type

```
=A5
```

Excel knows that you are referring to cell A5. How does it know this? Because you have begun the entry with the = sign, Excel knows that the cell is not going to contain text. Hence, the A5 must be a cell reference and not a text entry.

However, any time you are ready to type a cell reference, you can, instead, point to the cell using the mouse or arrow keys as the following Quick Steps explain.

Pointing to a Cell

1. Enter all elements of the formula up to the reference, including the = sign and any functions.	Your entry appears in the formula bar.
2. Use the arrow keys to move to the cell you are referencing. Or just click on the desired cell with the mouse.	When you use the arrow keys while Excel is expecting a cell reference, Excel enters "Point" mode. The word `POINT` appears on the status line at the bottom of the screen and a dotted cell highlight (called the *marquee*) will reflect the cell to which you are pointing. Figure 3.6 shows an example.
3. Enter the + sign or any other operator.	The marquee returns to the active cell awaiting your next point action, and the operator appears next to the previous cell reference.

4. Use the arrow keys again to point to the next cell.

   The marquee highlights the cell.

5. Press Return to complete the formula.

□

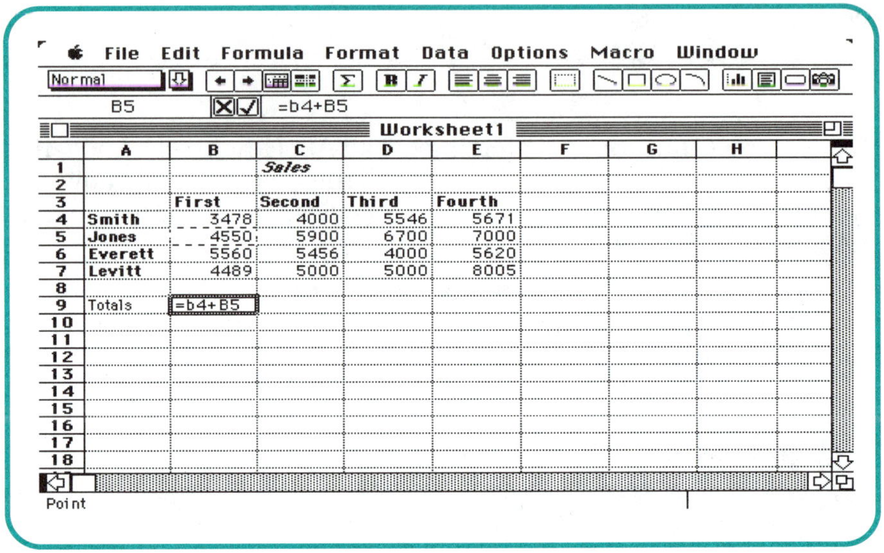

Figure 3.6 Using the ↑ to point to a cell while entering a formula.

Remember, you can use the pointing action any time you would normally type a cell reference. When using functions like SUM that require a range reference, you can also point. To point to a range reference, first enter this much of the function:

```
=SUM(
```

Next, point to the upper-left cell of the range, and then drag to the lower-right corner. The marquee will stretch to encompass the entire range. Press) (right parenthesis) and then Return when finished.

Using the Auto Sum Button

You can simplify the task of summing rows and columns by using the Auto Sum button on the Toolbar. Simply highlight the range of cells containing the values to be summed. These cells must be in a contiguous range. Include one extra cell to the right (if a row) or at the bottom (if a column) of this range. **Make sure the pointer is in the empty cell.** Press Tab or Return to move the pointer. Now click on the Auto Sum button and Excel automatically inserts the SUM function into the extra blank cell, using the rest of the range as the argument for the function. Press Return to accept the sum. This is an excellent timesaving tool.

Changing Column Widths

The *column width* is the number of numeric characters that will fit into a column. Thus, if the column width is eight, eight characters will fit into the cell.

As you enter data into a column's cells, you might find that an entry exceeds the width of its cell. This is often the case with text entries. When the cell immediately to the right of an "over-stuffed" cell is empty, Excel allows the entry to spill over to the adjacent cell. Figure 3.7 shows an example.

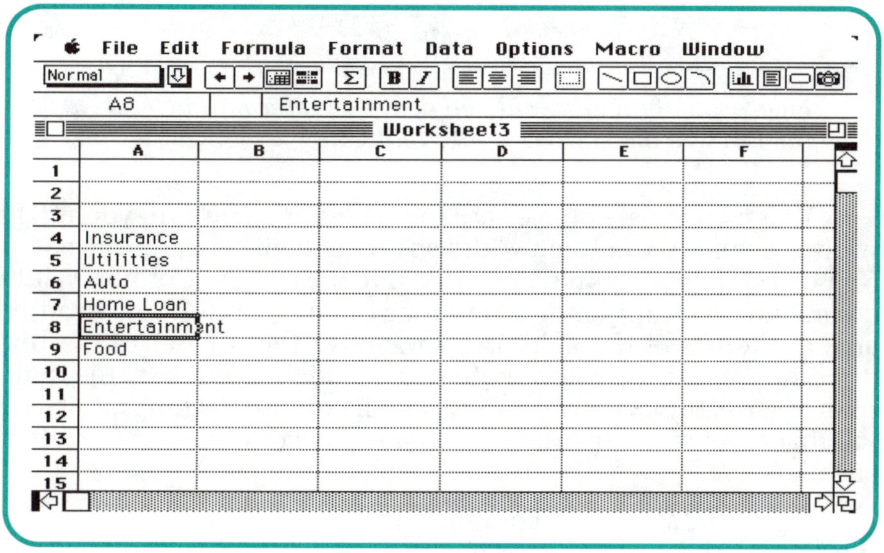

Figure 3.7 When a cell's entry does not fit into the cell, it will cover up the adjacent cell, provided the adjacent cell is blank.

Note that the entry is not split between the two cells. It is contained entirely in the original cell (cell A8 in Figure 3.7). The contents of cell A8 are simply allowed to appear in cell B8. However, if cell B8 contains an entry, the contents of A8 will not cover up that data. Instead, Excel will display as much of the information as possible. Figure 3.8 shows an example.

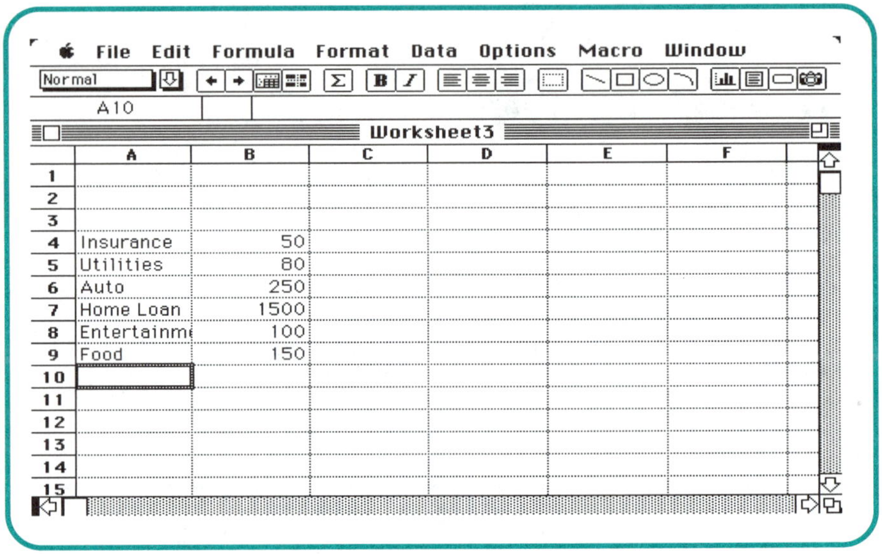

Figure 3.8 If an adjacent cell contains information, entries to the left will not spill over into that cell.

When your data entries are too wide for a column, you might want to change the column width so that it displays the entire entry. You can change a column's width using the Format-Column Width command, or simply move the mouse pointer to the row heading area at the top of the column. Now move the pointer to the line dividing the column you want to widen and the column to the right. In the figure, this is between the A and B column headings. Click on the line and drag to the right to expand the column or to the left to shrink it.

Figure 3.9 shows the column from Figure 3.8, now widened for the information previously too wide to fit into the column.

You can change the widths of all columns at one time by pressing Shift-Command-Space and then using the Format-Column Width command. Pressing Shift-Command-Space highlights the entire worksheet as shown in Figure 3.10.

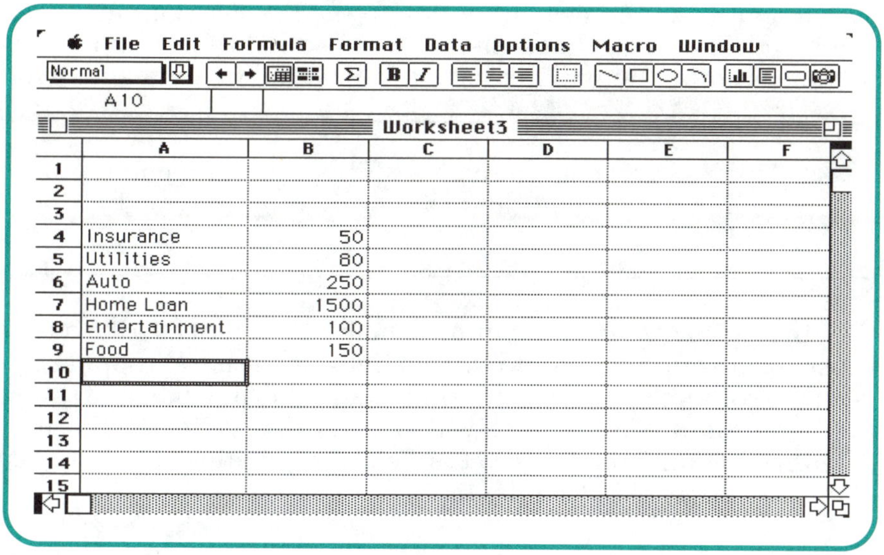

Figure 3.9 Changing a column's width using the Format-Column Width command.

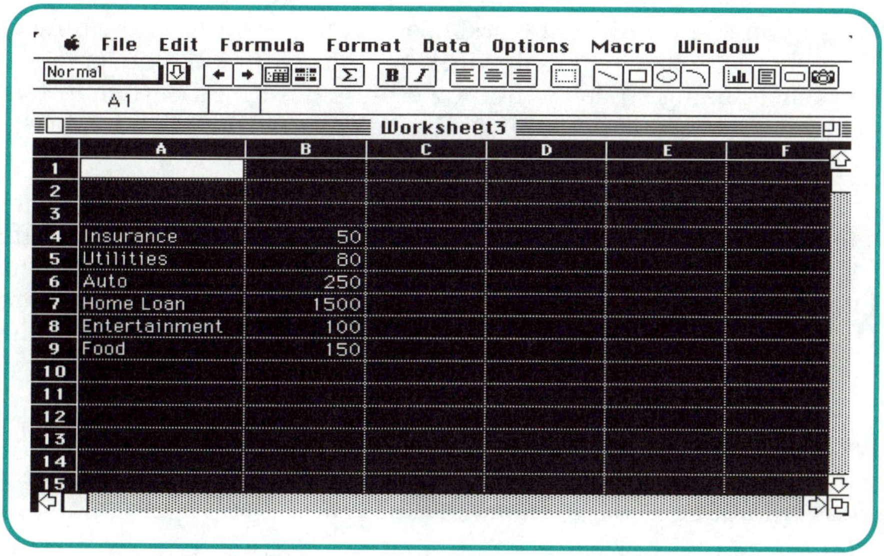

Figure 3.10 Highlighting the entire worksheet for column-width changes.

If you select the Best Fit option in the Format-Column Width command, Excel will choose the column width that best fits the data in that column. You will not have to adjust the width manually.

> **Tip**: You can choose the Best Fit option for a column by double-clicking on the column dividing line next to the column heading.

Instead of widening a column to make the text fit into it, you can cause the text to "wrap" onto several lines in its cell. Wrapping will keep the column width the same but change the height of the row so that more lines can be displayed. This is done with the Format-Alignment command. Choose the Text Wrap option. More on text alignment appears in Chapter 5.

Saving a Worksheet

When you begin building worksheets, you'll want to know how to save them to save yourself work in the future. If you create a worksheet using some of the procedures described earlier in this chapter, you can save your experiments at any time using the File-Save command.

The first time you save a worksheet, you will be asked to enter a name. When you enter a name for the worksheet, you can specify a specific folder if desired. Simply click on the desired folder in the Files listing to open it. If other folders appear in this folder, you can click on them to open them too. Finally, press Return to save the worksheet into the currently open folder.

If you've saved a worksheet before, Excel will update the old file with any changes you've made since the last time you saved. The worksheet will be stored on disk and will remain in view on-screen. You will not be asked to name the file.

There may be times when you want to save a file under a new name, even though you've saved it under a different name before. This technique is useful for making a copy of the file. Both copies of the file will be stored on disk. Saving a worksheet under a new name requires only a simple variation on the File-Save procedure. Just select the command File-Save As instead of File-Save. Then you can enter a name for the new file.

> **Tip**: Periodically saving your work with the File-Save command is a good idea. In case of a power failure or other catastrophe, a recent copy of the file will be stored on disk. Of course, you should also make backup copies on floppy diskettes from time to time.

Closing a Worksheet and Exiting Excel

Saving a worksheet does not remove it from the screen. This requires closing the worksheet. Whether you've saved a worksheet or not, you can close it using the File-Close command. If the worksheet does not require saving, it will be removed from the screen. If you have made changes to the worksheet, you will be asked if you want to save the worksheet before closing. You can opt to save the changes or not. Either way, the worksheet will be removed from the screen. (You can press Esc at this point to return to the worksheet, canceling the File-Close command.)

Closing a worksheet does not exit Excel. After closing all worksheets, Excel displays only the File, Edit, and Window menus. To quit Excel, use the File-Exit command.

What You've Learned

This chapter has provided the essentials for starting worksheets. You now know how to enter data into a worksheet, save the data, and use it again later. You can begin to experiment with various formulas that calculate the data stored in other cells of the worksheet. Remember, when you change the data in the referenced cells, the formulas will recalculate and present new values. Following are some important points:

- The File-New command begins a new worksheet.
- To re-use a previously saved worksheet, use the File-Open command and locate the desired file.
- Excel distinguishes between four types of data: text, numbers, dates, and formulas. Formulas usually calculate the numbers found in other cells.
- Formulas must begin with an = sign and contain cell references and operators.
- Excel's worksheet functions perform special calculations and can often be used in place of complex formulas.
- The Auto Sum button automatically creates column or row totals for you.
- You can type cell and range references or point to them whenever you would normally type them.
- Use the Format-Column Width command to change the widths of columns throughout the worksheet.

- Use the Best Fit button to have Excel choose the best column width for the data.
- Use the File-Save command to save a new or existing worksheet. If the worksheet already exists on disk, Excel will replace the old copy with the new one.
- To change a worksheet's name while saving, use the File-Save As command.
- The File-Close command removes a worksheet from the screen.

Chapter 4

Changing Your Worksheet Data

In This Chapter

- *Selecting data*
- *Deleting, moving, editing, and copying data*
- *Using absolute cell references*
- *Inserting and deleting cells*
- *Using cell notes*

This chapter describes various ways you can change your worksheet data. You can edit the information in a cell, move data to other locations on the worksheet, copy information, and more. These procedures will save you much time and effort when you build worksheets. You'll have the freedom to alter what you have done.

Selecting Data

A great number of Excel's commands require that you select data on the worksheet before entering the command. The command you select then applies to only the selected data. For example, to move data from one location to another requires that you first select the data to be moved and then enter the commands for moving the data. You'll find that many of the commands in this chapter and the next require data selection. So, the first thing to discuss is how to select data on the worksheet. Excel lets you use the mouse or keyboard to select data, as you will see in this chapter.

Selecting a Cell

You've already seen how to select a single cell. Just click in the desired cell, or move the cell pointer to it using any of the pointer movement commands discussed in Chapter 3. By definition, the active cell (the one on which the cell pointer is located) is selected. This means that you have at least one cell selected at all times. In fact, unless you select a range of cells, commands will often apply to the active cell because it's already selected.

Selecting a Range of Cells

Often, you'll want to select more than one cell at a time so that you can apply commands to *blocks* of the worksheet. For example, you might want to change the font of a group of cells at one time. Figure 4.1 shows a selected range of cells.

To select a range with the mouse, click on the first cell and hold the button; then drag the mouse to the last cell and release the button. The range between the two cells will be highlighted. Another method is to click the mouse in the first cell and release the button. Then hold the Shift key down while you click in the last cell.

The range will remain selected until you move the cell pointer again (without holding the Shift key). Try this to unselect the range.

The following Quick Steps explain how to select a range of cells using the keyboard.

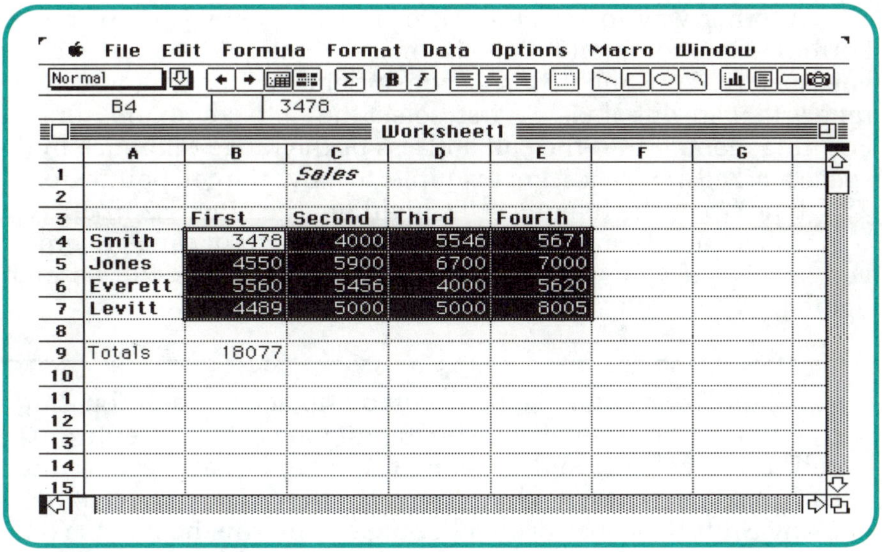

Figure 4.1 A selected range of cells appears as a highlighted block.

Selecting a Range of Cells with the Keyboard

1. Move the pointer to the first cell of the desired range, which is the upper-left corner of the range. — In Figure 4.1, you would move to cell B4.
2. Hold the Shift key down and press the arrow keys. Use the appropriate arrow keys to extend the selected area. — The highlighted range of cells grows in the direction of the arrow.
3. When the desired range is selected, release all keys. — The range is now selected.

Remember that a range of cells in a worksheet can be referenced by its first and last cells, separated by a colon. For example, the range of cells in Figure 4.1 is called B4:E7 because the upper-left cell is B4 and the lower-right cell is E7.

Another way to select a cell or range of cells is by using the Formula-Goto command. This command highlights any cell or range you specify. You might find it convenient for jumping to cells or ranges that are out of view. First, select the Goto command from the Formula menu. Enter the cell address or the range reference in the space marked `Reference`. For example, to move the cell pointer to cell Z25, type `Z25` as the reference. To highlight the range Z25:Z30, type `Z25:Z30` as the reference. Excel jumps to the cell or range reference you specify. If you specify a range, the entire range will be highlighted.

> **Tip**: Excel offers several automatic selections. You can select a column of cells by moving the cell pointer to any cell in the column and pressing Command-Spacebar, or you can click the mouse on the column heading. Then select a row using Shift-Spacebar or by clicking on the row heading. You can also select all cells in the worksheet at one time by pressing Shift-Command-Spacebar or by clicking in the upper-left corner where the column and row headings meet.

Selecting Several Ranges

There may be times when you want to perform a command on cells that are not adjacent. Perhaps you would like to change the font of a row along the top of the worksheet and a column along the side. To make the change to both ranges, you need to select both ranges at the same time as shown in Figure 4.2.

Selecting multiple ranges is an extension of the procedure for selecting a single range. First, select a single range as described in the previous section; then press the Command key while you select the second range as you did the first. Because you pressed Command, the first range remains selected as you select another.

You can use this procedure to highlight as many ranges as you like. As shown in Figure 4.2, the ranges can be different sizes and shapes and can be in different parts of the worksheet.

The following Quick Steps show how to select multiple ranges using the keyboard.

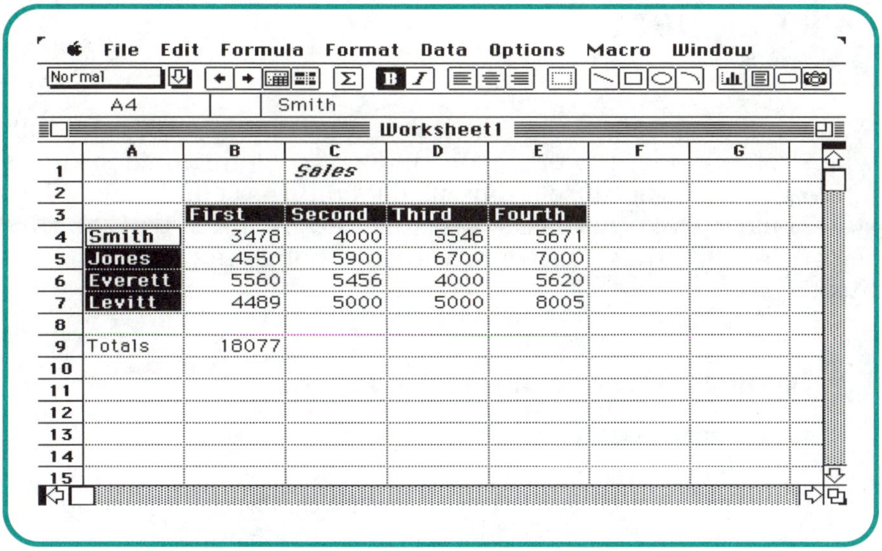

Figure 4.2 Selecting multiple ranges.

Selecting Multiple Ranges with the Keyboard

1. Select a range using the steps listed in the previous section.

   The selected range is highlighted.

2. Press Shift-F8.

   The status line shows the word `ADD`, indicating that you are adding to the currently selected range.

3. Move the pointer to the beginning of the other range. Don't use the Shift key at this time.

   The currently selected range remains selected, and the pointer moves.

4. Press Shift with the arrow keys to highlight the next range in the usual way.

   The new range is highlighted, and the first range remains highlighted. □

Deleting Data

Removing data from the worksheet is a common need, especially when you build large worksheets. In Excel, deleting data is known as *blanking* cells because removing data returns cells to their blank state. Like many other tasks, deleting data requires that you first select the cells that you want to blank. Following are the Quick Steps.

Deleting the Contents of a Cell or Range

1. Select the cell or range that you want to delete.
2. Select the Edit-Clear command (or Command-B).

   The dialog box shown in Figure 4.3 appears.
3. Press A to select the All option; then press Return.

   The All option clears all data from the selected cell or range, including entries, formatting options, and notes attached to the cells. □

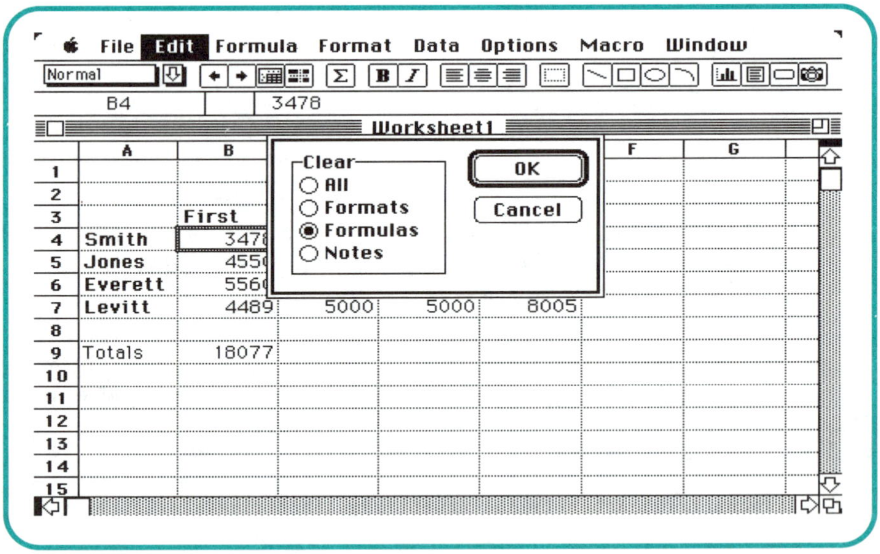

Figure 4.3 The Edit-Clear dialog box.

Tip: If you change your mind about deleting information, you can use the Edit-Undo command to retrieve your data. Make sure you use this command immediately after deleting the information, or you might risk losing the data. Edit-Undo revokes only the most recent command performed.

Remember that you can clear the entire worksheet by first selecting all cells with the command Shift-Command-Space, and then using the Edit-Clear command.

Naming Cells and Ranges

You've seen how formulas often require references to cells and ranges. In fact, cell and range references are the keys to worksheet calculations. However, using references can be inconvenient. Often, you have to look over the worksheet to find the cell or range that you want to reference or even "scroll" through the worksheet to find data that's not in view.

By *naming* cells and ranges that you use in formulas, you can easily refer to each reference by its name. The name is easier to remember than the reference. For example, suppose you use the SUM function to add a column of values, and the formula reads =SUM(A1:A10). If you were to give the range A1:A10 the name *JANUARY*, you could add that column with the function =SUM(JANUARY). Using the name is easier than using the range reference.

Another advantage to range names is that they don't change when you insert or delete worksheet rows or columns. This benefit will become more clear when you read about inserting rows and columns later in this chapter.

Once you name a cell or range, you can use the name over and over throughout your worksheet formulas. To name a range, follow these Quick Steps.

Naming a Range with Formula-Define Name

1. Select the cell or range that you want to name.

   Use the commands listed earlier in this chapter to select the range.

2. Select the Formula-Define Name command (or Command-L).

   The dialog box shown in Figure 4.4 appears.

3. Enter the desired range name in the space labeled *Name*; then press Return. Or you can press Add and then name another cell or range.

   If a name already exists in the Name box, it will be removed when you begin typing. The existing name is Excel's quess at what the name should be. It comes from the label (if one exists) in the first cell of the range. If you like this name, simply press Return to accept it. □

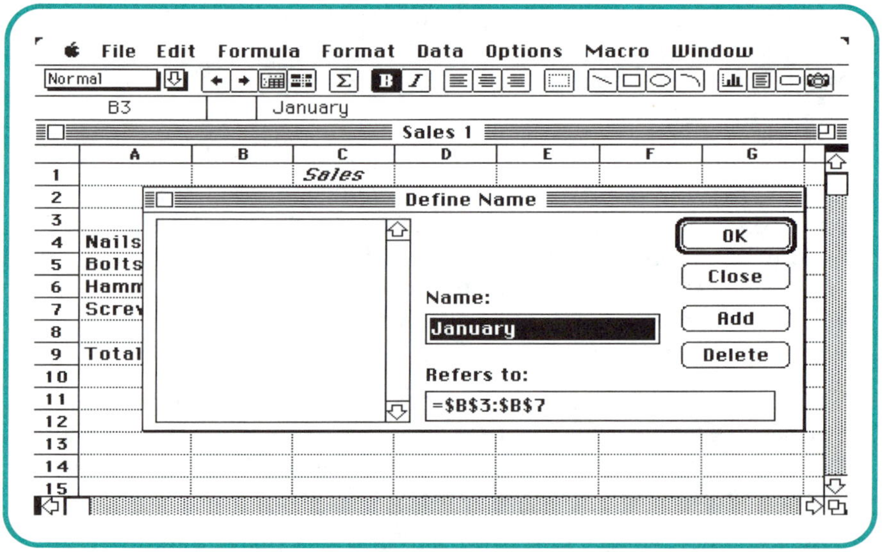

Figure 4.4 The Define Name dialog box.

Notice that the Define Name dialog box shows you a listing of all defined range names in the worksheet. The list includes the name you define, plus a few extras that appear as the result of certain operations you perform.

To use a range name in a formula, simply enter the name exactly as you typed it when you defined it. Do not use quotation marks for the reference. If you type the name incorrectly or if the name does not exist on the worksheet, Excel displays the message `#NAME?` in the cell to indicate it does not know the name you intend for the reference.

If you cannot remember a range name, simply use the Formula-Paste Name command to display the listing of existing names. After you find the name you're looking for, press Esc to exit the dialog box, or press Return to insert the highlighted name into the active cell.

> **Tip**: Now that you have named a cell or range, try using the Formula-Goto command to jump quickly to the named reference. Select Formula-Goto and then highlight the desired name from the list provided. When you press Return, Excel immediately highlights the range on the worksheet. This is an excellent way of moving to specific locations on the worksheet.

Finally, here are a few pointers to remember about range names:

- Each range name must be unique to an area of cells. If you use the same range name in a second location, the range name "moves" to that second location. The first range no longer has that, or any, name.
- Upper- and lowercase letters do not matter when using range names in formulas.
- Range names must begin with a letter and can contain letters, numbers, the period, and the underscore character. Range names that look like cell references will be rejected. For example, don't name a range *A5*.
- Any part of one named range can be part of another, different named range.

Moving Data

Sometimes you may not want to completely erase data from the worksheet but instead move it to another location. You can move data using a simple two-step process. First, you cut the information from its original location and then paste it into the new location, as described in the following Quick Steps.

Using Cut and Paste to Move Data

1. Select the cell or range that you would like to move.
   Highlights the cell or range.
2. With the range highlighted, select the Edit-Cut command or press Command-X.
   Excel places the marquee around the area to be moved. Figure 4.5 shows an example.
3. Move the pointer to the first cell of the new range into which you want to place the data. Do not select the range, just move to the upper-left corner of it. Be careful. If other data appears in this new area, it will be replaced by the moved data.
   The original range remains selected.
4. Press Command-V or use the Edit-Paste command.
   The highlighted data moves into the new location. Figure 4.6 shows an example. □

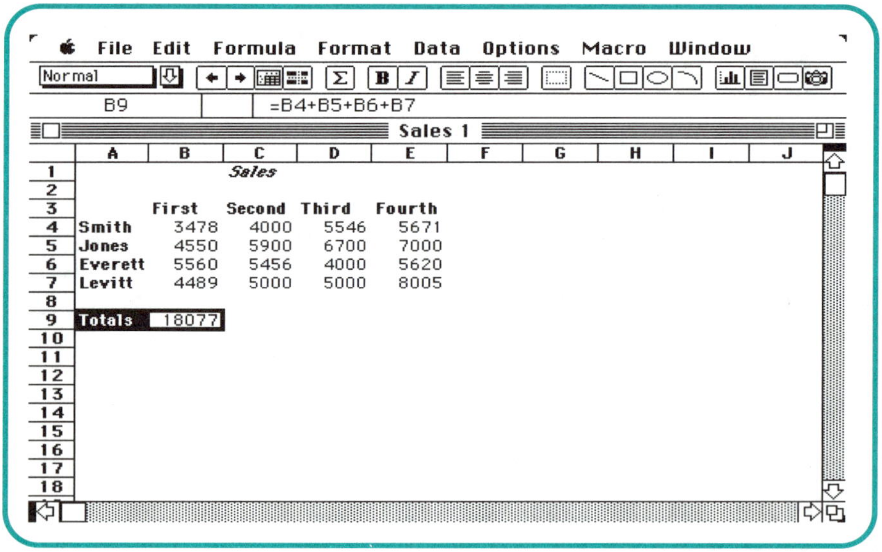

Figure 4.5 Cutting information with the Edit-Cut command.

> ▶ **Note**: Gridlines have been removed from some of these figures so that you can see the changing contents more easily. To learn how to remove gridlines from your worksheet, see "Changing the Worksheet Display" in Chapter 5.

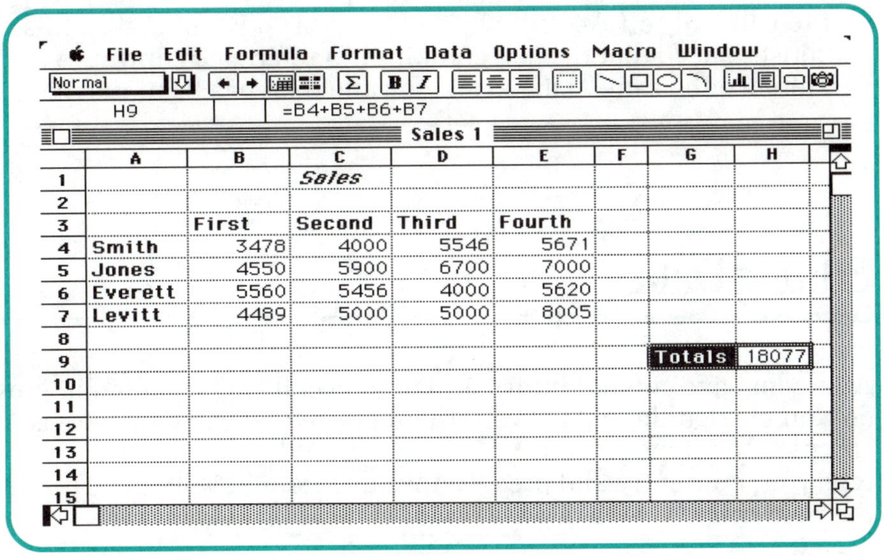

Figure 4.6 The result of moving data.

You can tell Excel to insert new cells when you paste data into the worksheet. This causes existing information to move over and allow room for the pasted data. To do this, use the Edit-Insert Paste command instead of the Edit-Paste command in Step 4 of the preceding Quick Steps.

When you move cells that contain cell references, the references remain exactly as they were in the original location. Take another look at Figure 4.5 and notice that the formula in cell B9 is showing in the formula bar. The formula contains a reference to another cell. When the data in cell B9 is moved as shown in Figure 4.6, the formula and its reference remain the same. The fact that references do not change might not surprise you, since it is probably what you would expect to happen. However, there are times when you want cell references to adjust to new locations. The section "Copying Data" later in this chapter describes how to move data so that cell references adjust.

> **Note**: If you cut and **move** a cell that has a reference to another cell, the reference will remain the same when **pasted** to a new location. The cell continues to reference the same data. However, if you cut and **paste** a cell that is being referenced by another cell, the reference changes to reflect the new location of the referenced cell. For example, suppose cell A4 contains a reference to cell A1. If you cut cell A1 and **paste** it to cell H5, cell A4 will now reference H5. Excel makes this adjustment so that the cell containing a reference continues to reference the same data, even after the data has been **moved**.

Editing Data

After you have entered information into a cell and accepted it, how do you change the data? Well, there are two ways. One way is to completely retype the entry. Simply move the pointer to the cell, type your new entry and press Return to accept it. When you accept the new entry, it replaces the old one.

The second way to change the data is to edit the data currently in the cell. You can change the existing entry and then save the changes you make. These changes are carried out in the formula bar using a series of editing commands.

First, move the pointer to the cell that you want to change. The contents of the cell appear in the formula bar. Click the mouse pointer in the formula bar, where the data appears. This places a flashing cursor inside the formula bar. Figure 4.7 shows an example. Next, use the editing commands to change the data in the formula bar. Editing commands are listed in Table 4.1. Press Return to accept the changes or Esc to reject them. If you accept the changes, Excel updates the information in the cell.

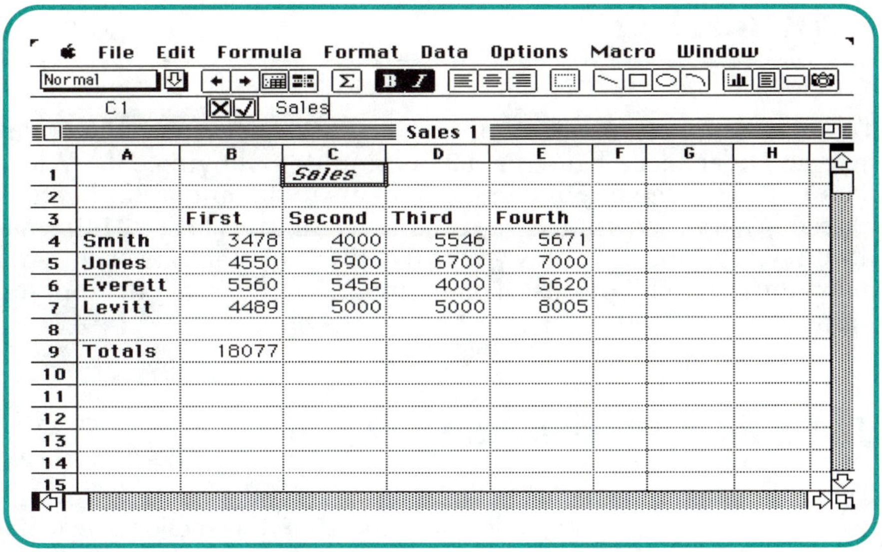

Figure 4.7 Placing the cursor in the formula bar.

Table 4.1 Editing Commands

Key	Result
Option-← or →	Moves one character left or right
↑ or ↓	Moves one line up or down (if there is more than one line)
Delete	Removes the character to the right of the cursor
Backspace	Removes the character to the left of the cursor
[type]	Type to insert new text at the cursor position
Option-Home	Moves to the beginning of the entry
Option-End	Moves to the end of the entry
Return	Accepts the changes
Esc	Rejects the changes

Copying Data

To avoid retyping information on the worksheet, you can copy it over and over again. Copying data is similar to moving data. When data is copied, the original entry remains intact and a duplicate is placed in a new location. Excel offers several ways to copy information. This section will show you three different methods of copying data. Plus, it will discuss some important facts about copying formulas.

The Edit-Copy Command

Using the example in Figure 4.8, suppose you want to copy the headings `First`, `Second`, `Third` and `Fourth` from the 1991 section over to the 1992 section. This would save you the time of retyping those headings for the 1992 totals. You can use the Edit-Copy command to copy the headings, as described in the following Quick Steps.

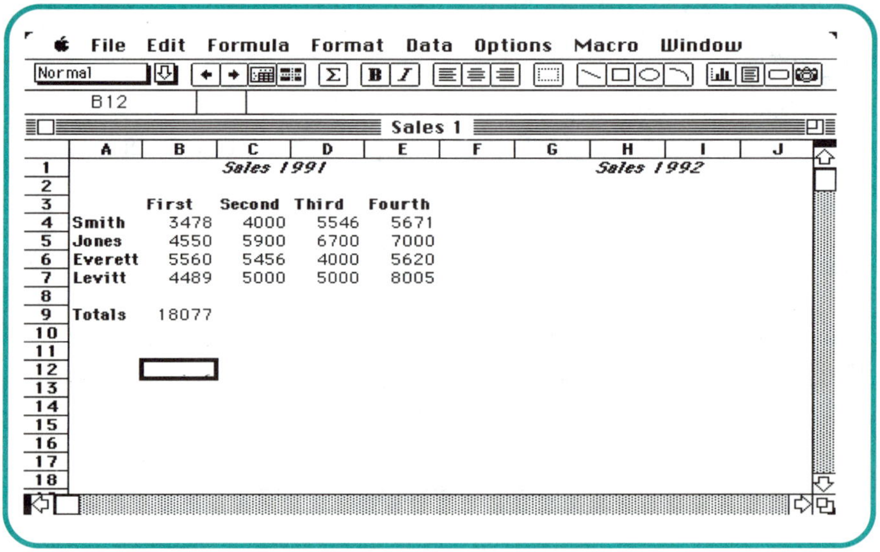

Figure 4.8 A sample worksheet ready for copying.

Copying with the Edit-Copy Command

1. Select the range of cells that you want to copy.	In Figure 4.8, you would select the range B3:E3.
2. Select the Edit-Copy command (or Command-C).	The copy marquee will surround the highlighted range, as shown in Figure 4.9. Notice the message in the status bar at the bottom of the screen.
3. Move the pointer to the first cell in the range that will receive the copy. This should be the upper-left corner of the range.	The marquee will remain on the original information.
4. Press the Enter key (on the numeric keypad) to copy the data to the new location.	The original data will remain in place and a copy will appear at the pointer location. Figure 4.10 shows the result.

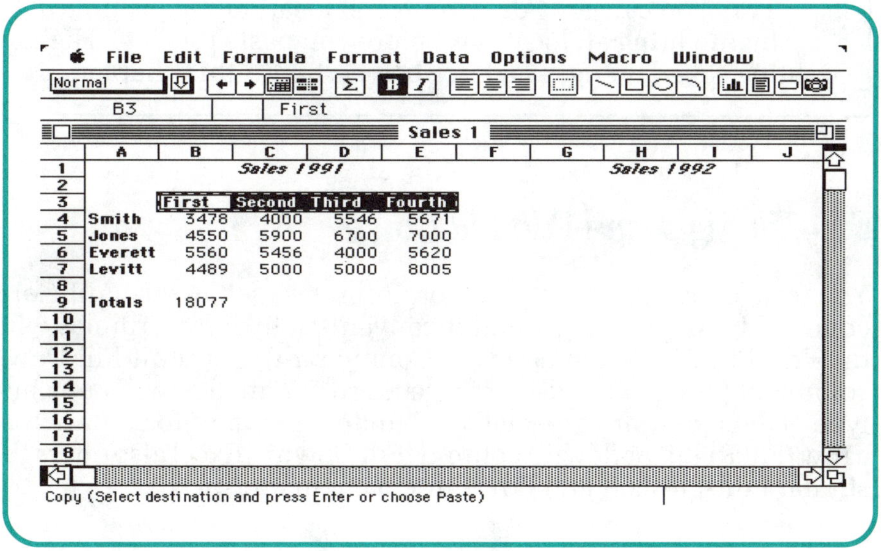

Figure 4.9 Copying the highlighted range using Edit-Copy.

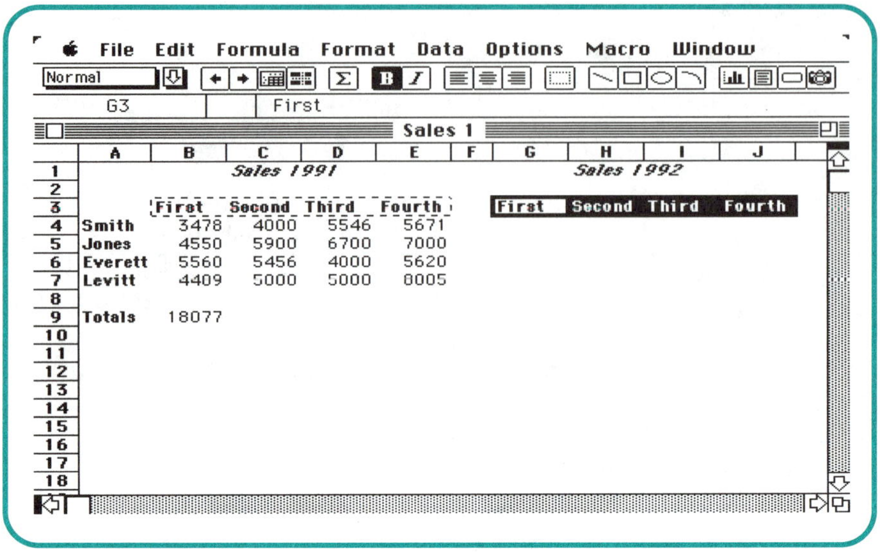

Figure 4.10 The worksheet after copying data to the new location.

> ▶ **Tip**: You can copy data to several locations at one time by highlighting all locations before you paste the data. Highlighting several ranges is described earlier in this chapter.

Edit-Fill Right and Edit-Fill Down

You can copy numbers, text, or formulas using the Edit-Copy command. But you might find it convenient to copy formulas with the Edit-Fill Right command (or Command-B) and Edit-Fill Down command (or Command-D). While these commands will copy any type of data, they are especially useful for copying a formula across a row (Fill Right) or down a column (Fill Down). (Excel also offers the similar Edit-Fill Left and Edit-Fill Up commands.)

To use Edit-Fill Right or Edit-Fill Down, start by moving the pointer to the cell with the formula that you want to copy. Using the mouse or key commands, highlight the range into which you want to copy the formula. This range must include the original cell, plus cells to the right or down that will contain the copies. Figure 4.11 shows an example.

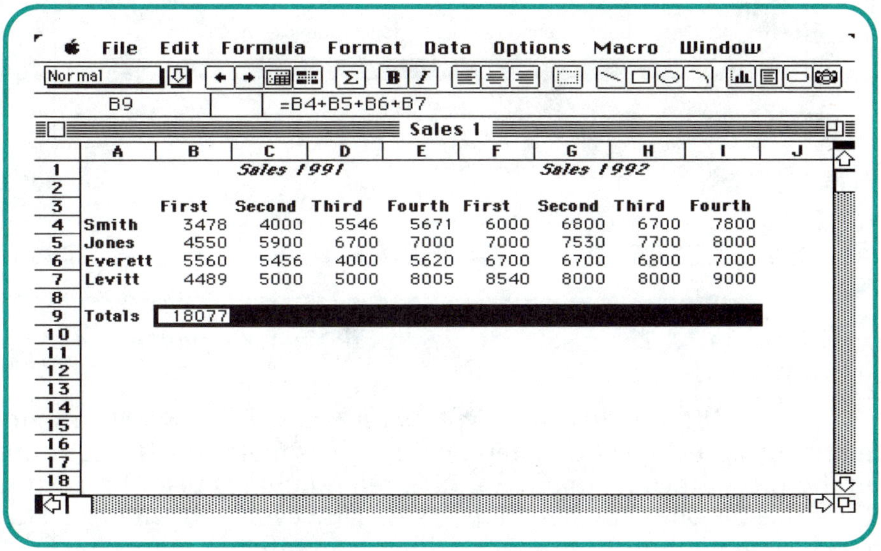

Figure 4.11 Highlighting the range to copy, including the original cell.

Select the Edit-Fill Right or Edit-Fill Down command. The formula in the first cell is instantly copied to the remaining cells in the highlighted range. Figure 4.12 shows the result.

As you can see, these commands are especially useful for copying formulas, but you can use them to copy any data from one cell to many adjacent cells. When copying a formula, keep in mind that cell references will adjust for each copy's new location. For example, the new formulas in Figure 4.12 produce the totals of their respective columns, not the total of the first column. If you examine the formulas that were copied, you'll notice that each has been adjusted to total the column where it's located. The formula in cell C9 is `=C4+C5+C6+C7`. The formula in D9 is `=D4+D5+D6+D7`.

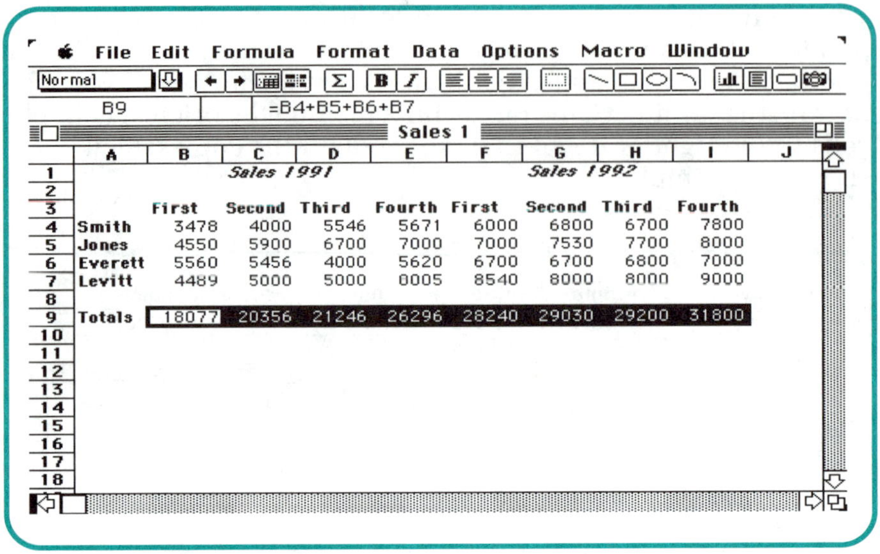

Figure 4.12 The result of the Edit-Fill Right command.

A condition called *relative referencing* allows Excel to automatically adjust formula references (such as matching the columns in the preceding example). Relative referencing is useful for situations like the one shown in Figure 4.12. However, you might find the need to prevent this automatic adjustment when you use the Edit-Copy or Edit-Fill Right command. Preventing relative referencing is discussed in the section "Using Absolute Cell References" later in this chapter.

> ▶ **Tip**: As you learned earlier, the Cut command does not use relative referencing like the Copy command. If you want to move data using the Cut and Paste procedure, but you want relative referencing, use the Copy command instead of the Cut command. Then, remove the extra copy from the original location.

The Option-Enter Technique

There is one more way to copy information. You might find this technique the most convenient for many situations. You can copy information as you enter it by pressing Option-Enter to repeat the data in other cells. The following Quick Steps show you how.

Q Copying with Option-Enter

1. Select the range of cells where you want to place the data. The entire range should be empty. — The range is highlighted, and the first cell is active.
2. Enter the number, text, or formula into the active cell. — The data you enter appears in the formula bar.
3. Press Option-Enter to accept the formula. — Copies the entry to all cells in the highlighted range. □

The result of using Ctrl-Enter is similar to the results from the Edit-Fill commands, but you can perform this copy technique as you enter the first formula, rather than afterward.

Using Absolute Cell References

You've seen how cell and range references adjust when you copy formulas. This is called relative referencing, and it is a useful feature that saves you from typing formulas over and over.

Most cell and range references are relative unless you make them *absolute*. (When you define a name for a range or reference, the default is absolute referencing.) An absolute reference does not change when the formula is copied to another cell. To make a reference absolute, simply insert dollar signs between the row and column references, as in the following examples:

$A$1	Absolute column and row
$A1	Absolute column but relative row
A$1	Relative column but absolute row
$A$1:$C$3	Absolute range reference

Notice that references can be partially relative and partially absolute. These mixed references are useful for special types of copying needs where the row reference may change, but the column reference will remain absolute (or vice versa). You may not find an occasion to use mixed references.

Take a look at a basic absolute reference. For example, look at the worksheet shown in Figure 4.13. This worksheet calculates the total price of three different items given each item's price per carton (entered into column C) and a desired quantity (entered into cell B3). Simply change the quantity value in cell B3 to calculate the total income from an order. The formula for the total in cell B6 is `=C6*B3`. This multiplies the carton price of the item by the given quantity.

Copying the formula =C6*B3 to the remaining cells in column B would produce errors. While the new formulas in cells B7 and B8 should reference the respective carton prices from column C, both formulas should reference exactly the same quantity amount from cell B3. This requires that the reference to cell B3 be absolute. Figure 4.14 shows the correct reference contained in cell B8 after making the reference to cell B3 absolute before copying.

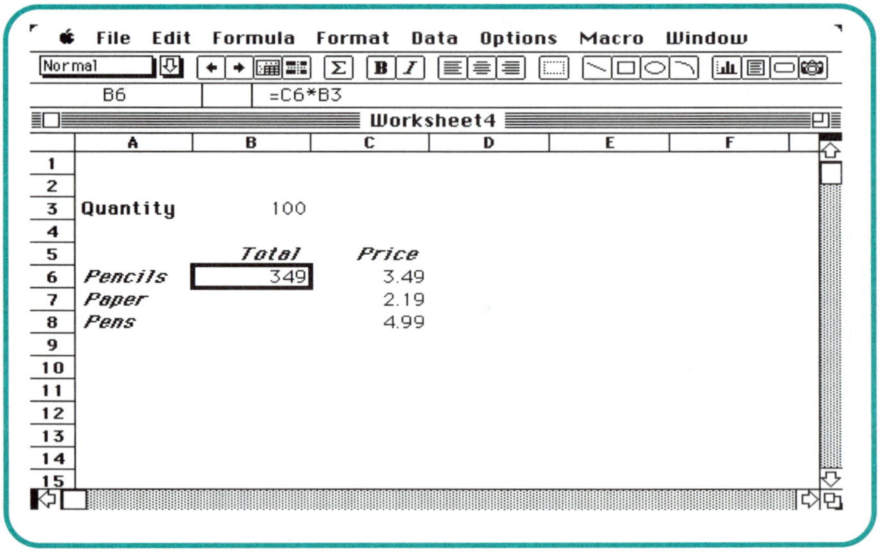

Figure 4.13 A simple worksheet example of relative referencing.

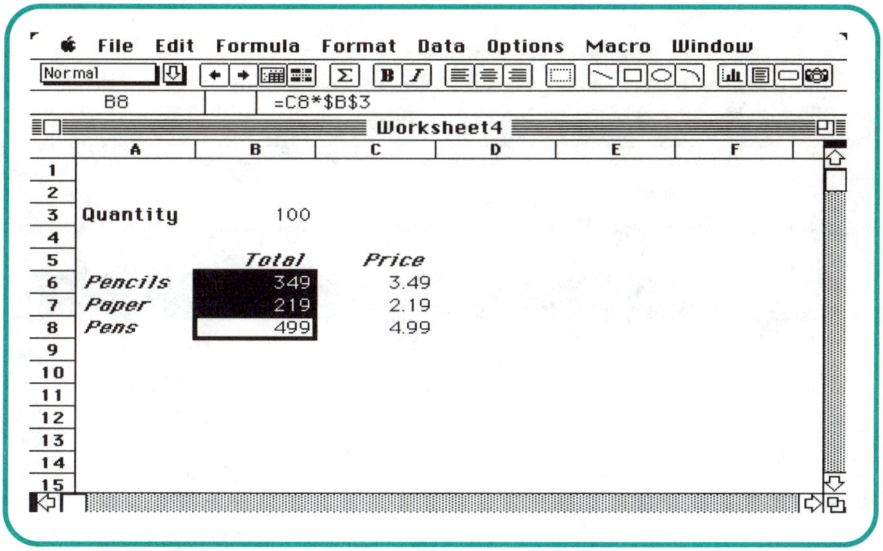

Figure 4.14 Copying with absolute references.

Remember that relative cell references change only when they are copied, not when they are moved with the Cut and Paste procedure. All references are absolute when moved.

Inserting and Deleting Cells

You can add rows and columns to your worksheet or remove them when needed using the Edit-Insert command (Command-I) and Edit-Delete command (or Command-K). Often, inserting extra columns or rows is necessary to make room for additional data or formulas. When you insert a row, for example, all rows below it will shift down to make room. When you delete rows, all rows below the deleted ones shift up to fill the space. Likewise, you might find the need to delete rows or columns from a worksheet to close up some empty space.

For example, to use Edit-Insert, start by moving the pointer to the row where you would like to insert a new row. Press Shift-Spacebar to highlight this row. If you want to insert more than one row, press Shift-↓ to highlight more. Highlight as many rows as you want Excel to insert. Figure 4.15 shows a worksheet ready for inserting.

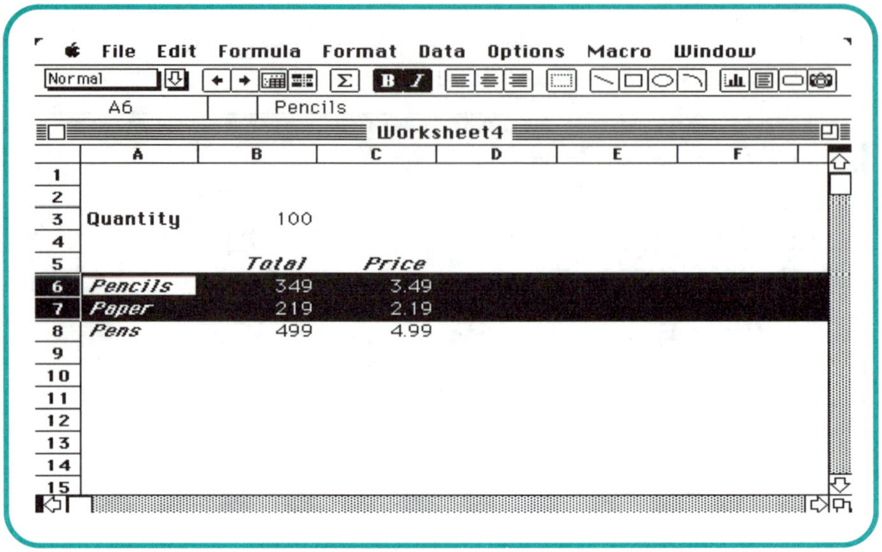

Figure 4.15 Worksheet rows highlighted for the insert command.

You can also accomplish this by clicking on the row heading number (on the left border of the worksheet), holding the mouse button down, and then dragging down to highlight as many rows as you like. Release the button when finished.

Select the Edit-Insert command. Excel inserts as many rows as you have highlighted and shifts all existing rows down to make room. Figure 4.16 shows the result.

Of course, you can perform the same process for columns by highlighting columns instead of rows.

To delete instead of inserting, use the steps above to highlight the unwanted rows or columns; then enter the Edit-Delete command. If you make a mistake, use Edit-Undo immediately after deleting to retrieve the rows or columns.

When you insert rows and/or columns, Excel adjusts cell references that are affected by the change to assure that the formulas continue to produce the intended values. For example, a formula might refer to cell B4 prior to inserting a row. After you insert a row above cell B4, this cell becomes B5, and the reference to it automatically changes to B5.

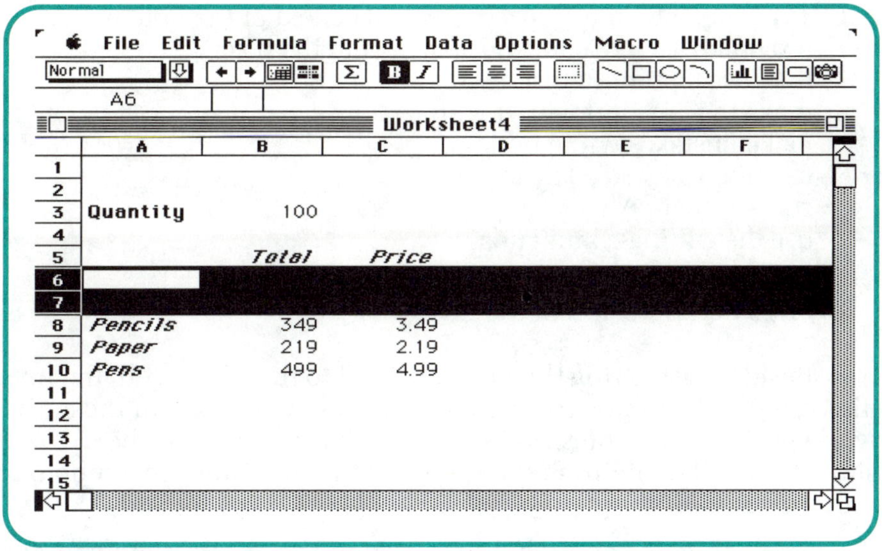

Figure 4.16 The result of the Edit-Insert command.

Applying Cell Notes

Cell notes are a valuable tool when using worksheets. If you create worksheets to share with others, cell notes are almost a must for helping other operators use your worksheet properly. But cell notes also can be practical for your own, private worksheets. Cell notes can help remind you of the purpose behind formulas or of the information that you are supposed to enter in various locations. Or cell notes can provide detailed information about values used in a worksheet. The following Quick Steps explain how to add a note to a cell.

Adding a Note to a Cell

1. Move the pointer to the desired cell.
2. Select the Formula-Note command.

Excel presents the dialog box shown in Figure 4.17.

3. Type the note in the space provided. To move to a new line, use Option-Return to move the cursor down. If you make mistakes while typing, use the Backspace key to correct them. Also, you may use the editing commands listed in Table 4.1.

   The text of the note will fit into the box.

4. Press Return to accept the note. □

Besides displaying the note attached to the active cell, the note dialog box lists all notes that have been added to cells in the active worksheet. These notes appear in the Notes in Sheet box. Excel shows the cell containing the note and the first line of each note to remind you of its contents.

You can edit any note by moving to the appropriate cell and selecting the Formula-Note command again. This displays the cell's note in the dialog box where you can change it. You can also select one of the notes in the Notes in Sheet listing to view the entire note, even if the pointer is not on that cell. After making changes, remember to press Return to accept them or Esc to reject them.

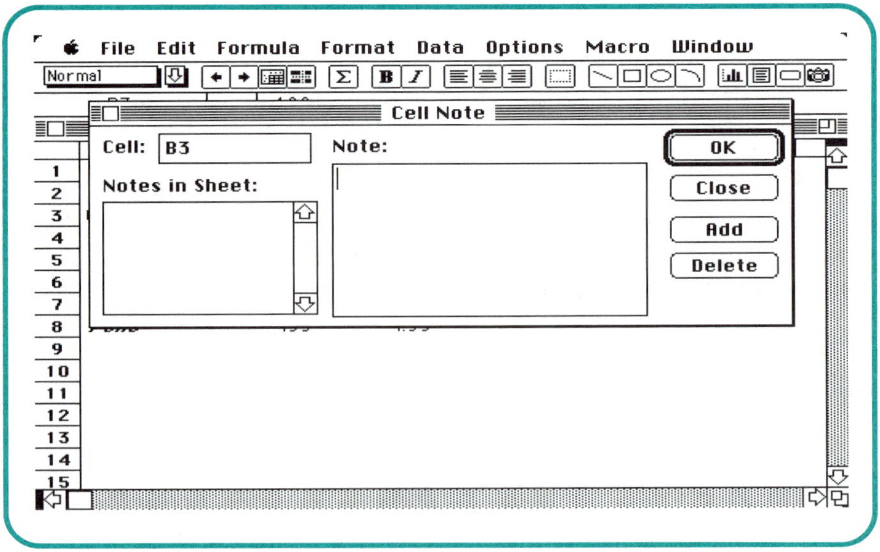

Figure 4.17 Adding a cell note.

You can display a cell's note using the Window-Show Info command. Start by moving the pointer to the desired cell. Select the Window-Show Info command. This brings up the Info display as shown in Figure 4.18.

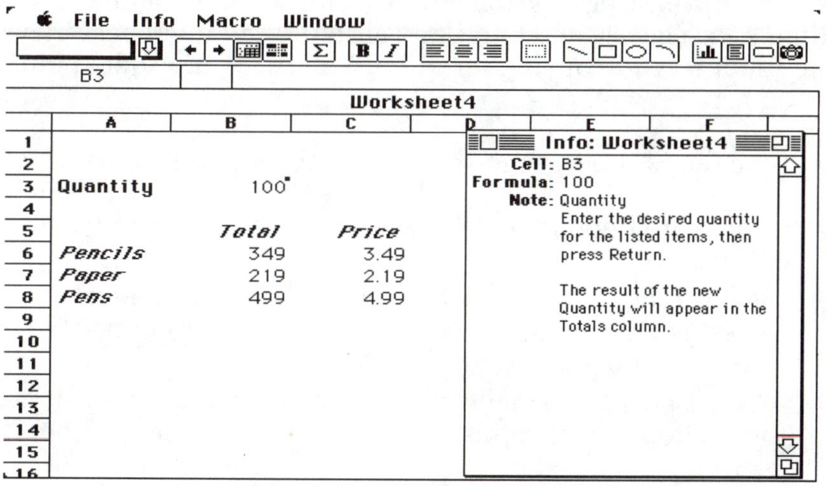

Figure 4.18 The Window-Show Info display.

This Info window shows various information about the active cell, including its note, any formula in the cell, and the cell's address. Since this display is a window and not a dialog box, you can change its size, shape, and position as you would any window.

> ▶ **Tip**: While the Info window is active, you can choose other information to display by using the commands in the Info menu.

Excel will mark each cell that contains a note, so you can easily see that a note exists when looking at the worksheet. This is done with the Options-Workspace-Note Indicator command. Cells with notes will receive a small mark in the corner. Double-clicking on a cell with that mark will activate the Info window.

What You've Learned

This chapter provided details about editing information in the worksheet using various editing commands. It also showed you how to copy, move, insert, and delete data using various commands in the Edit menu. The use of relative and absolute cell references plays an important role in copying formulas. Following are some points to remember:

- Use the Shift key with the cursor movement keys to select ranges of cells, or click and drag with the mouse. Selected ranges are highlighted and are available for various commands.
- Select a row by pressing Shift-Spacebar and a column by pressing Command-Spacebar. Select all cells at once by pressing Shift-Command-Spacebar.

- Ranges are referenced by their first and last cells, separated by a colon. These represent two opposite corners of the range, as in A1:D4.
- Use the Edit-Clear command to delete information in selected cells.
- To move data from one location to another, use the Cut and Paste commands.
- Click in the formula bar to edit the contents of a cell. Then use the various editing commands.
- When copying a formula, cell references contained in that formula will be copied relative to their new locations.
- You can copy data with the Edit-Copy command, the Edit-Fill Down command, or the Edit-Fill Right command.
- You can prevent the relative copying of cell references by making references absolute. To make a reference absolute, add dollar signs to its column and row references, as in $A$1.
- To insert or delete rows or columns of cells, use the Edit-Insert and Edit-Delete commands after selecting the appropriate rows or columns.

- Cell notes are useful for providing detailed information about a cell's contents. To add a note, move to the desired cell and select the Formula-Note command.
- Display a cell's note using the Window-Show Info command.
- Mark all cells containing notes by using the Options-Workspace-Notes Indicator command.

Chapter 5

Enhancing the Appearance of Data

In This Chapter

- *Changing fonts, sizes, and styles*
- *Special characters*
- *Aligning data*
- *Formatting numbers, dates, and times*
- *Rounding numbers*
- *Changing the worksheet display*
- *Adding borders to cells*
- *Storing format sets*

This chapter deals with enhancements you can make to the appearance of data on the worksheet. You can manipulate fonts, alter the color of data on-screen, and make various other formatting changes. Here you can learn about many of Excel's formatting options to make your worksheets more attractive and readable. You'll find many of these features useful for all your worksheets.

Changing Fonts, Sizes, and Styles

A font is a style of type such as boldface or italic in a particular typeface and size. Excel uses any installed fonts in your system, and you can switch between them at any time. Figure 5.1 shows some typefaces.

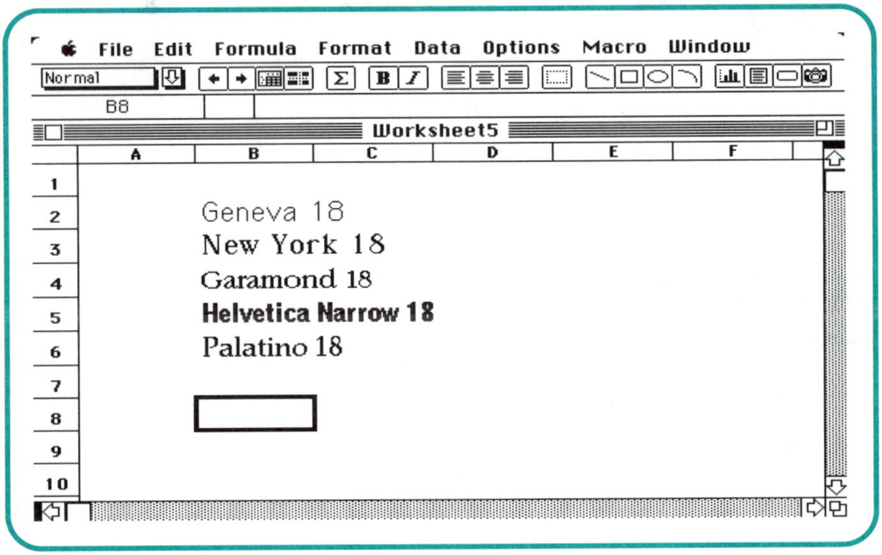

Figure 5.1 Excel's built-in fonts.

Typefaces can be displayed at various sizes and in various styles. Styles include boldface, italic, underline, and strikeout. Fonts apply to individual cells or groups of cells. You can change a cell's font at any time. To apply a particular font to a cell or block, use the following Quick Steps.

Q Changing Fonts

1. Highlight the cell or range you want to format.
2. Select the Format-Font command. — The Font dialog box appears (see Figure 5.2).

3. Choose the desired font from the Font list.
   Its name appears in the Edit box below the list. Check the Printer Fonts box to add your printer's built-in fonts to the list.
4. Choose the desired size from the Size list.
   The size appears in the Edit box below the Size list.
5. Check any of the desired Style options to apply the style.
   One click applies the option (checked) and another click removes it (unchecked).
6. Choose the desired color from the Color list.
   The chosen color appears in the Color list.
7. Click the OK button or press Return.

□

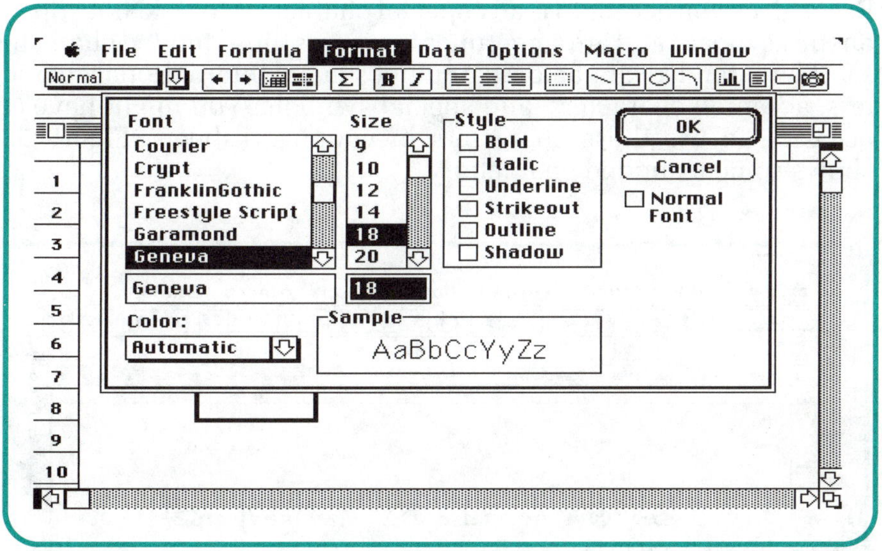

Figure 5.2 The Fonts dialog box.

After you click OK, the font, size, style, and color you selected will be applied to the highlighted range.

Note that all worksheet data begins in the default font, which is Geneva 10 point. This is a good font for most of the data in your worksheets. However, you can change this font at any time.

Bold & Italic Buttons

Because boldface and italic print are so common, Excel offers a quick and easy way to apply these styles to your worksheet data. Simply click on the appropriate button on the Toolbar at the top of the screen. The highlighted cells will immediately be formatted with bold and/or italic. To turn these styles off, highlight the cells and click on the buttons again.

Using Special Characters

Excel gives you access to many special characters that do not appear on the keyboard and are sometimes known as the extended character set. The extended character set includes many international characters, accented characters, and special symbols. You might have an occasion to use these characters in your worksheets. Figure 5.3 shows some extended characters.

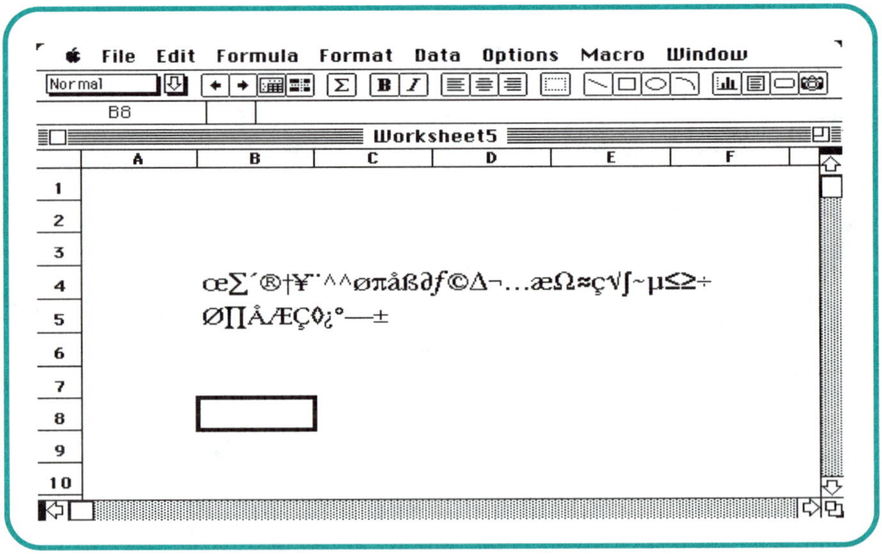

Figure 5.3 Some special characters.

Each font has its own extended characters, but many fonts have similar ones. Usually, you can access these characters by pressing the Option key as you type another letter. The Option-Shift combination creates even more extended characters.

Aligning Information in a Cell

When entered into a cell, numbers and dates automatically align with the right side of the cell. Similarly, text aligns itself with the left side of the cell. While these alignments suit most needs, you can change the alignment of information at any time. Simply highlight the cells you want to align; then click on the desired alignment button in the Toolbar. Alternatively, you can highlight the desired cells and then use the Format-Alignment command as described in the following Quick Steps.

Q Aligning Cells with Format-Alignment

1. Select the cell or cells that contain the data you want to align.
2. Select the Format-Alignment command. — The Alignment dialog box shown in Figure 5.4 appears.
3. Choose the desired alignment from the list and press Return to make the change. — The selected data conforms to the alignment you choose. □

Following are explanations of the various alignment options:

General	Aligns numbers and dates with the right side of the cell and text with the left side.
Left	Aligns selected data with the left side of the cell.
Center	Centers data within the cell.
Right	Aligns data with the right side of the cell.
Fill	Repeats the data to fill the entire width of the cell.

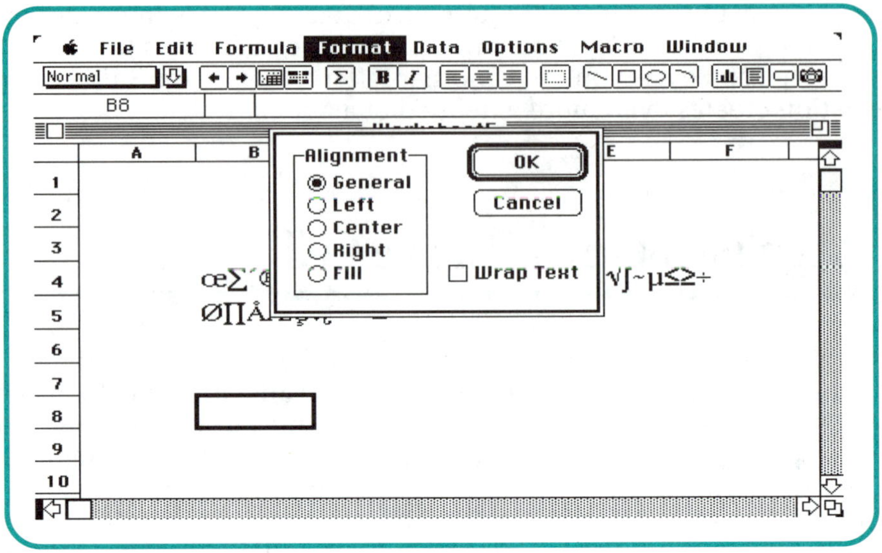

Figure 5.4 Alignment options.

Remember that the current cell widths affect alignment. The wider the cell, the more dramatic any alignment selections will appear.

You can remove the alignment you've added to a cell or range by changing it back to the General alignment setting. Alternatively, you can use the Edit-Clear command and choose the Formats option from the Clear dialog box. This clears only the alignment, fonts, and other formatting attached to the cell.

When you copy or move aligned data, the alignment is copied or moved along with the rest of the data. You can prevent copying alignment by using the Edit-Paste Special option with the Formulas or Values option to paste the data into the new location.

Number Formats

In Chapter 3 you saw how number entries can begin with or include special characters, such as $ % – and (. Some of these symbols actually change the format of the value you enter, although they don't change the value itself. Table 5.1 shows some examples:

Table 5.1 Symbols Affecting Number Formats

You type	Excel displays	Actual value in cell
5.999	5.999	5.999
$5.999	$6.00	5.999
–$5.999	($6.00)	–5.999
(5.999)	–5.999	–5.999
5%	5%	0.05
5 1/2	5 1/2	5.5

As you can see from the table, entering a dollar sign along with a value adds the dollar symbol, rounding to two decimal places and displaying negative numbers in parentheses. This is a traditional dollar-value format. When you add a percent sign to the end of the value, Excel displays the value as a percentage and converts the percentage value to a decimal equivalent. The decimal equivalent of 5% is .05. You can enter fractions by typing a "/" symbol, but be sure to include fractions only after entering an integer, as in 5 1/3. Type a zero if no integer value is needed, as in 0 1/3. Be sure to include a space after the integer.

But dollar values and percentages are not the only formats you can use for numbers. They are simply the ones you can control *as you type the value*. You can set the format of any existing values on the worksheet using Excel's Format-Number command as the following Quick Steps describe.

Formatting Values with Format-Number

1. Select the cell or range that contains the data you want to format.	
2. Select the Format-Number command.	Excel presents a list of formats available for your data, as shown in Figure 5.5.
3. Choose a format from the list and press Return.	The selected data conforms to the chosen format. ☐

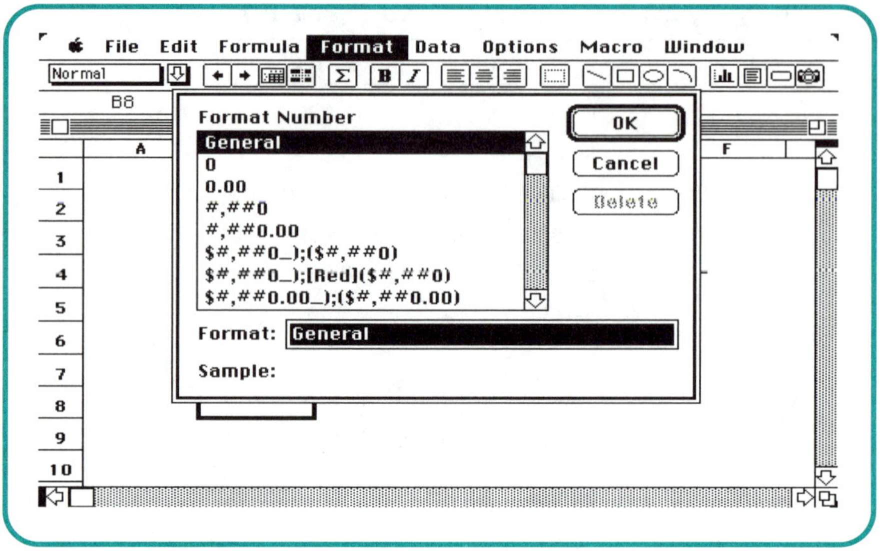

Figure 5.5 Excel's number formats.

The items in Figure 5.5 look pretty obscure, don't they? Without some background it's difficult to tell what each of these formats does. The list contains three groups of formats: for numbers, for dates, and for times. For example, look at the number formats in this list (the other formats will be covered later). Table 5.2 shows the various formats listed in the Format-Number dialog box and their effect on worksheet values.

As you can see, these formats include many ways to display numeric values. Notice that a semicolon divides some of these formats into two parts: the first part for positive numbers, the second for negative numbers. Later this chapter explains how you can customize these formats to control how zero values and text values are displayed when entered into a cell.

Excel provides a shortcut method for selecting the most common formats. First, highlight the cell or range containing the data to be formatted; then press one of the following key combinations to get the format listed beside it (be sure to press Ctrl with the Shift key to get these "shifted" characters):

Ctrl-~	General
Ctrl-!	0.00
Ctrl-$	$#,##0;($#,##0)
Ctrl-%	0%
Ctrl-^	0.00E+100

Table 5.2 Excel's Number Formats

Format	Positive Display	Negative Display	Zero Display
General	3595.5	–3595.5	0
0	3596	–3596	0
0.00	3595.50	–3595.50	0.00
#,###0	3,596	–3,596	0
#.###0.00	3,595.50	–3,595.50	0.00
$#,##0;($#,##0)	$3,596	($3,596)	$0
$#,##0;[RED]($#,##0)	$3,596	($3,596)*	$0
$#,##0.00;($#,##0.00)	$3,595.50	($3,595.50)	$0.00
$#,##0.00;[RED]($#,##0.00)	$3,595.50	($3,595.50)*	$0.00
0#	359550%	–359550%	0%
0.00%	359550.00%	–359550.00%	0.00%
0.00E+l00	3.60E+l03	–3.60E+l03	0.00E+l00
# ?/?	4 5/6	–4 5/6	0
# ??/??	4 5/6	–4 5/6	0**

*Displays in red, if available

**Uses different alignment than previous format

You'll probably find the shortcuts for changing formats easiest, and the five formats selected with the shortcuts are the most commonly used of all. Hence, you can avoid using the Format-Numbers listing almost entirely.

In addition to formatting data already in the worksheet, you can preformat a block of blank cells using one of the number formats. Whenever you enter a value into one of the preformatted cells, it will automatically apply to the format you selected.

To erase a format that has been applied to a cell or range, select the cell or range and enter the Edit-Clear command. When the dialog box appears, select the Formats option and press Return. This procedure removes any formatting attached to the cells, including font formatting. To remove only number formatting, select all the cells and choose the General format.

When you copy or move cells that have been formatted, the formatting stays with the data. If you want to copy the data without the formatting, use the Edit-Paste Special command to paste the data into the new location (instead of Edit-Paste or Return). Then, select the Formulas or Values option and press Return.

Date and Time Formats

Chapter 3 described how you can enter dates in a few different ways so that Excel will accept the date and display it in a particular format. You can enter dates as shown in Table 5.3.

Table 5.3 Entering Dates

You type	Excel displays
12/1/91	12/1/91
12-1-91	12/1/91
1 Dec 91	1-Dec-91
1-Dec-91	1-Dec-91
1 December 1991	1-Dec-91
December 91	Dec-91
1 December	1-Dec
1 Dec	1-Dec
12/1	1-Dec
12-1	1-Dec

Although you should enter all dates using one of the formats in Table 5.3, you can change the way Excel displays the date if you like. First, enter the date using one of the formats shown in Table 5.3. Next, select the cell containing the date and then choose one of the date formats from the Format-Numbers listing. The date formats appear below the list of number formats. Date formats and an example of each are listed in Table 5.4.

Table 5.4 Date Formats

Format Listing	Example
m/d/yy	1/23/91
d-mmm-yy	23-Jan-91
d-mmm	23-Jan
mmm-yy	Jan-91

As you can see, each of the date formats in Table 5.4 can be achieved when you enter the date in the first place. Just choose the associated entry format. However, it's nice to know that you can change any date at any time.

Like dates, times can be entered into Excel using one of several entry methods. Table 5.5 shows the time formats you can use.

Table 5.5 Entering Times

You type	Excel displays
15:35	15:35
4:35	4:35
4:35:15	4:35:15
4:35 pm	4:35 PM
4:35:15 am	4:35:15 AM

Excel assumes the 24-hour time format unless you enter the `am` or `pm` designation. Like date formats, time formats are most easily achieved by entering the time in the correct way. However, you can change the format of a time by highlighting the desired cell and using the Format-Time listing. The time formats are listed in Table 5.6.

Table 5.6 Time Formats

Format Listing	Example
h:mm AM/PM	9:35 PM
h:mm:ss AM/PM	9:35:15 PM
h:mm	21:35
h:mm:ss	21:35:15

Hiding Values of Zero

Worksheets often have zeros all over the place as the result of calculations or unentered information. Formulas often display a zero when referenced cells are blank. These zeros can make a worksheet look confusing and cluttered. Figure 5.6 shows a worksheet with several columns where data has not been entered. (This is just a modified version of the previous example.) Therefore, the cells with the formulas that total the empty columns produce zeros. In such a case, you might want to suppress the zeros.

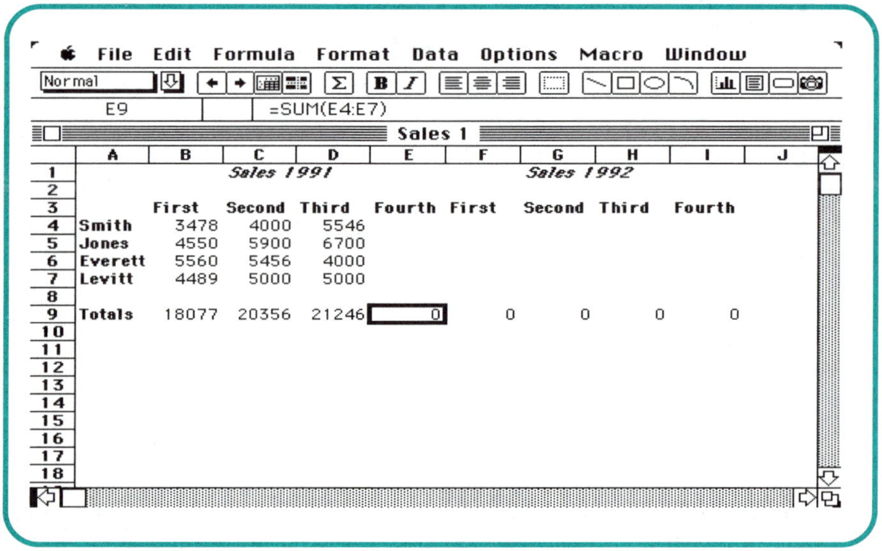

Figure 5.6 Example of formulas that produce unwanted values of zero.

You can make all values of zero appear as blank cells by using the Options-Display command. After selecting this command, the dialog box in Figure 5.7 appears. You have several choices at this point. This time, select the Zero Values option. (Other options in the Options-Display dialog box are discussed later in this chapter.) Press Z to remove the check mark from the option, causing the zero values to display as blanks on the worksheet.

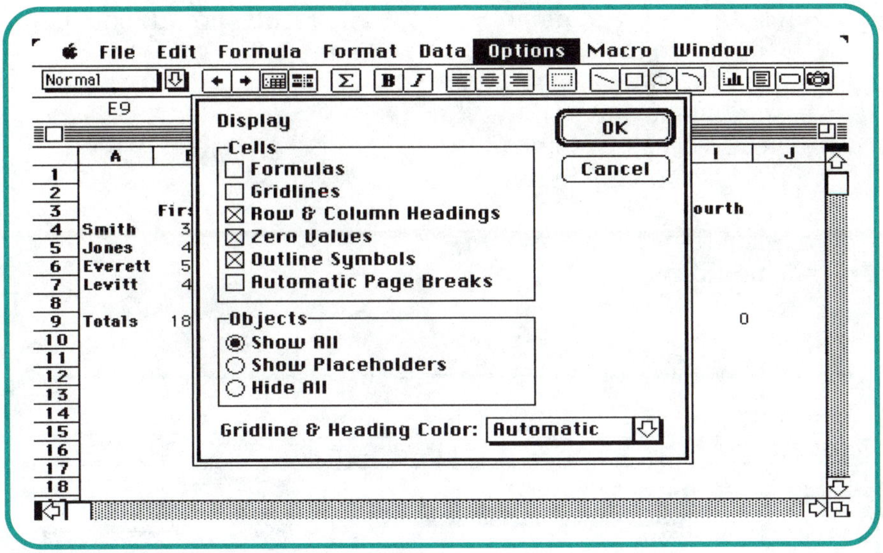

Figure 5.7 The Options-Display dialog box.

The result is that all zeros contained in this worksheet are invisible. Making all zero values invisible can clean up the appearance of the worksheet for printouts and display purposes. However, you might find the need to suppress only some of the zero values in a worksheet, leaving others alone. In this case, you can use a special formatting technique to affect only selected cells. The following Quick Steps explain this process.

Q Suppressing Zeros in Specific Cells

1. Select the cell or range that you want to change.
2. Select the Format-Numbers command.
   The Format-Numbers dialog box appears.
3. Press the Tab key to highlight the Format entry box at the bottom of the dialog box.
   Excel highlights the format currently applied to the selected cells. Unless you've changed it, this will be the General format. The screen should look like Figure 5.8.

4. Press the → key to move the cursor to the end of the entry. Now type `;-GENERAL;`, assuming the entry shows the General format. If some other format is showing in the dialog box, see the explanation that follows for the modification you need to make.

The result should look like Figure 5.9.

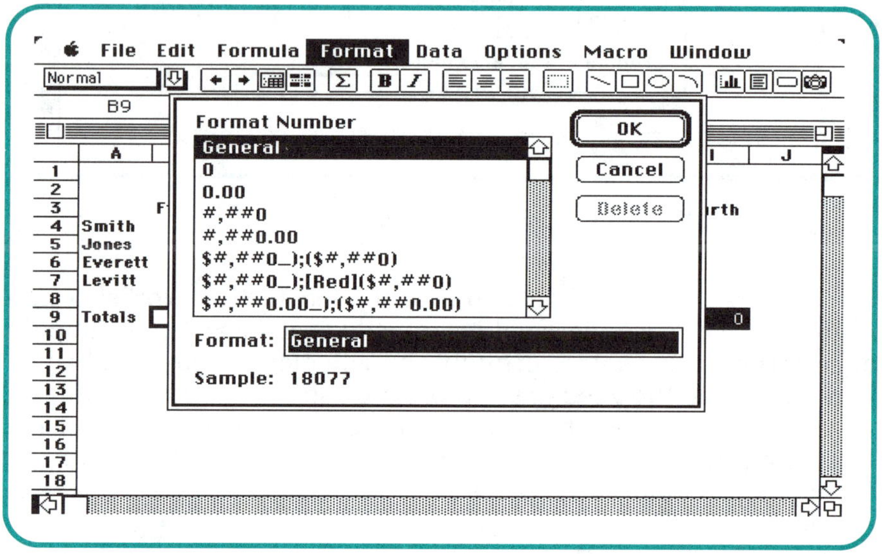

Figure 5.8 Ready to change the current format in the Format-Numbers dialog box.

In the preceding Quick Steps, you actually modified the General number format so that it displays zeros differently than other values (in this case, it doesn't display them at all). Number formats are divided into parts that are separated by semicolons. If a format has only one part (no semicolons), it applies to all values. If a format has two parts (one semicolon), the first part applies to positive values and zeros, and the second part applies to negative values. If the format has three parts (two semicolons), the first part applies to positive values, the second part to negative values, and the third part to zero values. In these steps, you've added two parts to the General format: a negative version of the General format and a blank version (nothing following the second semicolon).

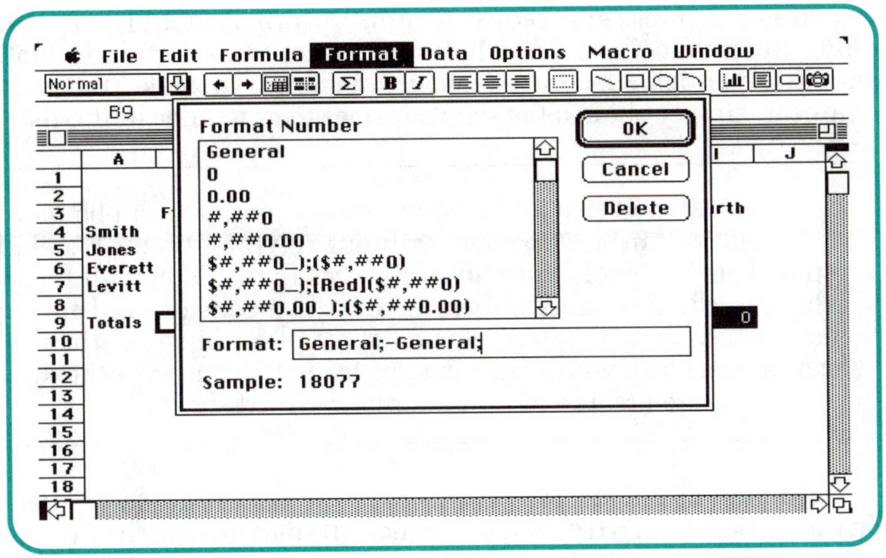

Figure 5.9 Modifying the General format so that it suppresses zeros.

You can modify any of the existing number formats in this way. Some of the formats already have two parts, in which case you need only add the third. Remember that semicolons divide the format into parts.

Making Data Invisible and Other Custom Formats

Modifying number formats can be useful for making them suppress zeros. However, you might be interested in creating some completely original number formats for special purposes. One example is to create a format that makes all values invisible to hide information on a worksheet.

Perhaps a worksheet contains entries that are confidential but needed for making calculations. You can hide the values from view without removing them from the worksheet using the ;;; number format. Just select the desired data, choose the Format-Numbers command, press the Tab key to highlight the entry area, and type the format as ;;; (three semicolons). The entire format should consist of only three semicolons. Press Return to accept the custom format, and the highlighted data becomes invisible. To make the data reappear, simply change the data's format to any other in the list.

> **Tip**: All modified and custom number formats can be re-used within a worksheet without retyping them. Excel remembers all special formats and stores them along with the others in the Format-Numbers listing. Your customized formats appear at the bottom of the list, so you can select them again and again. If you create a custom format for one worksheet, you have to re-create the format on other worksheets.

Another useful format controls the way phone numbers appear on the worksheet. To try this out, enter a 10-digit number in any cell of the worksheet. Most likely, Excel will convert the number to scientific notation because it's so large. Next, select the Format-Numbers command, press the Tab key, and then type the format as follows: `(###)###-####`. Then press Return. You might have to expand the column width to see the result. Try formatting 9-digit numbers into Social Security numbers with the format `###-##-####`.

Changing the Color of Data

As a final formatting technique, examine how to change the color of specific data in the worksheet by customizing an existing format. (Of course, you'll need a color computer system to benefit from this modification.)

To change the color of data, simply type one of the following color codes at the beginning of each section of the desired number format: `[black]`, `[white]`, `[red]`, `[green]`, `[blue]`, `[yellow]`, `[magenta]`, `[cyan]`. For example, to modify the general format so that all values appear in blue, type

```
[blue]General
```

If the format contains two or three parts, enter the color code in front of each part, as in

```
[blue]General;[blue]-General;
```

You can add these color codes to any new or existing format using the procedures described in the previous sections. To change the color of a text entry, you must enter one of the custom formats listed in Table 5.7. (Of course, you can change the color code used in Figure 5.6.)

Table 5.7 Entering custom formats with color.

You type	Excel displays
General;–General;General;[blue]	Displays numbers in the General format and text in blue
;;;[blue]	Makes all numeric entries invisible and text entries blue
General;–General;;[blue]	Displays positive and negative numbers in the general format, zeros invisible, and text blue
[blue]General;[blue]–General; [blue]General;[blue]	Displays everything in blue

Another way to change colors of data is to use the Format-Font command and select a color in the Color list. This procedure is described earlier in this chapter.

Rounding Numbers

Though Excel can store up to 15 decimal places for a value, many of Excel's built-in number formats round numbers to two decimal places. For example, if you enter the value $45.899 into a cell, Excel displays $45.90. Excel uses a dollar format to display the value with two decimal places and a dollar sign. Remember that the value in the cell has not been changed. The value is merely displayed to look like it has been changed. The cell's actual value is still 45.899, and any references to this cell's value will receive the value 45.899. In short, formatted values are not rounded at all; they only appear to be rounded.

All of Excel's number formats use either two or no decimal places. The exception is the General format, which uses as many places as needed for a value. For example, the two percentage formats are 0% and 0.00%. The first percentage format displays the number with no decimal places and the second displays with two. If you wanted to display percentages with one decimal place, you would have to modify one of the percentage formats. Using the format modification procedures described earlier, you would change one of these formats to read 0.0%. Likewise, you can modify formats to display as many decimal places as you like. If a format has several parts, remember to modify each part.

But if number formats merely display numbers as if they were rounded without really rounding, how do you round numbers so that their values are changed? Well, there are two ways. One way is to tell Excel to round numbers to the values that are displayed. In other words, you can make the number match the display. The value changes for all numbers in the worksheet at one time.

First, use number formats throughout the worksheet to make the numbers appear as you would like them. Then, use the Options-Calculation command and, at the dialog box that appears, press P to check the Precision as Displayed option. Press Return when finished. Excel warns that your data will *permanently* lose its accuracy before changing the values. If you give the go-ahead, all values throughout the worksheet are changed permanently to match their displayed values.

The second way to round a value does not operate on the entire worksheet at one time. Instead, you can use this method to round a single value in the worksheet. Simply enter the ROUND function into the cell by typing

```
=ROUND(value,places)
```

In place of the word *value* in the example above, enter whichever value you want rounded. In place of the word *places*, enter the number of decimal places to which you want the number rounded. To round the value 34.899 to two places, enter

```
=ROUND(34.899,2)
```

To round a value produced by a formula, enter the entire formula (without the equal sign) in place of the value. For example, cell A12 might contain the formula `=SUM(A1:A10)`, which produces the value 45.899. To round this value to two places, edit cell A12 and enter

```
=ROUND(SUM(A1:A10),2)
```

Notice that the entire formula without the equal sign is entered in the *value* position. The equal sign is not needed because formulas require them only at the beginning. For more information about the ROUND function and other functions, see Appendix B.

Changing the Worksheet Display

Excel offers several ways to change the overall worksheet display. You might find these changes make your worksheets more attractive. The changes can be made to any worksheet you like without affecting others. One of the most common changes is to remove the gridlines that bound the cells. Your worksheets often can look cleaner without the grids. Another change is to remove the row and column headings that appear at the top and left side of the worksheet. When you are creating a worksheet, these headings are useful for referencing cells. However, if you have finished constructing a worksheet's formulas, you may be able to do without headings. Worksheet display changes are fairly simple and straightforward. First, choose the Options-Display command to reveal the dialog box shown in Figure 5.10.

Now click on the Gridlines or Headings options to remove those elements. Press Return when finished. Figure 5.11 shows a worksheet with these elements removed. To replace these elements, repeat the process.

Note that you can also change the color of the headings and gridlines using the Gridline & Heading Color list in the dialog box.

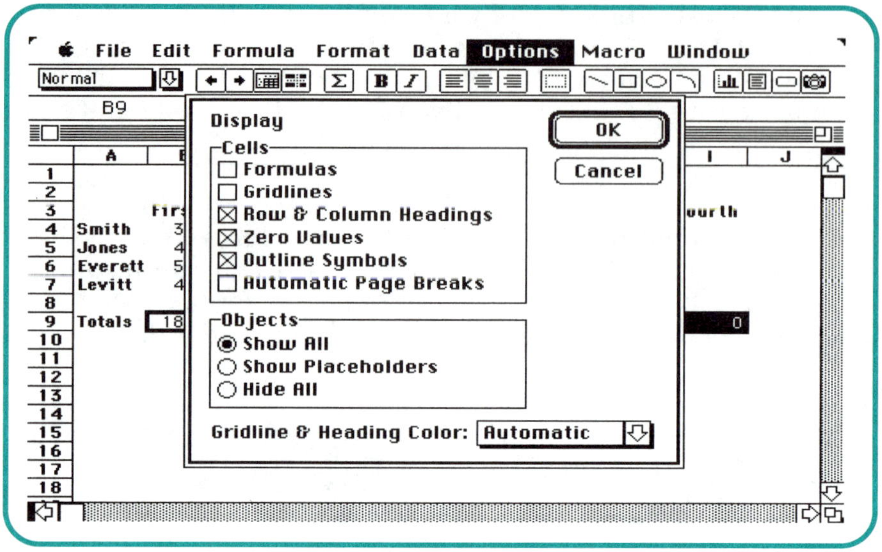

Figure 5.10 The Options-Display dialog box.

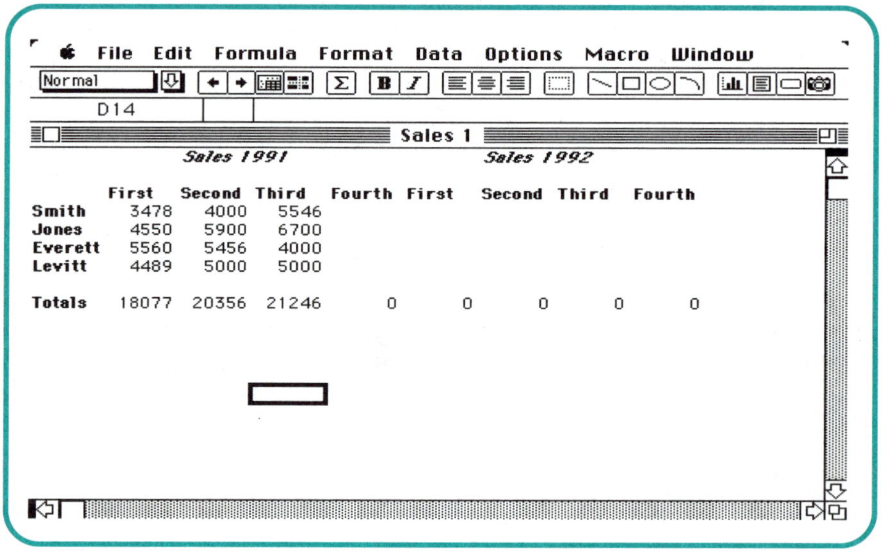

Figure 5.11 A worksheet with no headings or gridlines.

Adding Borders to Cells

One of the best ways to enhance the appearance of a worksheet is to add borders to the data on the worksheet. Using the Format-Borders command, you can add boxes around cells and ranges, and you can add emphasis lines anywhere on the sheet. Figure 5.12 shows a worksheet with various border lines added.

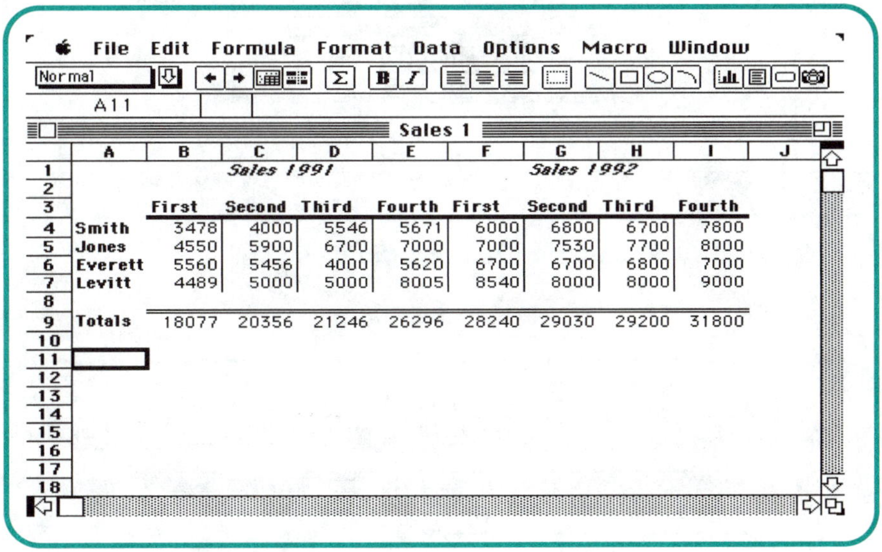

	A	B	C	D	E	F	G	H	I	J
1			Sales 1991				Sales 1992			
2										
3		First	Second	Third	Fourth	First	Second	Third	Fourth	
4	Smith	3478	4000	5546	5671	6000	6800	6700	7800	
5	Jones	4550	5900	6700	7000	7000	7530	7700	8000	
6	Everett	5560	5456	4000	5620	6700	6700	6800	7000	
7	Levitt	4489	5000	5000	8005	8540	8000	8000	9000	
8										
9	Totals	18077	20356	21246	26296	28240	29030	29200	31800	

Figure 5.12 An example worksheet with borders added.

To add borders to the worksheet, simply highlight the desired cell or range and then select the Format-Borders command. The dialog box in Figure 5.13 appears.

Simply click on the desired position and then on the desired line type. You can select a different line type for each side of the cell if desired.

Choose any number of options from the Format-Borders dialog box to add borders to the selected range. Choosing Left adds a border to the left side, choosing Outline adds a border to all sides, and so on. You can combine any number of these options for various results. The Shade option adds shading to the selected range. Figure 5.14 shows the various ways you can add borders.

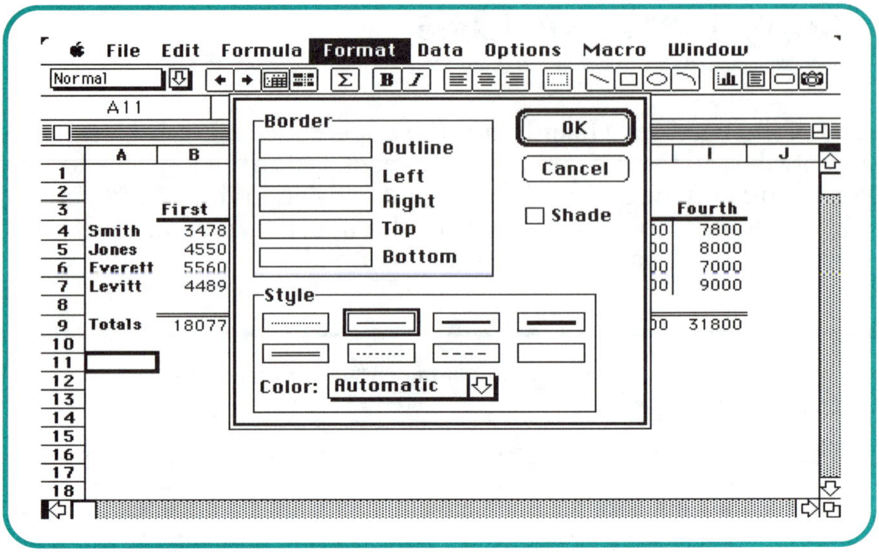

Figure 5.13 The Format-Borders dialog box.

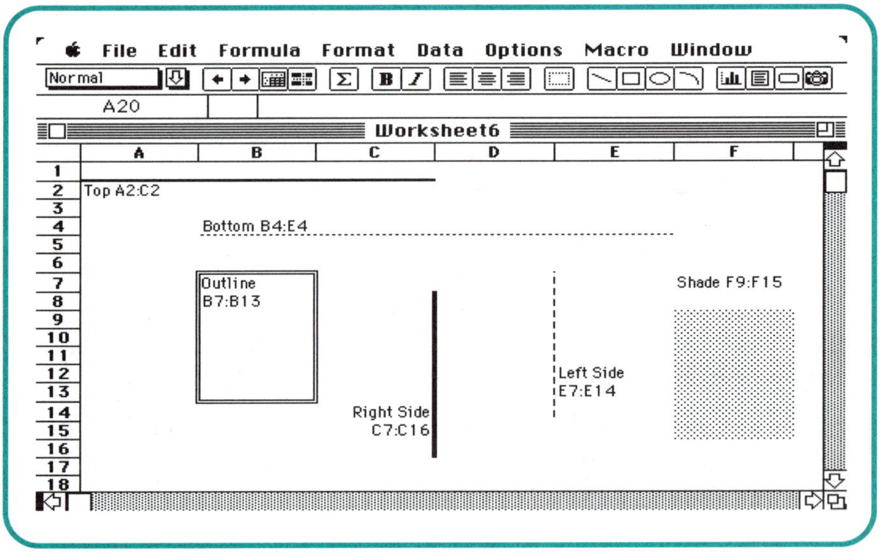

Figure 5.14 Various border additions.

You can combine border options with row height and column width options to get various effects. Experiment on your worksheets for best results.

Saving Format Sets

If you find yourself using the same set of formats on several cells, you will like Excel's custom styles feature. Using the Format-Styles command, you can save formatting options in sets, give those sets special names, and then re-apply the entire set of formats by selecting the name. Any combination of formatting options you use can be stored as a style. The following Quick Steps show how.

Q Saving Format Sets

1. Apply the desired formats using the options at the top of the Format menu.	This will apply the formats to the highlighted cell or range.
2. Select the Format-Style command.	The dialog box shown in Figure 5.15 will appear.
3. Enter a name for the combination of formats you've established. These formats are shown at the bottom of the dialog box. Press Return when finished.	The name will now appear in the Styles list on the Toolbar.
4. To use a pre-saved set of formats, choose the desired name from the Style list in the Toolbar. Using the keyboard, you can choose the style by using the Format-Style command and selecting the name from the dialog box's list.	All styles saved under the selected name will apply to the currently highlighted range.

□

Style sets are stored with individual worksheets. So, when you save the worksheet, the styles will be saved with it. Each worksheet can have its own set of named styles.

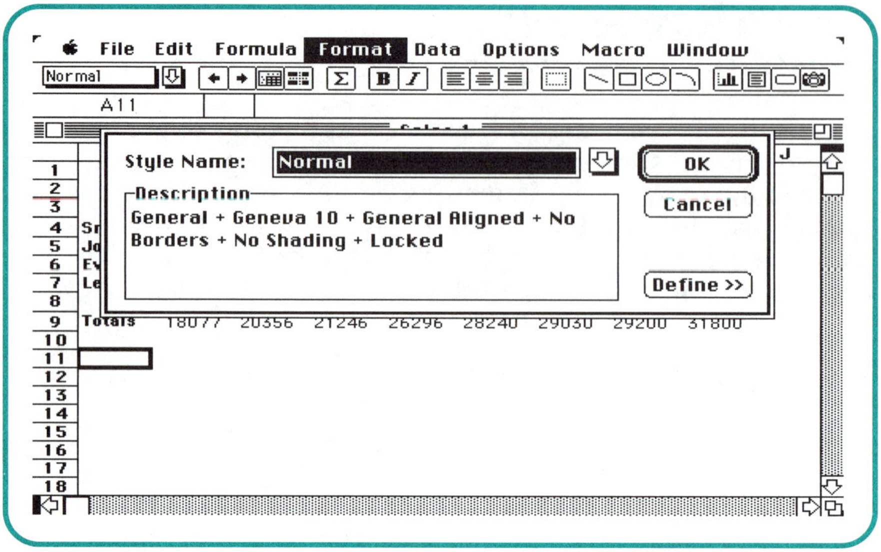

Figure 5.15 The Format-Styles dialog box.

What You've Learned

This chapter provided details about Excel's worksheet formatting commands. These commands let you enhance the appearance of data on the sheet by changing type fonts and styles. Various options in the Format menu provide these enhancements. The Options menu also contains commands for data formatting. Following are some of the formatting options to remember:

- You can choose a font using the Format-Font command.
- You can select a font's color using Format-Font.
- Align information in a cell with the Format-Alignment command or the alignment buttons.
- Excel's number formats are accessible from the Format-Numbers listing.
- Some formats appear to round numbers, but they just display rounded numbers without rounding the value of the data.

- You can hide zero values using a modified number format or the Options-Display command.
- You can make data invisible using the custom format ;;; in the Format-Numbers dialog box.
- Use the ROUND function to permanently round numbers off. Alternatively, use the Options-Calculation command with the Precision as Displayed option to round numbers throughout the worksheet.
- To remove the gridlines that appear on the worksheet or the column and row headings, use the Options-Display command.
- Use the Format-Borders command to add borders, lines, and boxes to various areas of the worksheet. This command will also provide shading for selected areas and let you choose a border color.

Chapter 6

Drawing

In This Chapter

- *Using graphics in Excel*
- *Drawing objects*
- *Editing object patterns*
- *Using text boxes*
- *Using outside artwork*

There's an artist in everyone. Excel's new graphics features may bring out the artist in you. In this chapter you will learn how to use Excel's drawing tools to create simple illustrations on your worksheet. You also can use these features to annotate your graphs and worksheet data. This chapter will show you how, using the mouse, you can draw four different types of objects: Lines, Ovals, Rectangles, and Arcs. You'll also discover how to edit these basic objects by changing their patterns, outlines, shapes, and positions. Finally, you'll learn how to bring in graphics from external programs and add them to your worksheets.

Graphics in Excel

So maybe you're not an artist, but you will still find Excel's new graphics features easy to use and useful for your worksheets and graphs. You've seen how Excel lets you paste a graph onto the worksheet when you copy it from a graph sheet. In addition, Excel lets you draw right onto the worksheet by using several drawing tools. These tools create graphic objects which you can combine to create pictures and annotative elements on the worksheet. Figure 6.1 shows an example of some graphic objects on a worksheet.

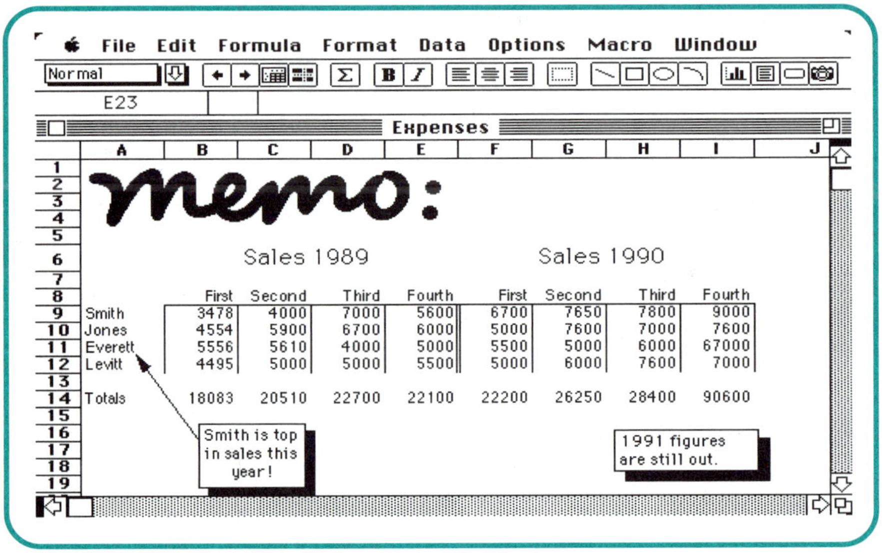

Figure 6.1 Some drawings on a worksheet.

These simple graphic objects reside "above" the data on the worksheet so that they "overlap" the data. In other words, drawings are made on an invisible "layer" that is above the worksheet layer. Because of this, drawings always cover up worksheet data below (unless you create transparent objects as described later). As shown in the figure, you also can copy outside illustrations into Excel, such as those created with the MacPaint program. Now, take a look at the basic steps to drawing in Excel.

Using the Drawing Tools

Excel offers four drawing tools and a few extra tools for manipulating your objects. These are located on the Toolbar. Figure 6.2 shows the Toolbar and the drawing tools covered in this chapter.

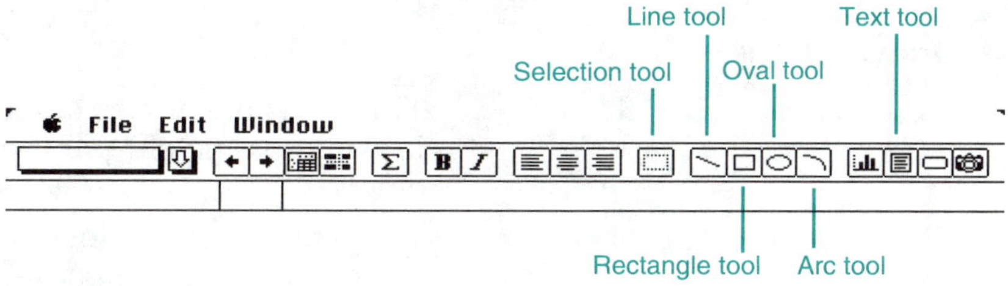

Figure 6.2 The Toolbar and its drawing tools.

Line Tool—Use this tool to draw lines, dotted lines, and arrows. Click on the tool, then click and drag on the worksheet to create the line.

Rectangle Tool—Use this tool to draw rectangles on the worksheet. Click on the tool, then click and drag on the worksheet. Your initial click determines one of the corners of the rectangle.

Oval Tool—Use this tool to create circles and ovals. Draw this object as you would a rectangle.

Arc Tool—Use this tool to create curved lines and arcs. The arc is drawn across two points as a quarter-oval. The relative distance between your click and release points determines the size and shape of the arc.

Text Tool—Use this tool to place a text box onto the worksheet. Draw this box as you would a rectangle. Then you can type any text into this box and format it with various fonts and styles.

Selection Tool—Use this tool to select, or highlight, an object or group of objects so that you can move or edit them.

Lines, Rectangles, Ovals, and Arcs

Drawing these four objects requires the same basic movement of the mouse. First, you select the object tool; then you click and draw on the worksheet to create the object. The position of your "click" point and your "release" point (after dragging) create the object. Following are the Quick Steps.

Q Drawing Objects

1. Select the desired tool from the Toolbar. — This turns the mouse pointer into a "cross hatch" pointing device.
2. Click onto the worksheet and hold the mouse button down. — This sets the first point of the object—often the upper-left corner.
3. Drag the mouse to another location, such as down and to the right. — The object will appear between the two points.
4. Release the mouse.

> **Tip**: If you hold the Shift key down while you draw an object, it will be drawn to specific restrictions. Lines will be drawn only vertically, horizontally, or at a 45-degree angle; ovals will be drawn as perfect circles; rectangles will be drawn as perfect squares; and arcs will be perfect quarter circles.

Text Box

You create text boxes just like you create rectangles, but these boxes have a special quality. They can contain text. After you create the text box, the cursor will be blinking inside. You can now begin typing text as shown in Figure 6.3.

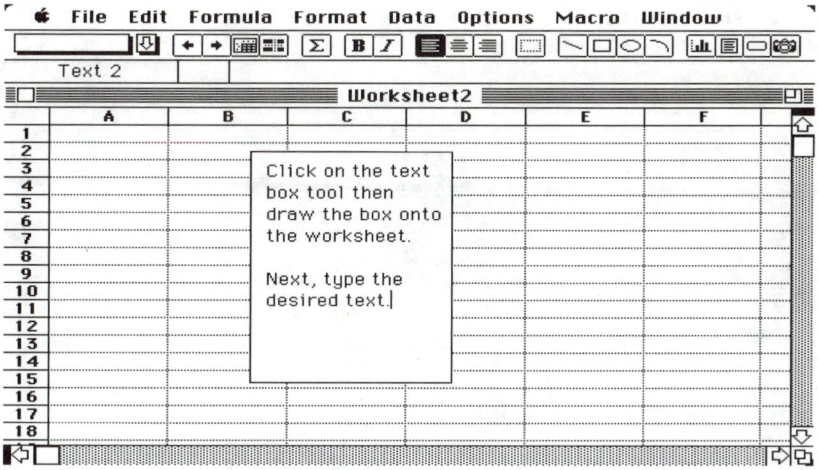

Figure 6.3 Placing the cursor in a text box.

Selecting Objects

Before you can move or edit an object, you must select it. That's what the Selection Tool does. Just click on the tool, and then click and drag on the worksheet to draw a rectangle that surrounds the desired object(s). Figure 6.4 shows an example.

When you release the mouse button, the object(s) inside the selection rectangle will be highlighted. You can confirm this by spotting the selection markers that appear on the edges of the object(s). After you select an object, you then can move it, copy it, or edit it.

> ▶ **Tip**: You also can select objects by simply clicking on them while the mouse pointer is an arrow. To select several objects this way, simply hold the Shift key down while you click on all the desired objects.

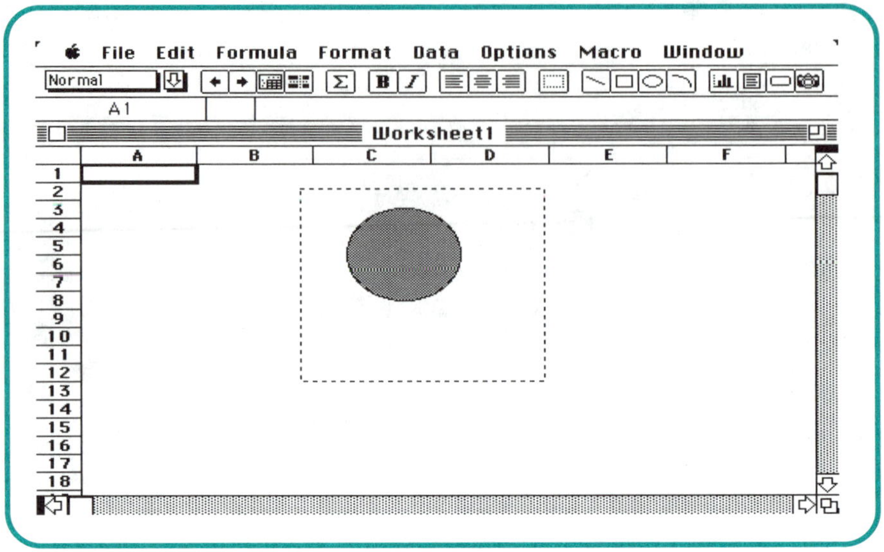

Figure 6.4 Surrounding an object with the selection rectangle.

Moving and Sizing Objects

To move an object, you must first select it as described previously. Then you can move the mouse to the border of the object until you see the familiar mouse arrow appear. Now click and drag the object to any location you like.

If you click directly on a selection marker (little squares) that appears on the border of the object, then you can manipulate the size and shape of the object. Just click on the marker and drag it to another location to change its position; the object will adjust. Figure 6.5 shows an example of the object from Figure 6.4 in its new shape.

Objects are normally "attached" to the worksheet cells that they cover. This means that when you adjust the width of a column or row containing a graphic object, the object will change its size and shape to reflect the cell change. This change is usually good, since many graphics are drawn on the worksheet to correspond to specific cells. However, if you want to detach objects from their underlying cells, select the object and use the Format-Object Placement command. Next, choose the Don't Move or Size with Cells option.

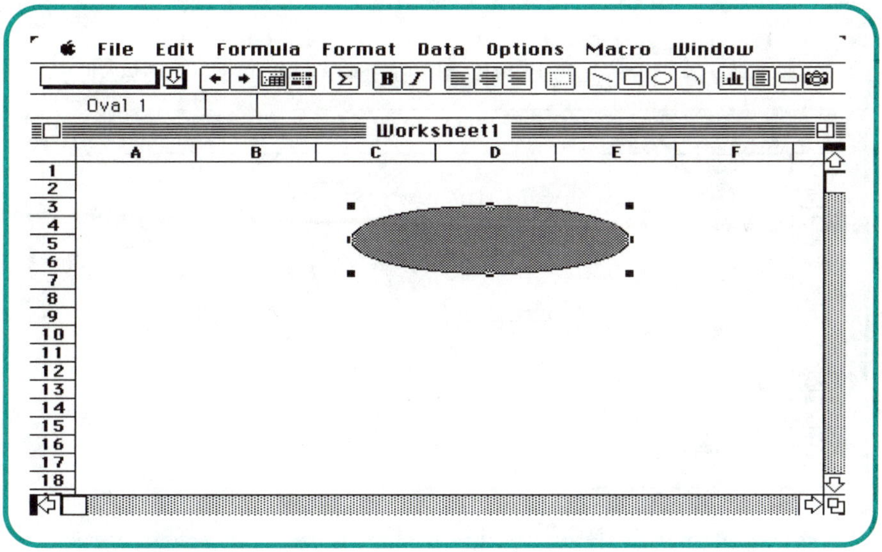

Figure 6.5 Changing the size and shape of an object.

Overlapping, Deleting, and Grouping Objects

Objects overlap each other. When you draw an object in the same general location of another, the new object will cover up the previously drawn object. You can use this capability to strategically create special effects—but you may need to change the overlapping order of objects if you don't happen to draw them in correct sequence. Figure 6.6 shows some overlapped objects.

You can bring any object to the top of the others by selecting it and then choosing the Format-Bring to Front command. The Format-Send to Back command sends it to the back of the pile. Remember that objects, even when in the back, are always on top of the worksheet data.

You also can group objects so that they respond as a single object. This procedure is similar to selecting several objects at the same time, but grouping objects keeps them together as a single object until you ungroup them. You group objects by selecting them and then choosing the Format-Group command. To make the objects independent again, highlight the grouped object and select Format-Ungroup.

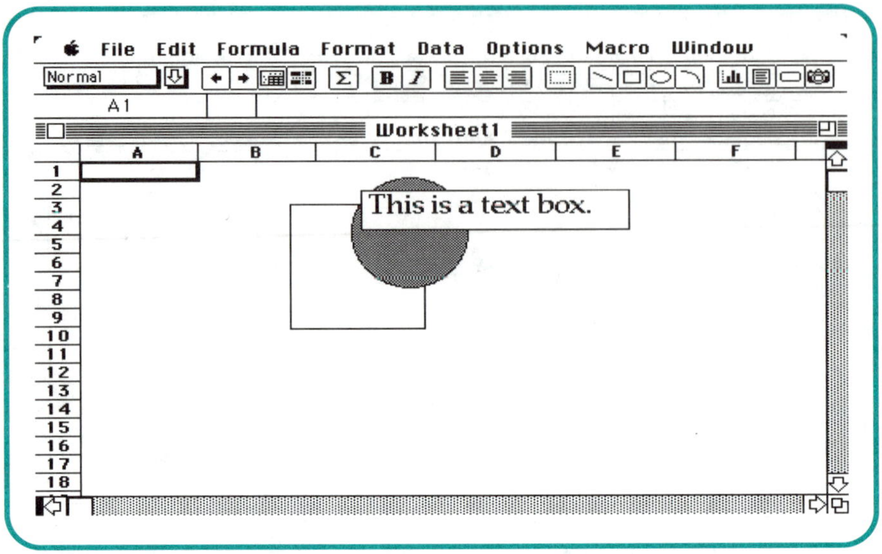

Figure 6.6 Overlapping objects.

> ▶ **Tip**: You can place grouped objects into other groups if desired. Remember that objects will be ungrouped in the same order—so objects may require several ungroup commands before they are entirely separated.

To delete an object, click on it to select it, and then press the Del key. You can delete grouped objects this way also.

Changing Patterns and Lines

You can change the pattern filling an object and the type of line that surrounds the object if you like. First, select the object and then use the Format-Patterns command. Alternatively, you can double-click on the desired object. The dialog box in Figure 6.7 appears.

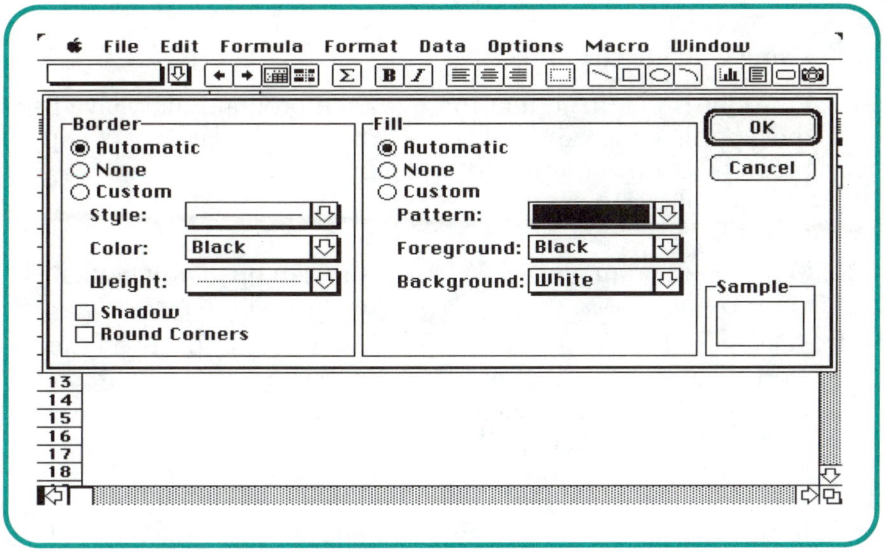

Figure 6.7 The Format-Patterns dialog box for rectangles.

Note that this dialog box will be slightly different for lines and text boxes because these objects have unique properties. Simply choose the options you want to apply and press Return. Notice that the patterns are divided into the border and the interior of the object.

When changing the patterns of lines, you can also add arrow heads to the lines to create arrows. These come in several types. You should experiment for best results. When formatting text boxes, you can select a font for the information in the box.

Using Outside Illustrations

Although Excel has its own drawing tools, you may find them lacking for creating sophisticated graphics. Or perhaps you would like to use clip art that has already been created for you. This is no problem in Excel. You can use graphics created from many different programs in your Excel worksheets, including Freehand, Super-Paint, and others. To include outside graphics, use the following steps.

Using Outside Graphics

1. Enter the program containing the graphic image and use the program's Copy command (or equivalent) to copy the image.

   Each program may have its own particular way of copying data.

2. Quit the program and enter Excel.

   You can open any worksheet or start with a new one.

3. Select a cell in the Excel worksheet indicating where you would like the image to appear, and then choose the Edit-Paste command.

   The image appears on the worksheet.

If the procedure is unsuccessful, you may have too little memory to keep the image on the clipboard while you switch programs. Figures 6.8 and 6.9 show the procedure using the Freehand program.

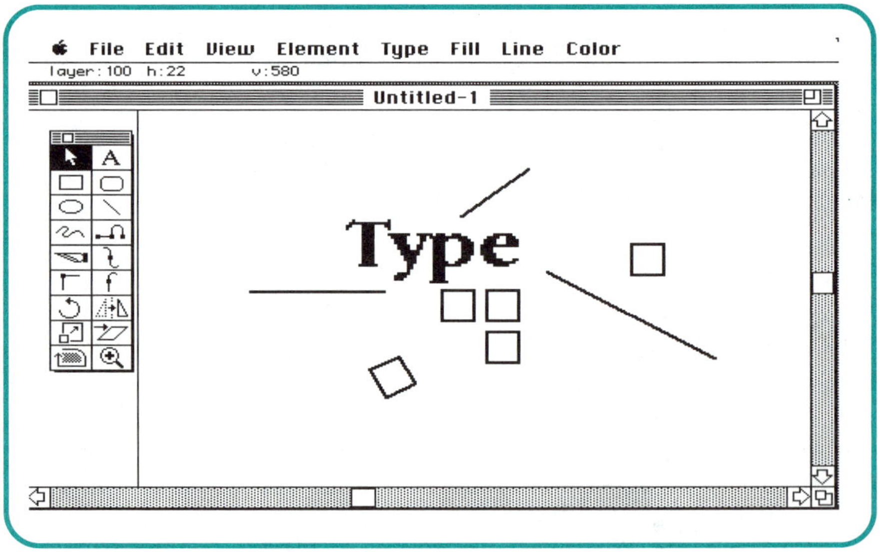

Figure 6.8 Copying an image from Freehand.

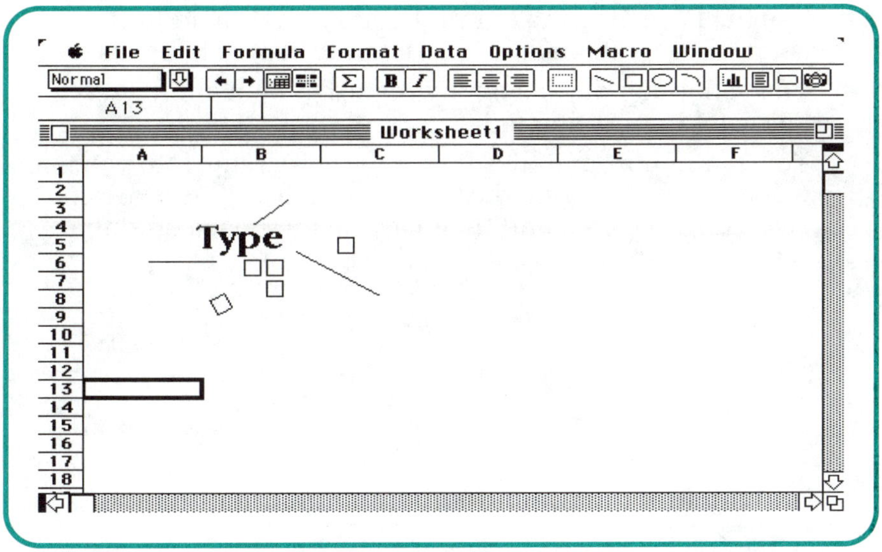

Figure 6.9 Pasting the image into Excel.

What You've Learned

This chapter provided essential instructions for using Excel's drawing tools. You learned how to draw objects on the worksheet, how to change their sizes and shapes, how to group them, overlap them, and edit them. Following are some points to remember:

- To draw an object, click on the desired object tool; then click and drag on the worksheet.
- Select an object by clicking on it or using the object selection tool.
- Select several objects by holding the Shift key down while you click on them.
- You must select an object before you can change its size, shape, position, or pattern.
- Use the Edit-Patterns command to alter an object's interior and border pattern.

- Use the Format-Bring to Front and Format-Send to Back commands to change the overlapping order of objects.
- You can group objects by highlighting them and using the Format-Group command.
- You can import graphics from other programs into your worksheet by copying the image from the other program, switching to Excel, and then pasting the image onto the active worksheet.

Chapter 7

Printing the Worksheet

In This Chapter

- *Overview of printing*
- *Adding and removing printers*
- *Changing printer connections*
- *Setting up your printer*
- *A basic printout*
- *Enhancing the printout*
- *Printing column titles*

Printing is an indispensable function for any program. In Excel, you can print your worksheets using a basic printing procedure, or you can enhance the printout using several print options. This chapter shows you how to print your worksheets using Excel's basic printing capabilities. Plus, you'll learn how to enhance the printout for special needs by adding page numbers, headers, footers, and more.

Overview of Printing

Excel's basic printing process is fairly simple. First, set up the format for your printout. Tell Excel what part of the worksheet you want to print with the Options-Set Print Area command. Add headers, footers, and page numbers, or change page margins using the File-Page Setup command. For long lists and tables, you might want to print column headings at the top of each page using the Options-Set Print Titles command. Finally, print the worksheet with the File-Print command.

This is the basic printing procedure discussed in this chapter. You might want to try out the steps listed throughout the chapter on a sample worksheet.

> **Tip**: All Macintosh applications access printers the same way. First, select the Chooser from the Apple menu and click on your printer in the Chooser's printer list. Then close the control panel. If your printer does not appear in the list, consult the printer manual for installation procedures.

Basic Printing

When you are ready to print, select the File-Print command. This command presents a dialog box of print options. These options may vary slightly, depending on your printer. Figure 7.1 shows the basic Print dialog box and its options. (The print quality is not an option in this dialog box because it is set up for a laser printer.)

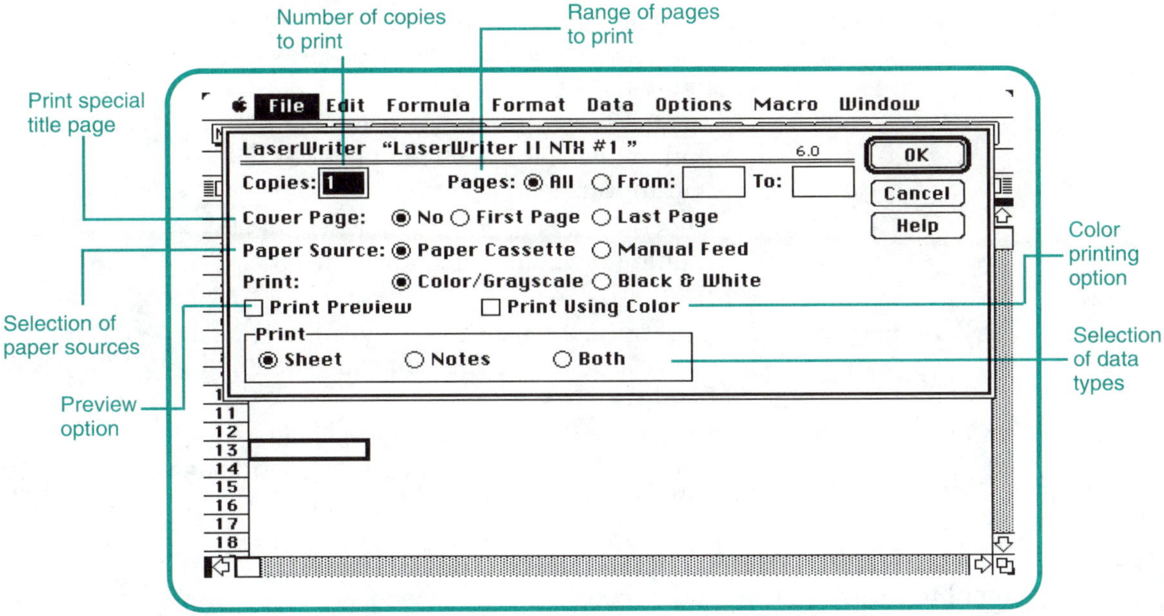

Figure 7.1 The Print dialog box.

The Print dialog box contains a few choices you can make before printing. Following is a list of these options:

Copies You can print multiple copies of each page with this option. Just enter the number of copies you would like to print in the space provided.

Pages This option lets you select the page(s) you want to print. You can specify the range or indicate that you want to print all pages.

Quality This option is available for most dot-matrix printers. It lets you print at various qualities. Draft quality provides faster performance. Draft prints the worksheet data using the printer's built-in font, which is often less attractive than other quality settings.

Cover Page This option lets you print a special title page at the beginning or end of the report. This option is available for laser printers only.

Paper Source	Available for laser printers, this option lets you feed paper from the paper tray or manually.
Paper Feed	Available for dot-matrix printers, this option lets you hand feed paper or use continuous-feed paper.
Print Using Color	This option is used for color printers to include the color selections with the printout.
Print Preview	This option causes the printout to appear on-screen so that you can examine it before printing.
Print	Select Sheet to print the worksheet, Notes to print the notes attached to the worksheet cells, or Both to print both.

After making your choices, choose OK to begin printing. Choose Cancel to return to the worksheet.

Previewing the Printout

With Excel, you can view each page prior to printing. To preview the printout, select the Preview option from the File-Print dialog box, and then press Return. The first page of the worksheet appears in a reduced image on the screen, as in Figure 7.2.

Several buttons appear at the top of the preview to give you control. If the printout consists of multiple pages, you can use the Next and Previous buttons to flip back and forth. The Close button returns you to the worksheet. The Print button begins printing to the printer directly from the Preview screen. The Zoom button enlarges the preview to its actual size so that you can examine the printout more closely. When already enlarged, the Zoom button reduces the view. You also can enlarge the preview by clicking on the area of the page that you would like to view more closely.

Use the Setup button to make your Page Setup selections. These selections are also available through the File-Page Setup command and are explained later in this chapter. Finally, the Margins button displays the page margins and tab settings on the Preview screen. You can adjust the page margins right on the Preview screen by dragging the lines to new locations.

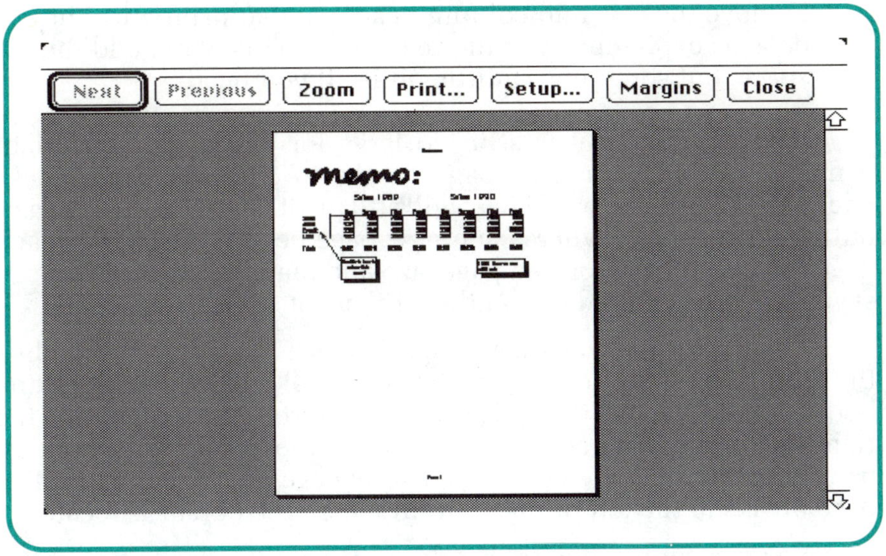

Figure 7.2 Example of the print preview feature.

Page Breaks

If your worksheet is too large to fit on one page, Excel splits the work on two or more pages. Excel makes the split based on your current page dimensions, margin settings, and cell widths. Excel always splits the worksheet at the beginning of a column (vertically) and/or row (horizontally), so the information in a cell will never be split between two pages.

If the automatic page breaks are not adequate for your worksheet, there are many ways to make adjustments:

- Change the page margins using the File-Page Setup command, as explained later in this chapter.
- Change the page orientation to Landscape to print the worksheet sideways on the paper. You can choose the Landscape orientation with the File-Page Setup command, also described later in this chapter.
- If the worksheet is too wide, decrease the widths of some cells if possible.

- Remove the row and column headings that print with the data, as explained later in the chapter. This won't add much space, but sometimes a little bit is all you need.

If your worksheet is still too large for one page, you might consider adding your own page breaks to override page breaks chosen by Excel. The worksheet will still print on two or more pages, but you can control where each new page begins. As long as each page fits into the prescribed page size and margin settings, you can set a page break anywhere on the worksheet.

There are three ways to set page breaks. First, you can establish the right-hand side of each page, letting Excel break the pages at the bottom. Simply move the cell pointer to the column designating the right side of the first page, move to the top-most cell in that column (row 1), and then choose the Options-Set Page Break command. The page breaks to the left of the column where the cursor is located.

You can continue to set breaks for the right side of all pages in the worksheet. Figure 7.3 shows an example of a page break set manually at column G and indicated by a dotted line. In the example shown in Figure 7.3, columns A through F are to the left of the manual page break and will print on one page. However, unless another page break is specified in the worksheet, all pages to the right of column G are determined by Excel.

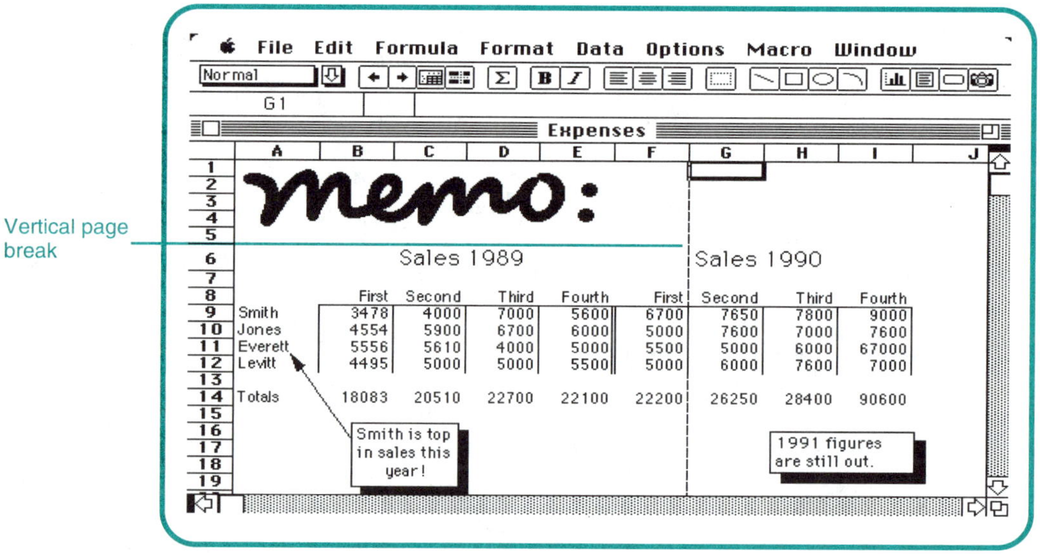

Figure 7.3 Setting a page break manually.

You also can set the bottom of a page by moving the pointer to column A of the row just below the last row you want to include in the page. For example, to break the page at row 45, place the pointer in cell A46. Next, select the Options-Set Page Break command.

Finally, you can set both the bottom and right side of a page by selecting the cell below and to the right of the bottom-right corner of the page. For example, to set the right side of a page at column G and the bottom at row 45, select cell H46. Then choose the Options-Set Page Break command. This technique affects only pages above and to the left of the cell you selected (to the left of column H and above row 46 in our example). For other areas of the worksheet, you must set additional page breaks or Excel will break the pages automatically.

Page breaks remain active until you remove them. Establishing new page breaks does not alter existing breaks; it simply adds to them. To remove a page break, reselect the column, row, or cell that was used to create the break and choose the Options-Remove Page Break command. This command appears only when the pointer is in the correct cell, row, or column.

> **Tip**: If you highlight two or more noncontiguous ranges for printing, Excel prints them on separate sheets. To print noncontiguous sections on the same sheet, use the Format-Column Width command to eliminate the unused or unwanted space between two areas of data. Simply enter a value of 0 for the columns to be eliminated. By modifying the worksheet in this way, you collapse it so that it fits on one page.

Selecting a Print Area

You probably will find the need to print specific sections of a worksheet, such as a range of cells. Although you can set the right and bottom page breaks to include the area you want to print, it's easier to single out the area as a separate page and then print that page. Highlight the range you want to print; then select the Options-Set Print Area command. When you select the File-Print command, Excel will print only the established print area. If the area is too large to fit on one page, Excel will break it into multiple pages.

You can highlight multiple ranges as the print area and Excel will print all the ranges at one time, each range on a separate page. Highlighting multiple ranges was discussed in Chapter 4. With all the ranges highlighted, choose the Options-Set Print Area command, and then print the worksheet. Each range will appear on a separate page in the order in which they were selected.

To remove the established print area, use the Formula-Define Name command to show all established range names on the worksheet. If a print area is set, the name `Print_Area` appears in the name list. (Excel automatically applies this name to the currently selected print area.) Select this name and press the Delete button to delete it. You can now establish manual page breaks or set a new print area.

Enhancing the Printout with File-Page Setup

There are many parts of the basic printout that you might want to change. For instance, Excel automatically prints the worksheet gridlines along with the data. Many people like to remove gridlines for the printout. You may also want to add a header and footer to the basic printout. The header consists of the name of the worksheet, and the footer is the page number.

The File-Page Setup command controls print enhancements. Take a look at these controls by selecting the File-Page Setup command. The dialog box like the one shown in Figure 7.4 appears.

> **Note**: Figure 7.4 illustrates the Page Setup dialog box for laser printers, such as the Apple LaserWriter. Depending on the printer, the options in this box may vary.

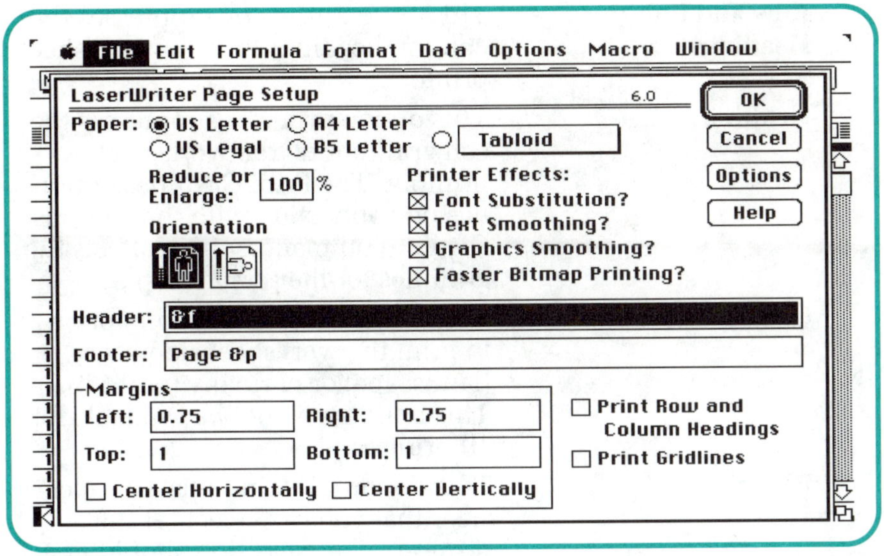

Figure 7.4 The File-Page Setup options.

The following list includes each File-Page Setup option and its purpose.

Header — This option adds a header to the top of each page in the printout. You can include any text plus special commands to control the appearance of the header. See "Adding Headers and Footers" later in this chapter for more details.

Footer — This option adds a footer to the bottom of each page.

Margins — Margin measurements control the top, bottom, left, and right margins of the page. Excel will include information with the next page if it does not fit within the specified margins. Margins are relative to the paper size currently set with the Printer Setup options. You also have options for centering the printout on the page.

Row and Column Headings	This option prints or suppresses the column headings for your worksheet printout.
Gridlines	This option prints or suppresses the cell gridlines on the worksheet printout. The Print Gridlines option has no connection with the Options-Display command, which affects the gridlines for the screen display.
Orientation	You can use the orientation option to print the worksheet sideways (landscape) or normally (portrait). This option may not be available for all printers.
Paper	This option contains a list of paper sizes that you can select for the printout. This selection should match the type of paper you currently have in the printer.
Reduce or Enlarge	Some printers let you reduce or enlarge the printout as it prints. Enter the desired enlargement or reduction here. Note that 100% is normal size. This option may not be available on all printers.
Fit to Page	This option prints the worksheet at full size to fit the size of the page. This is useful for printing graphics and charts. This option may not be available on all printers.
Printer Effects	Printer effects let you control various laser printer functions. Font Substitution tells Excel to substitute a laser font when nonlaser fonts are used in the worksheet. Text Smoothing helps the appearance of text. Graphics Smoothing can aid the appearance of graphics. Faster Bitmap Printing speeds up the printing of bit-mapped graphics. These options are usually activated.

Options	Select the Options button to see more printer effects, such as flipping or rotating the images.

Make the appropriate selections for the printout, and then press Return to accept your options. When you print the worksheet, your changes will be effective. Remember that the Gridlines option and the Row and Column Headings option affect the printout only, not the screen display.

Adding Headers and Footers

Using the Header and Footer options, you can add headers and footers to your printouts. A *header* is a line of text repeated at the top of each page, and a *footer* is a line of text repeated at the bottom of each page. Headers and footers can contain any text you like, plus commands for automatically entering the date, time, and page number. Other commands placed inside the header or footer control the placement and style of text in each.

To define a header and/or footer, select the File-Page Setup command. Then, enter text and any special codes into the Header space and/or Footer space. Special codes and their effects are as follows:

&L	Aligns the characters that follow with the left margin.
&R	Aligns the characters that follow with the right margin.
&C	Centers the characters that follow.
&P	Prints the page number.
&D	Prints the current date in the format 2/24/91.
&T	Prints the current time in the format 1:30:00 PM.
&F	Prints the current file name.
&B	Boldface.
&I	Italics.

The commands &L, &R, and &C align information in the header and footer. You can use one of these codes to align the entire header or footer or combine the codes to break up the header or footer into sections. Figure 7.5 shows some footer examples.

Example: `&R Chapter 1`
Printout:

Example: `&L Using Excel &R Chapter 1`
Printout:

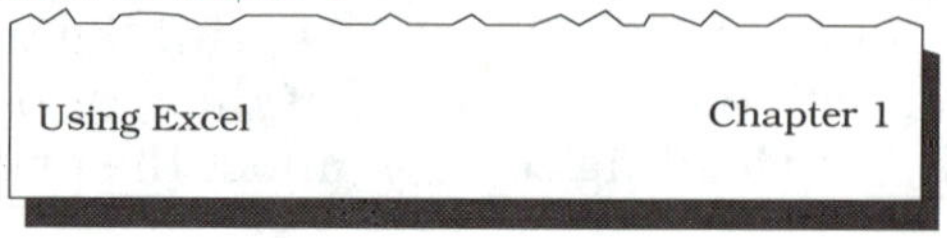

Example: `&L Using Excel &C &R Chapter 1`
Printout:

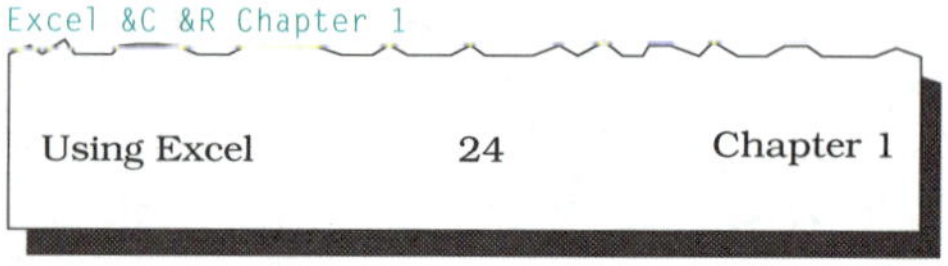

Figure 7.5 Examples of Excel footers.

Printing Column Headings

Worksheets are often set up with a row of titles or column headings above the columns of data to clarify what information is in each column. If the columns contain many rows of data, your printout might be several pages long, and you might want the column headings to print at the top of each page. While a header is a useful label for each page, you cannot align headers with worksheet columns. Stick to using the header to print the document name, the date, and other such information.

Excel can automatically print column headings at the top of each page and align the headings with the columns in the worksheet. All you have to do is specify which cells (probably a row or two near the top of the worksheet) contain the column headings. First, highlight the entire row (or rows) containing the column headings; then use the Options-Set Print Titles command. The selected rows are now set as the print column headings.

Suppose you wanted to print the worksheet shown in Figure 7.6 with the column headings at the top of each printed page. First, highlight the entire block of data that you want to print without including the headings. Use the Options-Set Print Area command to set this block as the current print area. Next, highlight the row containing the headings (row 3 in Figure 7.6) and use the Options-Set Print Titles command. (Remember, you can highlight a row using Shift-Space.) Finally, print the worksheet normally with the File-Print command. The column headings you selected (such as `Title`, `Author`, `Call No`, `Subj`, and `Date Pub` in Figure 7.6) will print above the appropriate column on each page.

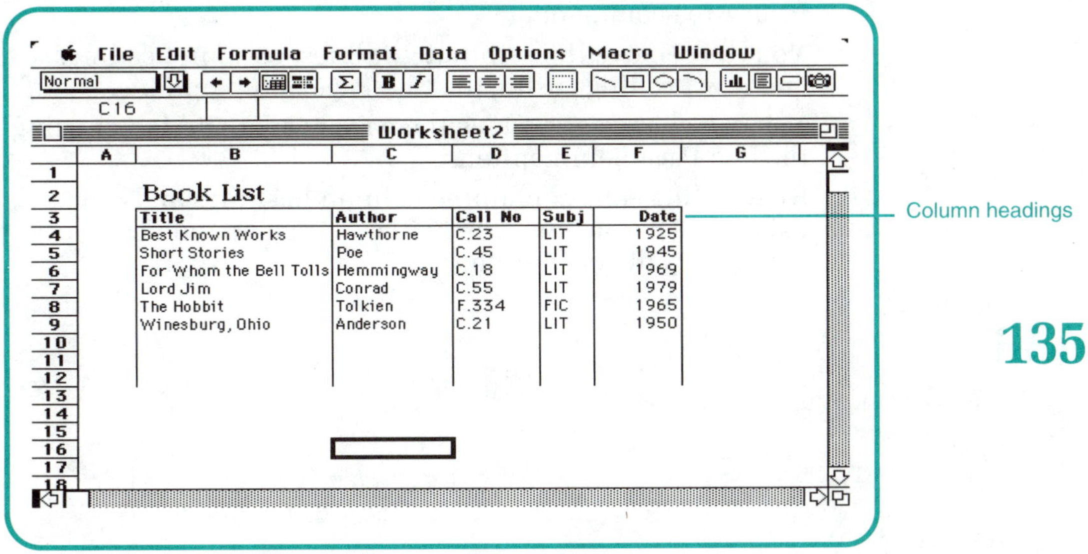

Figure 7.6 Worksheet with column headings.

To remove the print titles you've established, select the Format-Define Name command and remove the name `Print_Titles` from the list.

What You've Learned

This chapter provided details about printing worksheets. The chapter discussed printing a worksheet with the File-Print command and making various enhancements to the output using the File-Page Setup options. Following is a list of things to remember:

- You can preview a printout on-screen using the Preview option in the File-Print command or use the File-Print Preview command.
- Excel automatically breaks pages for the printout unless you manually set page breaks with the Options-Set Page Break command.
- To print a specific area of the worksheet, use the Options-Set Print Area command.
- You can remove the printout gridlines, column headings, and row headings using the File-Page Setup options.
- You can change or remove the page header and footer using the File-Page Setup options.
- By selecting cells containing column headings and then using the Options-Set Print Titles command, you can print column headings on each page.

Chapter 8

Charting Your Data

In This Chapter

- *Parts of a chart*
- *Charting your worksheet data*
- *Changing the chart type*
- *Creating combination charts*
- *Placing a chart onto the worksheet*

This chapter provides complete instructions for creating charts in Excel. First, it gives you a brief overview of the charting process. After this, the chapter explains some basic charting terminology used throughout the rest of the chapter and in Excel's commands and options. Details about creating charts follow. You'll find Excel's charting capabilities give you a lot of control in how you can present data.

Overview of Charting

You can make a lot of choices regarding the appearance of a chart in Excel, but the basic process for creating charts is the same. You begin with Excel's default (or automatic) chart and then modify it to your liking.

The process is easy. First, select the worksheet data that you want to chart, including any column and row headings that might apply. Select the File-New command and choose the Chart option. This opens a chart window with a column chart that reflects the data you selected in the first step. You can change to a different chart type using the Gallery options. Next, you can modify various elements of the chart, including the axes, titles, patterns, colors, legend, and so on. Add descriptive text to the chart if you like. When you're finished, save the chart with the File-Save command.

Charting is really as simple as that. Don't let all the charting commands and options make you think otherwise. By the end of this chapter, you'll be able to create any chart and control various aspects of that chart.

Parts of a Chart

Take a few moments to look over the parts of a chart as shown in Figures 8.1 and 8.2. Figure 8.1 shows a basic worksheet ready for charting. Figure 8.2 shows a basic column chart (sometimes called a bar chart) with various elements identified. The chart in Figure 8.2 was created from the data in Figure 8.1. An explanation of each of the chart elements follows.

Data series—The bars, pie wedges, lines, or other elements that represent plotted values in a chart are called the data series. For example, a chart might show a set of similar bars that reflects a series of values for the same item. The bars in the series would all have the same pattern. In Figure 8.2, there are two different patterns of bars. Each pattern represents a separate data series. As you can see, data series reflect the individual items being charted. For example, charting the sales for Store 1 versus Store 2 would require two data series—one for each store. Often, data series correspond to rows of data in your worksheet.

Categories—Categories reflect the number of elements in a series. You might have two data series to compare the sales of two different stores, and four categories to compare these sales over four quarters. Some charts have only one category, and others have several. Categories are often explained by the category labels below the axis. Categories normally correspond to the number of columns that you have in your chart data, with the category labels coming from the column headings. See Figure 8.2 for an example.

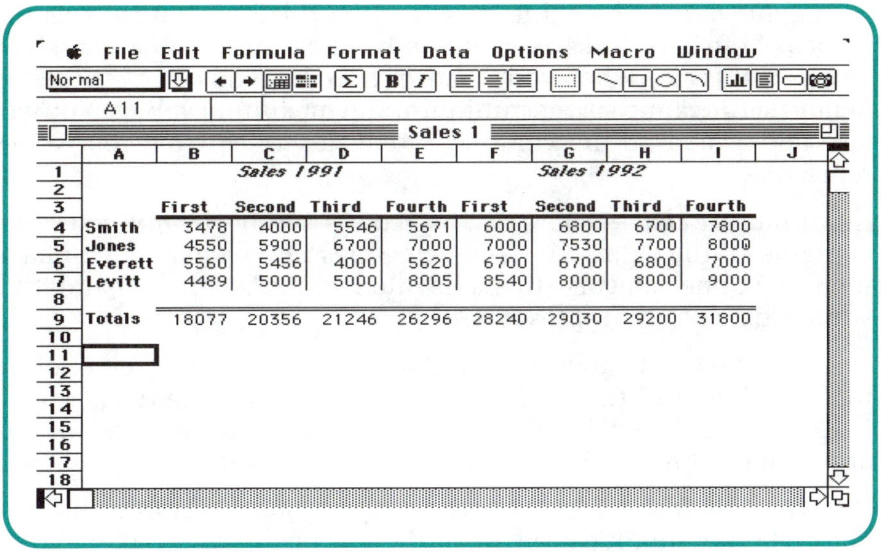

	A	B	C	D	E	F	G	H	I
1			Sales 1991				Sales 1992		
2									
3		First	Second	Third	Fourth	First	Second	Third	Fourth
4	Smith	3478	4000	5546	5671	6000	6800	6700	7800
5	Jones	4550	5900	6700	7000	7000	7530	7700	8000
6	Everett	5560	5456	4000	5620	6700	6700	6800	7000
7	Levitt	4489	5000	5000	8005	8540	8000	8000	9000
8									
9	Totals	18077	20356	21246	26296	28240	29030	29200	31800

Figure 8.1 An example worksheet for charting.

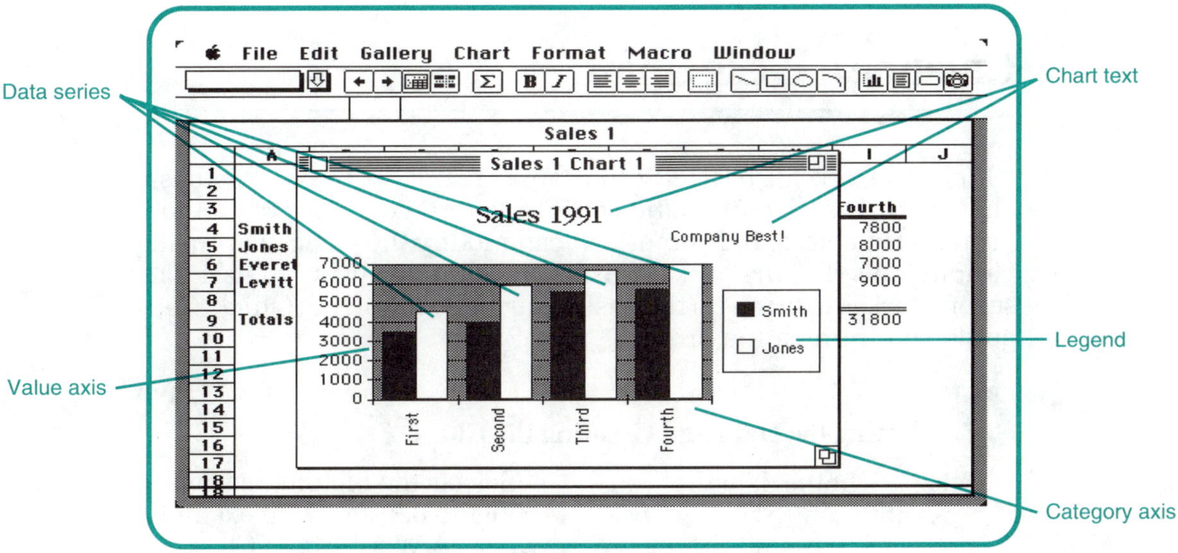

Figure 8.2 The parts of a chart.

Chart text—Chart text includes all the labels on the chart. Most chart text has to be added to the basic chart. You can control the appearance of labels by changing the type fonts and type styles. You can also add text to any part of a chart for explanatory purposes.

Value axis—The value axis is the vertical axis. It reflects the values of the bars, lines, or plot points. Excel automatically assigns values to this axis when you create a chart, but you can override the default settings and set the minimum and maximum values. You can also add a label to the value axis that describes what the values represent.

Category axis—The category axis is the horizontal axis that contains all the data series and categories in the chart. If you have more than one category, this axis often contains labels that define what each category represents.

Plot area—The plot area contains the actual bars, lines, or other representations of the data series. Everything outside the plot area helps explain what's inside the plot area. You can control the appearance of the plot area independently of other chart elements.

Legend—The legend consists of the series labels in your chart data. These will appear either at the left or top of the data. Excel matches the labels with the data series and provides a "key" to the chart.

Creating a Basic Chart

All charts start out basically the same. You have to create a basic chart with Excel's automatic settings before you can create more customized charts. If desired, you can modify the basic chart using various tools. The first task is to select the data you want to chart. The second task is to bring up the basic chart. The following Quick Steps guide you through the process.

Q Selecting the Data and Creating the Chart

1. Highlight the data that you want to chart. This can be several rows and columns if desired. Rows usually reflect the data series, and the columns reflect the categories. Be sure to include any row or column titles that apply.	Selects the highlighted area. Figure 8.3 shows an example. See "A Word About Chart Orientation" later in this chapter for details about the row/column order of a chart.

2. Select the File-New command. — Brings up a dialog box with three choices.

3. Select the Chart option; then press Return to open the new chart window. — The chart appears with Excel's default options set. Figure 8.4 shows the basic chart. □

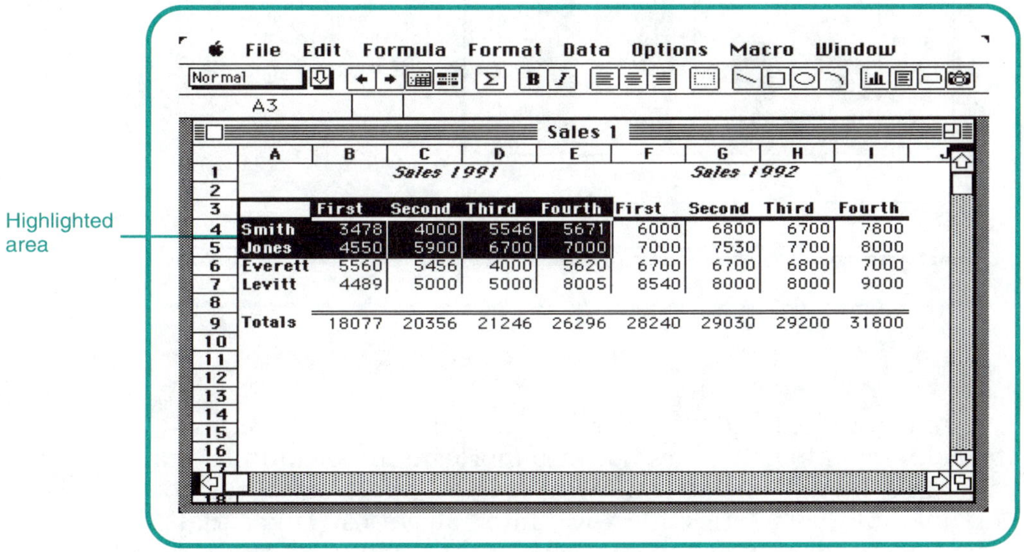

Figure 8.3 Highlighting the chart data.

> ▶ **Tip**: If you have an extended keyboard, Excel offers a shortcut to the charting procedure. After selecting the data, simply press F11 to create the chart.

> ▶ **Note**: Excel provides a tool for creating charts directly on the worksheet. You can "draw" a chart on the worksheet by highlighting the chart data and then clicking on the chart tool in the Toolbar (fourth tool from the right end). Next, click on the worksheet and drag the mouse to create a box. When you release the mouse button, the box will contain the chart. This chart is now part of the worksheet, and you can save the chart along with the worksheet data. To activate the chart menus, double-click on the chart in the worksheet.

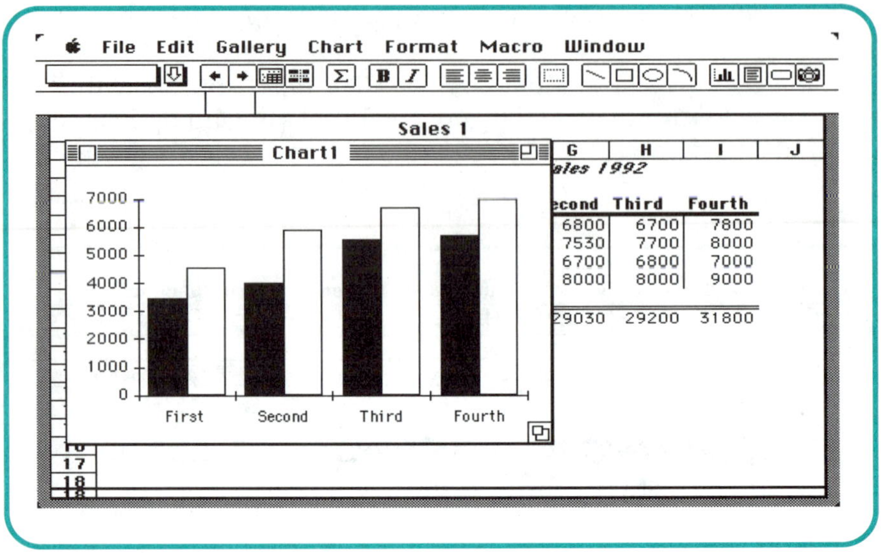

Figure 8.4 The basic chart.

In Figures 8.3 and 8.4, the rows translated into data series and the columns into categories because there are more columns than rows. In some instances, you might create a chart that turns your columns into data series and rows into categories. This situation would occur when you have more rows than columns. You'll find more about controlling chart orientation later in this chapter.

Changing a Chart's Values

A chart and the worksheet that created it are linked. You can make changes in the worksheet, and the changes will be reflected in the chart. The chart and the worksheet must both be open for the changes to be immediate. For example, suppose you return to the worksheet from Figure 8.3 and increase one of the values. After making a change to the worksheet, you don't have to do anything ... Excel has already updated the chart window. You can simply view the updated chart.

The automatic update feature is always active, but the chart and its worksheet must be open at the same time. The next section explains how you can open either the chart or worksheet by itself.

Opening, Saving, and Closing Charts

Before getting into various chart modifications, look at how to open, close, and save charts. Since you've already seen how to open, close, and save worksheets, this procedure will not seem like anything new. To save a chart, simply make sure that the chart window is in view, and then use the File-Save or File-Save As command just as you would save a worksheet. You'll be asked to name the chart and specify the folder in which it should be saved. You can close the chart window using the File-Close command or by clicking in the worksheet's close box in the upper-left corner.

Note that charts are not saved with the worksheets that created them. Rather, they become separate and independent files on disk. You can open a chart without opening the worksheet that created it. And you can open a worksheet without its charts. If you change the values in the worksheet when the chart is not open, the chart will not be updated automatically to reflect those changes. Worksheets and charts are separate files, although they are linked together. Excel knows which worksheets created which charts.

> **Note**: A new feature in version 3.0 lets you place a chart onto its worksheet along with the data. In this case, the chart is saved with the worksheet and not separately. You will learn more on this feature later in this chapter.

To open an existing chart, use the File-Open command just as you would on a worksheet, as discussed in Chapter 3. If the worksheet that created the chart is already open, Excel will automatically update the chart to reflect any changes you've made to the worksheet. If the worksheet is not open, Excel gives you the choice of updating the chart with the most current data from the worksheet, or leaving the chart as is. This message is shown in Figure 8.5.

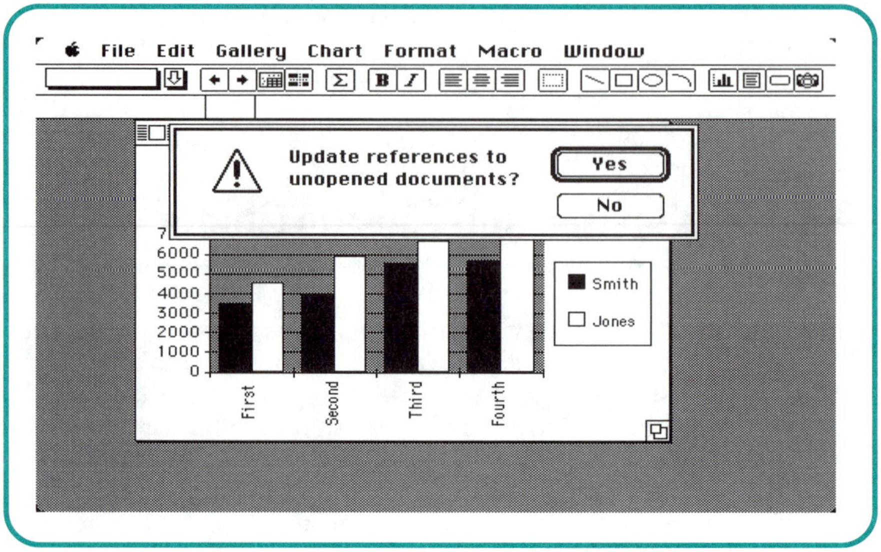

Figure 8.5 If you open a chart without the worksheet, Excel offers to update the chart.

If you choose to update the chart, Excel finds the worksheet and changes the chart to reflect any worksheet modifications. However, the worksheet will not be opened. If you choose not to update the chart, Excel will leave the current values alone. Following is a summary of these rules:

- After a chart is created from a worksheet, you can save it using the File-Save command.
- When a worksheet and its chart are open at the same time, changes made to the worksheet are immediately reflected in the chart.
- If a chart is not open, changes made to its worksheet are not reflected by the chart.
- If you open a chart without first opening the worksheet, Excel offers to update the chart with the latest version of the worksheet. This option is useful if the worksheet has been changed without the chart.

As mentioned earlier, Excel remembers which worksheets created which charts. However, if you change the name of a worksheet, delete it, or move it to a different folder, Excel may ask that you locate the worksheet so that it can reestablish the relationship between the chart and the worksheet.

A Word About Chart Orientation

There may be times when Excel produces a chart from a highlighted range, and the chart is "backward." The data series appears where categories should be and vice versa. Consider the example in Figure 8.6. This chart uses the same data as the chart in Figure 8.4, but the orientation has been changed. Rather than showing the salespeople as the data series and the quarters as categories, this chart shows the quarters as data series and the salespeople as categories.

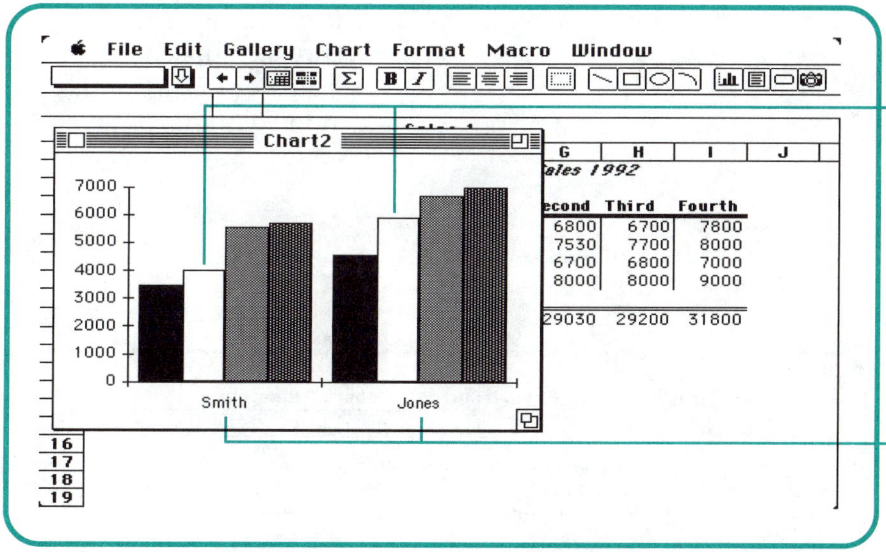

Figure 8.6 Changing the orientation of the chart in Figure 8.6.

If the orientation can be different like this, how does Excel know which orientation to use? Well, Excel makes a guess, based on your selected data. If you have more columns than rows, then the columns become the categories. If you have more rows than columns, then the rows become categories.

You can always change Excel's orientation for a chart if Excel's guess is wrong. Following are the Quick Steps to this procedure.

Changing a Chart's Orientation

1. Close the incorrect chart, responding No to the Save Changes dialog box.

   This should return you to the worksheet.

2. Highlight the chart data; then select the Edit-Copy command.

3. Open a new chart by selecting the command File-New, choosing the Chart option, and pressing Return.

   Brings up a blank chart window. The chart is blank because Excel knows you have copied the data.

4. Select the Edit-Paste Special command.

   The dialog box shown in Figure 8.7 appears.

5. Change the Values In option from Rows to Columns or from Columns to Rows, depending on its current setting. Then press Return. Simply change the setting to the opposite option.

   The chart appears in the window with its new orientation.

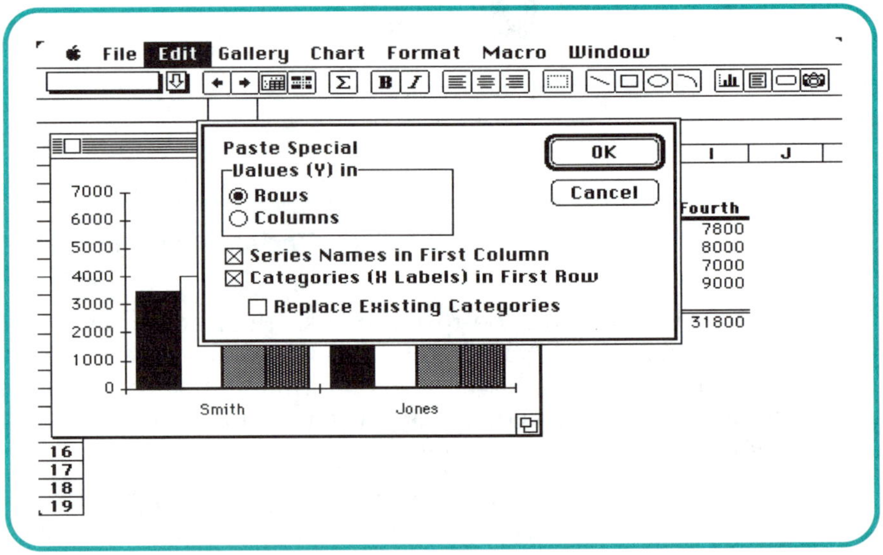

Figure 8.7 The Edit-Paste Special dialog box.

Changing a Chart's Size and Shape

Excel creates all new charts at a standard size and shape. This is another of the many defaults that Excel uses when creating new charts. You can, however, change the proportions of the chart. This process is as simple as changing the chart window. By changing the window proportions, you effectively change the proportions of the chart. Figures 8.8 and 8.9 show the sample chart with two different window proportions.

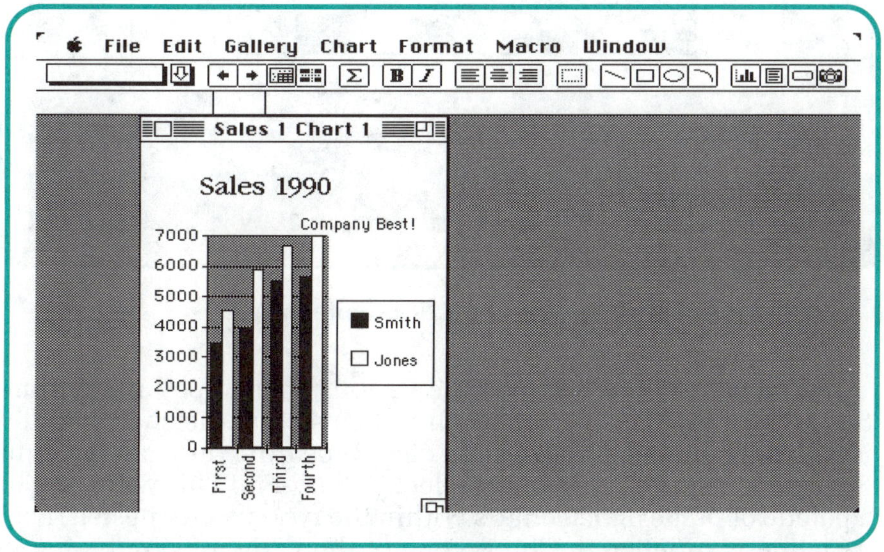

Figure 8.8 Making a chart taller than normal.

After changing the chart window, be sure to save the changes with the File-Save command. Later, when you print this chart, you can choose to keep the proportions you see on-screen or you can override them.

Changing the Chart Type

Excel offers several types of charts for your data. You'll find that certain chart types are best for certain situations. You'll learn how to change the chart type and get an overview of the chart types offered by Excel.

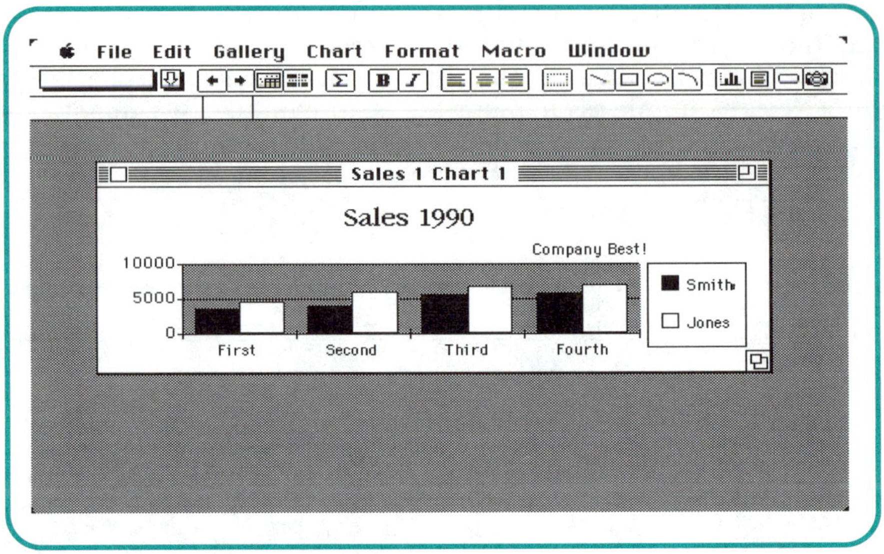

Figure 8.9 Making a chart wider than normal.

You can switch between the various chart types at any time. Simply display the basic chart on-screen so that the chart window is active. Then, select the desired chart type from the Gallery menu. For example, to get a pie chart, select Gallery-Pie. This will bring up a palette of predesigned charts within the type you requested. Each variation is numbered. Choose one of the variations by typing its number, and then press Return. The active chart will change to reflect your choice. Following is a list of the chart types offered in the Gallery menu and their variations.

Area Charts

Area charts are similar to stacked column charts in that they show how items combine to form a total. But area charts provide a more dramatic representation of the change in values over time. The top of the area chart reflects the total of all elements beneath it. Figure 8.10 shows an example of area chart format 1.

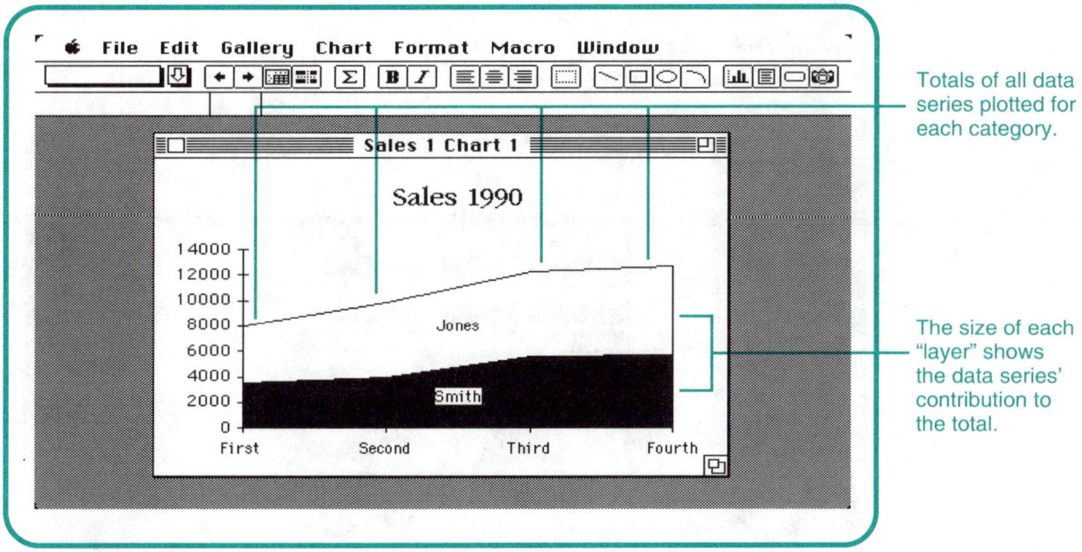

Figure 8.10 An example area chart.

To create an area chart, simply begin with the default chart provided by Excel; then select the desired format from the Gallery-Area command.

Bar Charts

Bar charts are horizontal representations of column charts and are often called histograms. Bar charts emphasize the performance of a group of items. Often, different patterns are not required for bar chart data series. Figure 8.11 shows an example of format 1.

Column Charts

Column charts show the relationships between items over a period of time. The columns make it easy to compare the values of items in each category. You also can get an idea of how an item has changed its value over the course of the categories, but area and line charts are best for viewing value trends. Column charts are best for comparing two or more items. Figure 8.12 is an example of column chart format 1.

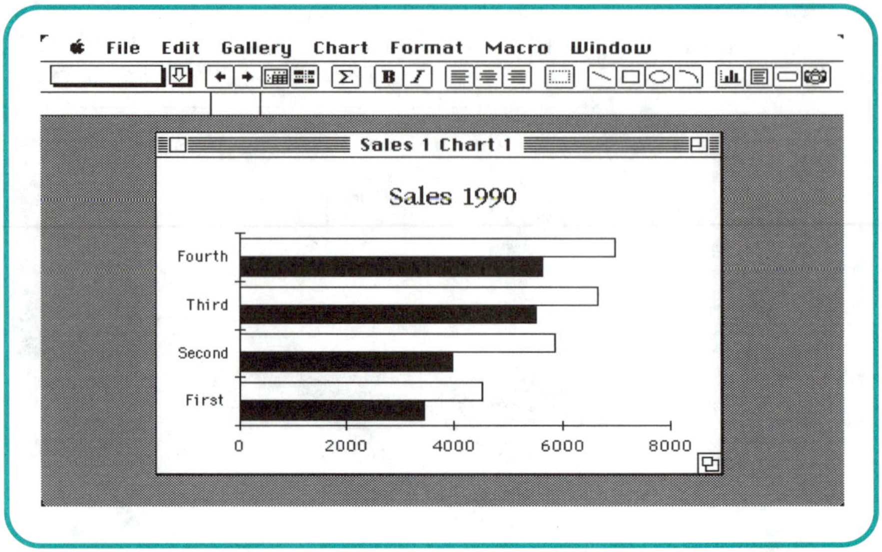

Figure 8.11 An example bar chart.

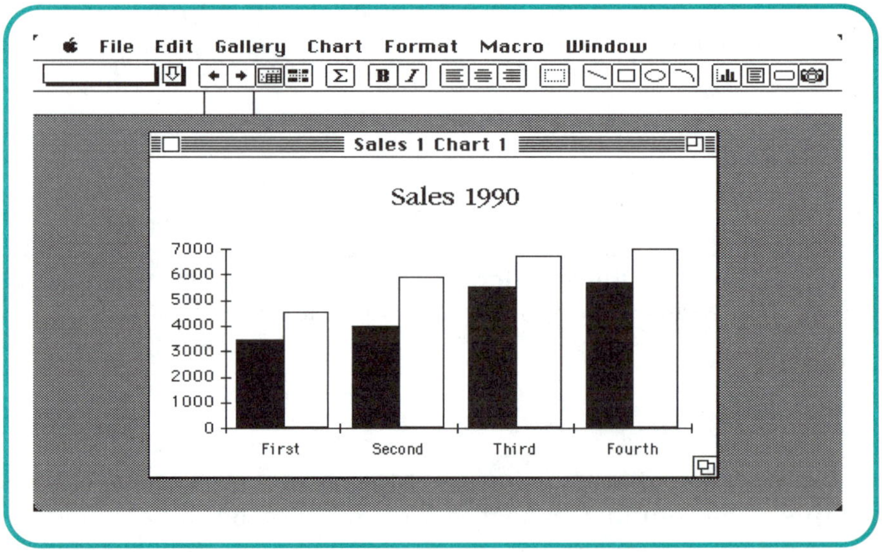

Figure 8.12 A column chart.

Column chart number 1 is the default chart in Excel. All new charts appear in this format. To change formats, simply choose one of the others from the Gallery-Column options.

Line Charts

Line charts are ideal for showing how one or more items have changed over time. The lines emphasize the change and not the comparison of one item to another. Line charts are also useful for plotting numerous categories of data for a few different data series. Figure 8.13 shows chart type 2 from the line charts.

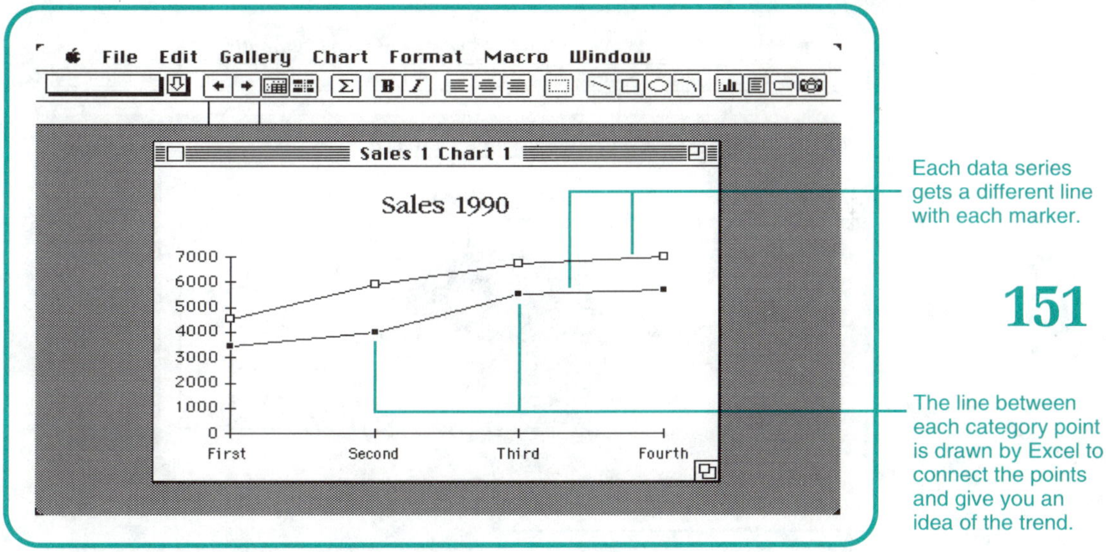

Figure 8.13 An example line chart.

After you have created a chart, simply choose the Gallery-Line command and select the desired chart format.

Format 7 is a special type of line chart, called a *hilo* chart. This format is used to show two values for each category. To create a hilo chart, select two rows of data (and as many columns as you like). The first row will represent the high value, and the second will represent the low value. Because this is a category-oriented chart, the data series have little bearing on the data.

Format 8 is called a *hilo-close* chart. It is similar to the hilo chart but uses three values for each category: a high, a low, and a closing value. Hilo-close charts are often used for stock market analysis. Be sure to select exactly three rows of data. The first row is the high, the second is the low, and the third is the closing value.

Pie Charts

Pie charts are the ideal way to show how each data series compares to the total. Pie charts can plot only one category of data, but each wedge of the pie represents a different data series. If you need to show more than one category, consider using a stacked column or area chart instead. Figure 8.14 shows pie type 3.

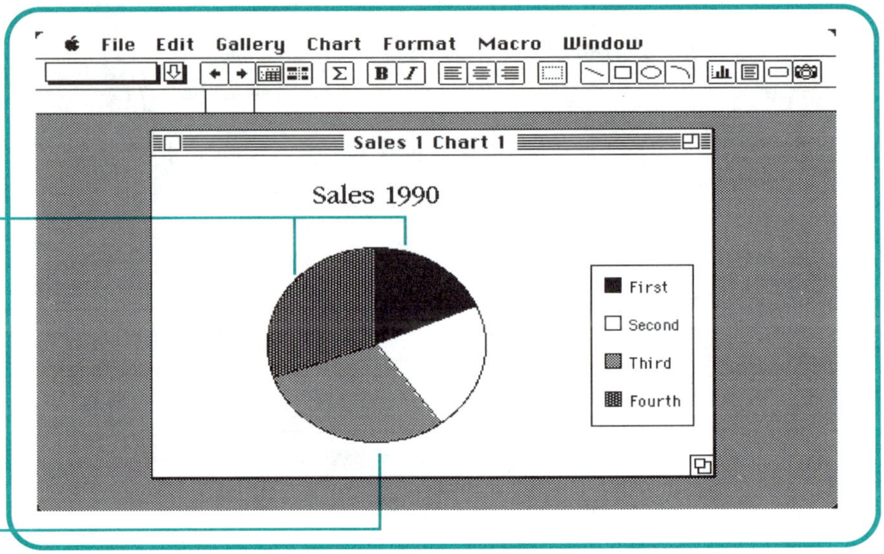

Figure 8.14 An example pie chart.

First, create a chart, which will appear as a column chart with only one category of data. Then, choose the Gallery-Pie command and select the desired format. If you select more than one category, the pie chart will use only the first.

Scatter Charts

Scatter charts are used to plot values on x and y axes. On a scatter chart, the category axis does not exist. Instead you have two value axes: one horizontal and one vertical. Excel plots the points on the x and y axes.

Creating a scatter chart requires a slightly different procedure than other charts. First, highlight two columns of information. These two columns represent the two values for each plot point. In other words, the values in both columns are used to plot each point. The first column represents the horizontal value, and the second column is the vertical value. The number of rows determines the number of points. Figure 8.15 shows an example.

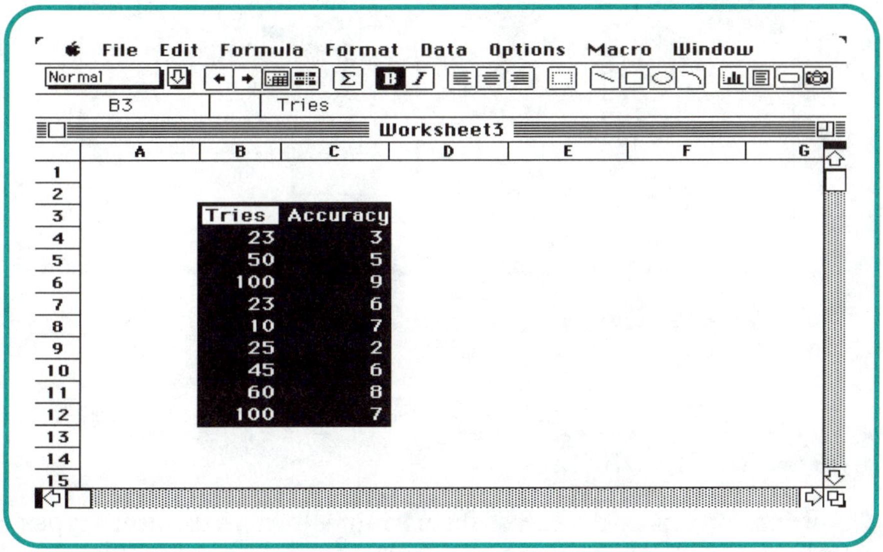

Figure 8.15 Highlight two columns for a scatter chart.

Next, enter the Edit-Copy command to copy the data. Choose the File-New command and select the Chart option to open a new chart. The chart window should be empty. Now select the Edit-Paste Special command and select the Categories in First Column option. If the first row of the selected data contains labels (as in the example), then select the Series Names in First Row option. Press Return when finished.

The final step is to select one of the scatter chart formats from the Gallery-Scatter menu. Figure 8.16 shows an example of format 1 using the data from Figure 8.15.

In this example, accuracy improves consistently with more tries.

Scatter charts show important "clusters" of plot points on an x-y grid.

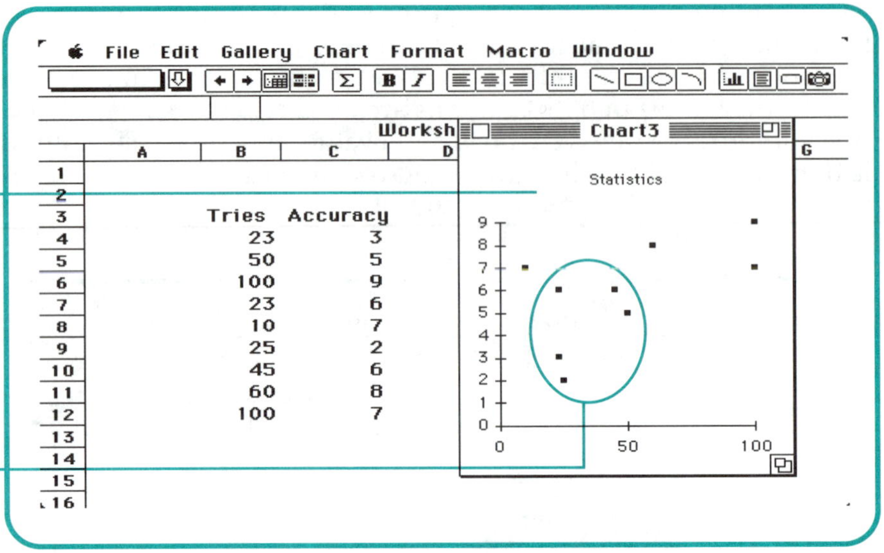

Figure 8.16 Example scatter chart.

Combination Charts

Combination charts display information using two different types of charts. Like all charts, combination charts begin as the default column chart. Then, when you select one of the combination formats from the Gallery-Combination menu, Excel splits the data series into two groups: a *main chart* group and an *overlay chart* group. Each group will get half of the data series in the chart. The main chart group gets the first half, and the overlay group gets the second half. If there is an odd number of data series, then Excel places the extra series in the main chart group.

The main chart group is formatted with one chart type, and the overlay group is formatted with a different type. Figure 8.17 shows an example of combination chart 4.

Remember that Excel splits the data series in half (or as close to half as possible). However, you might want to control how many series get into each group. For example, you might want only one data series in the overlay chart group and all the rest in the main group. You can control this split after creating the combination chart. Select the command Format-Overlay, and then change the First Overlay Series option. Enter the number of the series with which the overlay chart should begin. The overlay chart will contain this data series and all series after this one. For example, if you have six data series in the chart and you want only the last two in the overlay group, enter a 5 as the First Overlay Series value. This places series 5 and 6 in the overlay group.

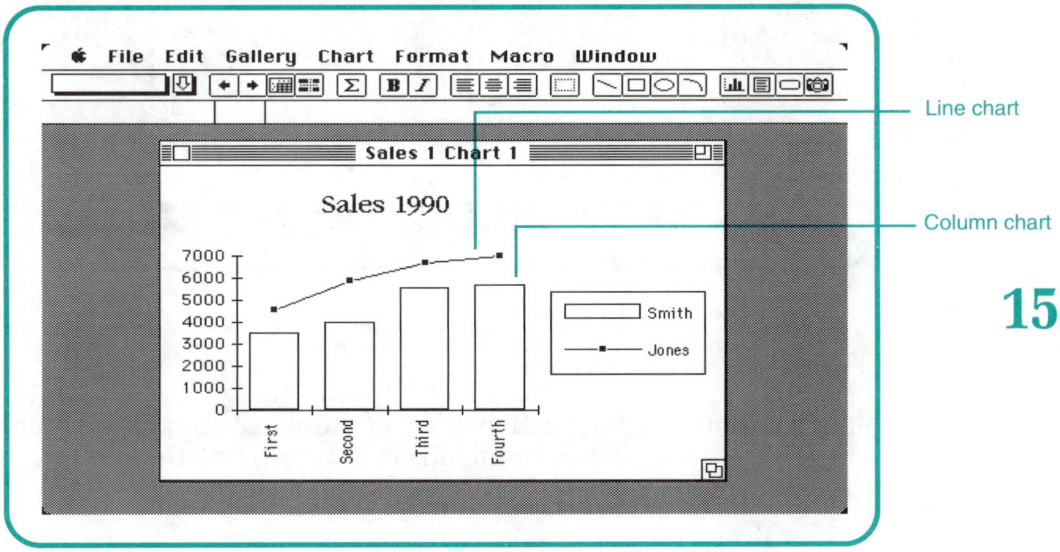

Figure 8.17 An example combination chart.

Note that a 3-D chart (discussed next) cannot be part of an overlay chart.

3-D Charts

Excel offers four 3-D chart types. These charts are similar to their 2-D counterparts, but they display the chart's data categories on a third axis, called the *depth axis*. This, plus the depth added to the data series markers, causes the 3-D effect. Each 3-D chart type comes with several preset styles that appear when you select the type from the Gallery menu. Figure 8.18 shows an example of a 3-D chart.

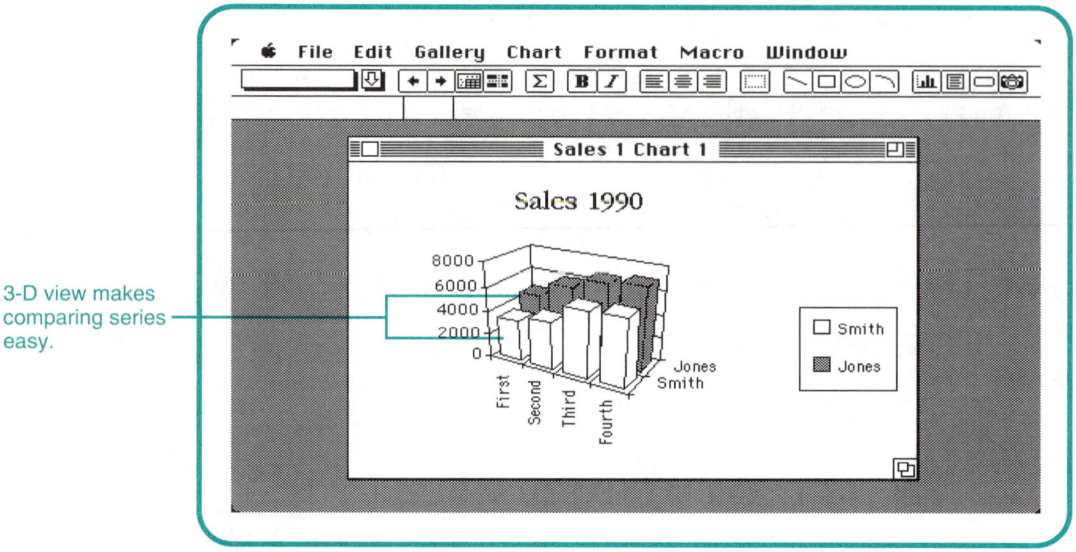

Figure 8.18 A 3-D chart.

3-D charts offer several special options that you use to control their position and perspective. Most of these 3-D options are found in the Format-3D View command, which presents the dialog box shown in Figure 8.19.

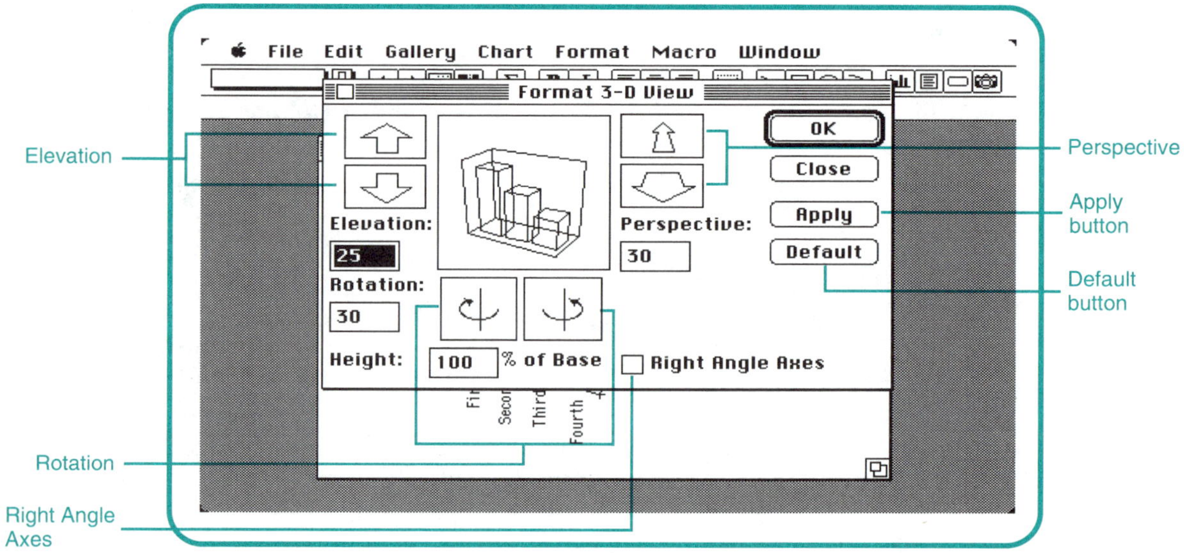

Figure 8.19 The Format-3D View dialog box.

Examine each of these options briefly. You should experiment with them for best results.

Elevation

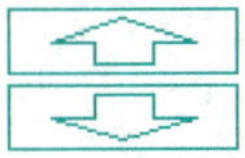

The elevation arrows (or the numeric setting) change the height at which you are viewing the chart—as if you are climbing a ladder to see the top of the chart. The higher the number, the higher you are on the "ladder." You can click on the Up and Down arrows or enter a number into the Elevation box.

Rotation

The rotation icons (or the numeric setting) affect the angle at which you are viewing the chart—as if you were walking around the chart or as if the chart were being rotated in front of you. Click on the icons or enter a numeric setting.

Perspective

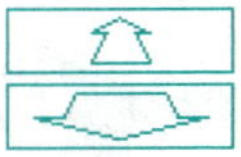

The perspective icons change the distance from which you are viewing the chart—as if the chart were being brought closer or farther away from you. Click on the arrows or enter a numeric setting.

Apply

This button applies the changes you've made to the chart without leaving the dialog box.

Default

This button changes the chart to the default 3-D settings.

Right Angle Axes

This button causes the axes to remain at right angles to each other at all times—ignoring the perspective setting.

Height

This setting controls the tallness of the chart in respect to the base. Enter the height as a percentage of the base. For example, a setting of 200% makes the graph twice as tall as it is wide.

Unless you click the Apply button, the settings you choose will apply to the chart after you press Return. You can change a chart at any time. For example, you can use another set of 3-D options to change the distance between the bars (or any data series markers). You can change the distance between a bar and the bar next to it. And you can change the distance between a bar and the bar behind it. These options appear in the Format-Main dialog box:

Gap Depth	This setting changes the distance between a bar and the bar next to it.
Chart Depth	This setting changes the distance between a bar and the bar behind it.

Placing Charts on the Worksheet

One of the best new features in Excel version 3.0 is the capability to place a chart onto the worksheet along with your worksheet data. This feature enables you to create full-page displays that include charts and numbers on the same page. To place a chart on its worksheet requires that you copy the entire chart and paste it on the worksheet. Following are the Quick Steps.

Q Adding a Chart to the Worksheet

1. Bring the chart window into view using the mouse or the Window menu.	
2. Select the Chart-Select Chart option.	The entire chart will be selected.
3. Select the Edit-Copy command.	
4. Bring the worksheet into view.	
5. Position the cell pointer at the desired location for the chart.	
6. Select the Edit-Paste command.	The chart will appear in the worksheet at the chosen location. Figure 8.20 shows an example of this. □

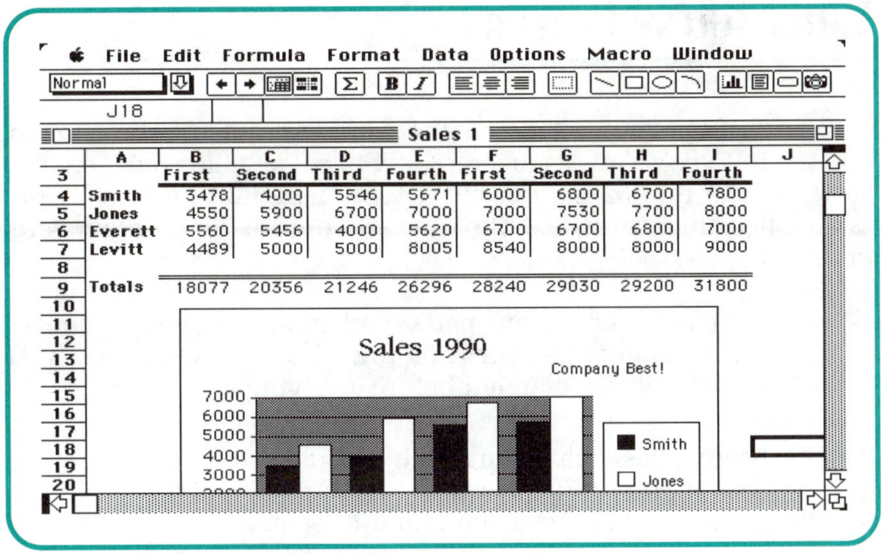

Figure 8.20 Adding a chart to the worksheet.

Note that the size of the chart window dictates the size of the chart in the worksheet. So, if you want to shrink the chart or make it taller, size the chart window before you copy the chart into the worksheet. You also can move the chart after it's on the worksheet by clicking on the chart and then dragging. You can resize the chart by dragging on its highlight boxes.

After you bring a chart into the worksheet in this way, the chart is no longer connected to the original chart window. It is, in fact, a completely separate copy of the chart. You can delete the separate chart file if you don't need it any longer. Therefore, if you make changes to the original chart (in the chart window), these changes will not affect the chart you copied into the worksheet. To make changes to the worksheet chart, you must double-click the mouse on the chart to bring up the chart options. Changes to the data that created the chart will affect both charts, however.

Finally, when you save the worksheet, you will be saving the chart along with it. This chart will appear on the worksheet until you remove it. You can remove a chart by clicking on it and then pressing the Delete key.

What You've Learned

In this chapter you've learned the fundamentals of the charting process in Excel. You discovered how to select chart data, create a basic chart, and change the chart type using any of Excel's pre-established chart formats. Following are some of the points covered in this chapter.

- Charts consist of various parts or elements. These elements can be highlighted by pressing the ↑ and → keys. Often, you must highlight an element before applying a particular command.
- To begin a basic chart, highlight the chart data on the worksheet, including row and column labels if applicable. Then use the File-New command to open a new chart window.
- When the chart window and the worksheet window are open at the same time, changes made to the worksheet are immediately reflected in the chart.
- If you make changes to the worksheet when the chart is not open, Excel will update the chart the next time it is opened when the worksheet is also open.
- If you open a chart without the worksheet open, Excel will ask if you want to update the chart to reflect the most current changes to the worksheet. Excel asks this even if you have not made changes to the worksheet.
- You can change the row/column orientation of a chart by using the Edit-Paste Special command.
- Changing the size and shape of the chart window changes the size and shape of the chart itself.
- Use the Gallery options to change the chart type.
- You can add a chart to the worksheet by using the Edit-Copy command to copy the chart and the Edit-Paste command to paste the chart into the worksheet.
- You can change the perspective and view of a 3-D chart by using the Format-3D View options.

Chapter 9

Customizing Charts

In This Chapter

- *Changing a chart's axes*
- *Changing the chart's patterns and colors*
- *Changing the category labels*
- *Annotating a chart with text and graphics*

Now that you know how to create all types of charts in Excel, you're ready to discover how you can customize and modify your charts. Excel gives you control over most of the chart's elements, including the axes, chart text, and series patterns and colors. This chapter will give you an overview of these changes and complete your education on Excel's powerful charting capabilities.

Changing Axis Scales

Excel automatically scales the value axis for your charts to best fit the minimum and maximum values being charted. However, you might need to customize the values along the vertical axis. You can set the minimum and maximum values, as well as the number of intermediate points along the axis. These intermediate points are called *major units* and *minor units*. You can set the vertical axis scale using the following Quick Steps.

Setting the Vertical Axis Scale

1. With the chart window active, press the ↑ key until the vertical axis is highlighted, or click on the axis.

   Figure 9.1 shows what the vertical axis looks like when it's highlighted. Notice the boxes at each end. Each time you press ↑ a different chart element is highlighted.

2. Select the Format-Scale command.

   The dialog box shown in Figure 9.2 appears. This box contains various options for changing the vertical axis. Each option is discussed following these steps.

3. Enter values for the desired options and press Return when finished.

   The chart will change to reflect the values you set. □

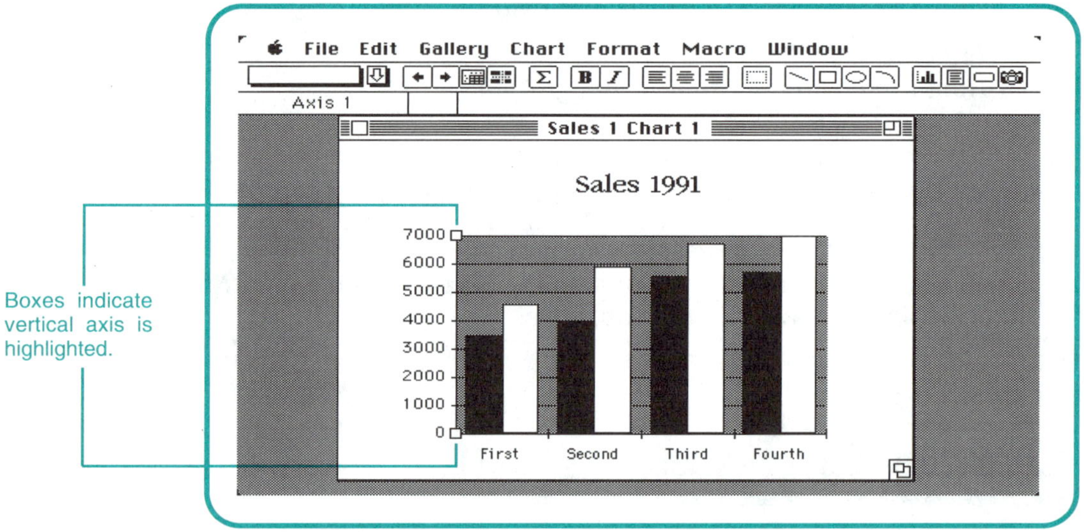

Figure 9.1 Selecting the vertical axis.

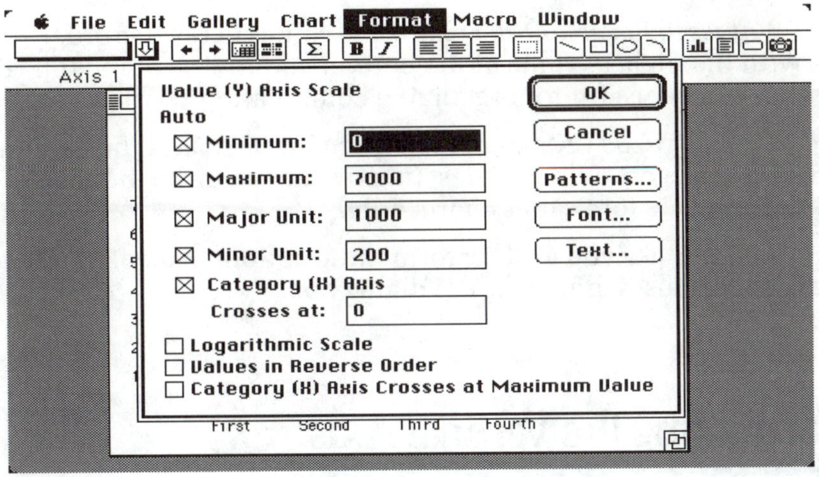

Figure 9.2 The Format-Scale options.

Following is a description of each option in the Format-Axis dialog box (for vertical axes):

Minimum specifies the low value on the axis. Values less than this minimum will not be visible on the chart.

Maximum specifies the high value on the axis. Values above this maximum will be out of view above the chart.

Major Unit specifies the number of divisions between the high and low values. Each division will be labeled numerically. Enter a number by which the maximum value divides evenly.

Minor Unit specifies the number of tick marks between the major units. Enter a number by which the major unit value divides evenly, or enter the same value as the Major Unit to display no tick marks. Minor unit tick marks are not labeled as are the major units. They are simply cross-hatch lines on the axis. Also, most charts start out with the minor unit tick marks set to invisible. You can make them visible using the formatting options discussed in the next section.

Crosses at specifies the horizontal position of the vertical axis—that is, the position along the category axis where the vertical axis appears. When using this feature on Bar charts, the category and value axes are reversed.

Logarithmic Scale changes the axis to a logarithmic scale.

Values in Reverse Order charts the values in reverse order—that is, with the highest value at the bottom and lowest at the top. This option can be useful for organizing combination charts.

Category Axis Crosses at Maximum Value makes the value axis cross the category axis at the last (maximum) value on the chart. This option appears for scatter charts only.

Buttons take you to other formatting options, except the OK and Cancel buttons, which exit the dialog box.

Formatting the Vertical Axis

164 Besides controlling the axis values and positioning the tick marks along the axis, you also can choose from a number of tick mark formats. After setting the values, choose the Format-Patterns command (make sure that the vertical axis is still highlighted when you select this command). The dialog box shown in Figure 9.3 appears.

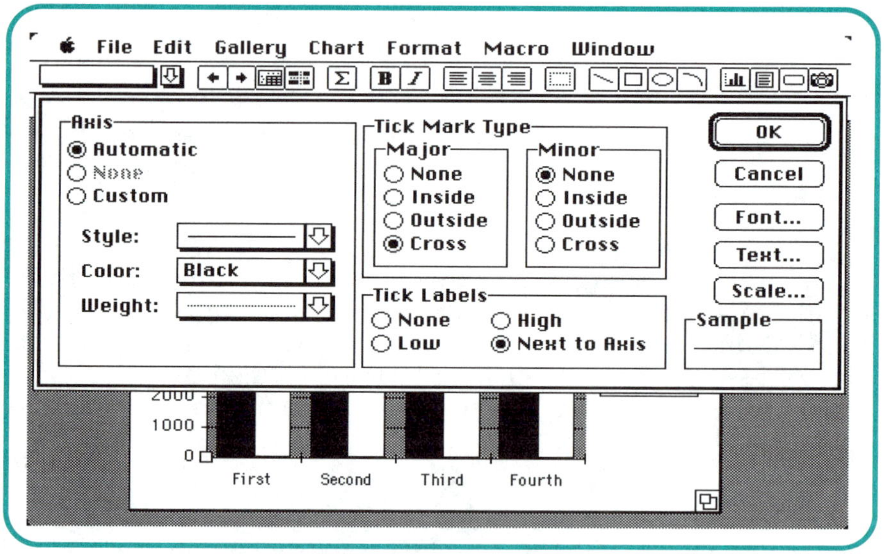

Figure 9.3 The Format-Patterns dialog box.

> ▶ **Tip**: You can access the Patterns dialog box by double-clicking on the axis or other chart element.

Notice that there are three major groups of options. The Axis options include the style, color, and weight of the axis line. The Tick Mark Type options include styles for the major and minor tick marks. The Tick Labels options control the appearance of the scale numbers that appear along the value axis.

Select the desired group of options by clicking on it with the mouse. Choosing the Automatic option lets Excel control the appearance of the axis line. Note that the minor tick marks are normally in the Invisible (None) position. This means that your Minor Unit changes in the Format-Scale command discussed earlier will not be visible. You can make the minor tick marks visible by choosing one of the other Minor options in this dialog box. Experiment with these settings for best results. Figure 9.4 shows a few different combinations.

Changing the Patterns of Data Series

Many people like to change the colors and/or patterns of the data series for special effects. While Excel's default patterns and colors serve the purpose of distinguishing one data series from another, you might find some patterns and colors more attractive than others. For example, you might want to remove all patterns and use only color. You change the pattern of a data series with the Format-Patterns command. You can choose from a number of patterns, including those already used by other data series in the same chart. The following Quick Steps give the details.

Q Changing the Data Series Patterns

1. With the chart window active, click on the desired data series to highlight it.

   A highlighted data series contains small white squares in each of the bars, pie wedges, or other plot elements as shown in Figure 9.5.

2. Select the Format-Patterns command.

   The Format-Patterns dialog box appears. This dialog box is slightly different from the Format Patterns box you used with the Axis. Excel changes the options based on the element you have highlighted. The dialog box is shown in Figure 9.6.

3. Select the desired options in the dialog box; then press Return to accept the changes or Esc to reject them.

   The data series you select will immediately reflect the pattern changes. Details about the pattern options are provided next. □

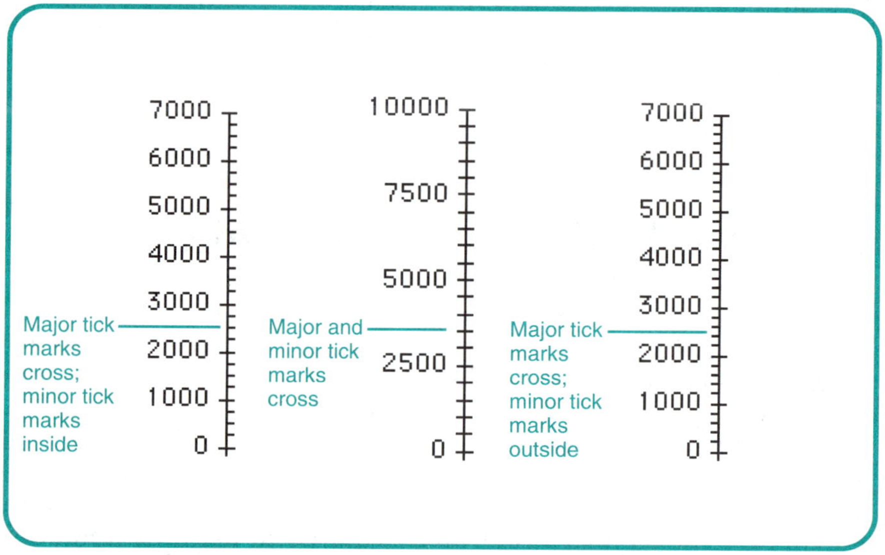

Figure 9.4 Some tick mark formatting examples.

The Format-Patterns options are divided into two groups for the data series. The Border options affect the perimeter of the highlighted element, including the style, thickness, and color of the border line. The Area options control the inside of the element, such as its pattern and color. Most of these options are self-explanatory.

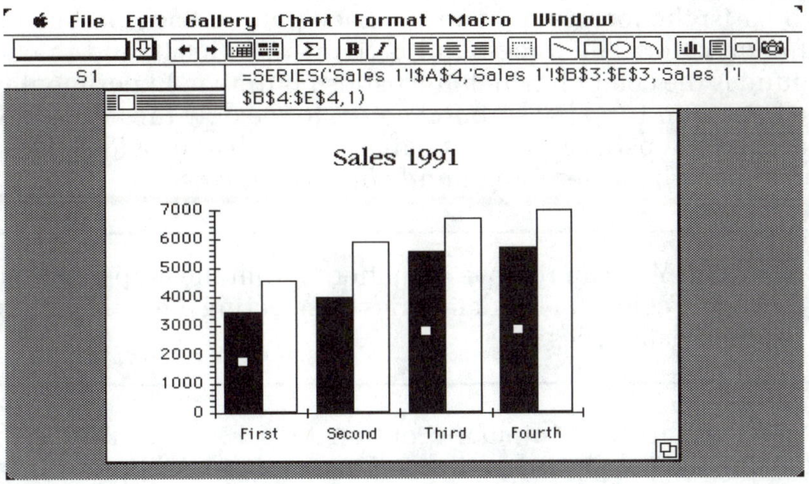

Figure 9.5 Selecting a data series.

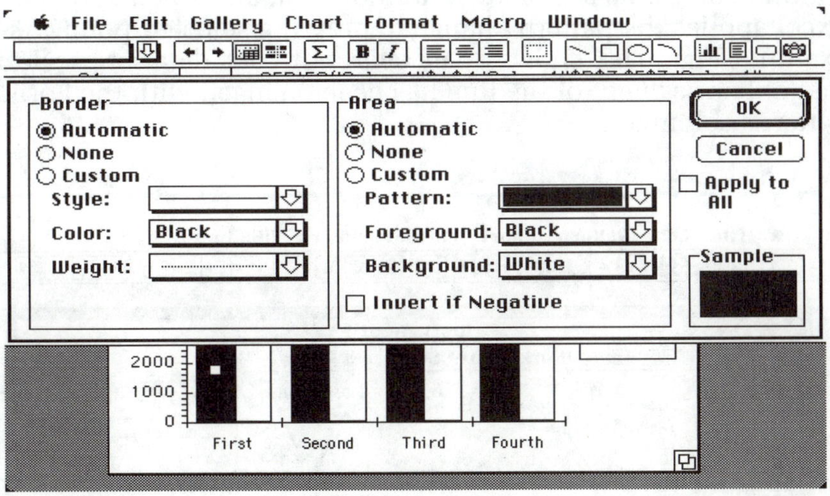

Figure 9.6 The Format-Patterns dialog box for data series.

If you have a color system, keep in mind that the patterns have two parts: the foreground and the background. Each part can be a different color. The foreground is the pattern itself, and the background is the color on which the pattern is drawn. Experiment with the foreground and background colors to see how these work. Note that the solid pattern (the first pattern in the list) provides the solid version of whichever foreground color you choose.

> **Tip**: You can remove all patterns from the graph and use only colors for the data series by selecting the solid pattern for each data series.

As usual, the Automatic option tells Excel to take care of choosing the colors and patterns. The Apply to All option is most useful when your chart contains only one data series. When a chart has only one data series, you can highlight only individual plot points. Therefore, when your chart contains only one data series, you must use the Apply to All option in the Format-Patterns dialog box to make your pattern changes apply to all the plot points in the column chart, line segments in a line chart, and so on. Otherwise, Excel applies the pattern change to only the selected point. As an example, Figure 9.7 shows a line chart with one data series. Notice that only a segment of the line has been changed with the Format-Patterns command.

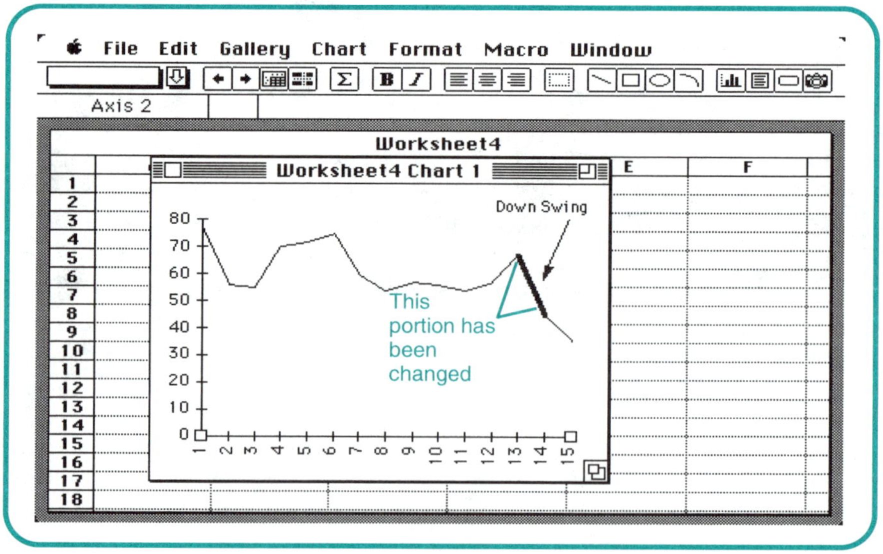

Figure 9.7 Changing a portion of a data series.

Changing the Category Labels

If you're not satisfied with the category labels that go with your chart, you can change them. You can use any text or value as a category label. Following are the Quick Steps to change category labels.

Q Changing the Category Labels

1. If the desired category labels are not already part of the worksheet, enter them into any worksheet range. Use the same number of labels as there are categories in the chart. Figure 9.8 shows an example.
2. Select the range containing the desired labels; then use the Edit-Copy command to copy this data. — Excel places the marquee around the labels.
3. Activate the chart window. Assuming the chart is open, you can use the Window menu to do this. — The chart, with its old category labels, should now be in view.
4. Select the Edit-Paste Special command. — The Paste Special dialog box appears.
5. Make sure that the Categories in First Row and the Replace Existing Categories options are checked. If your new category labels were in a column rather than a row, the Categories in First Row option will read Categories in First Column. Press Return when finished. — The category labels change, as shown in the example in Figure 9.9.

□

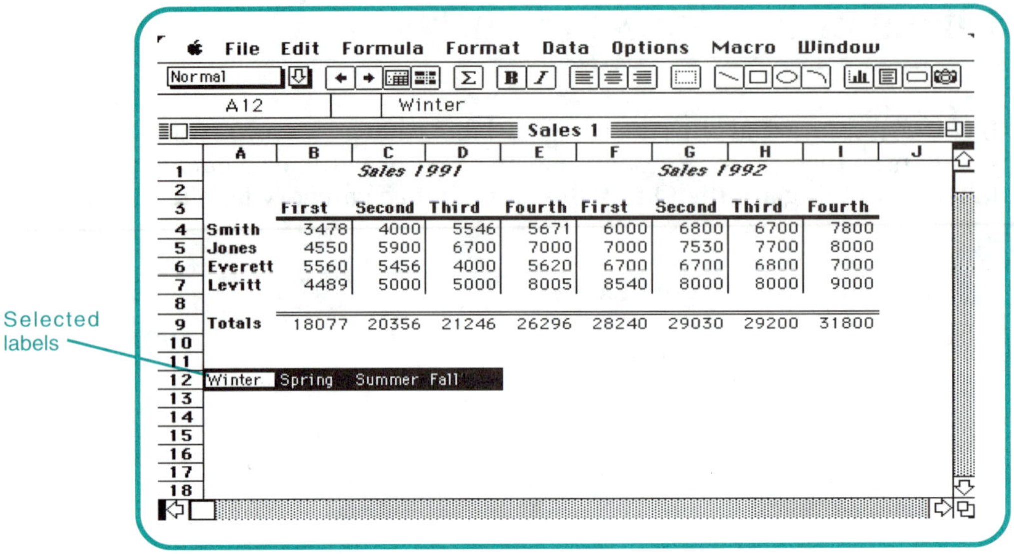

Figure 9.8 Adding new category labels to the worksheet.

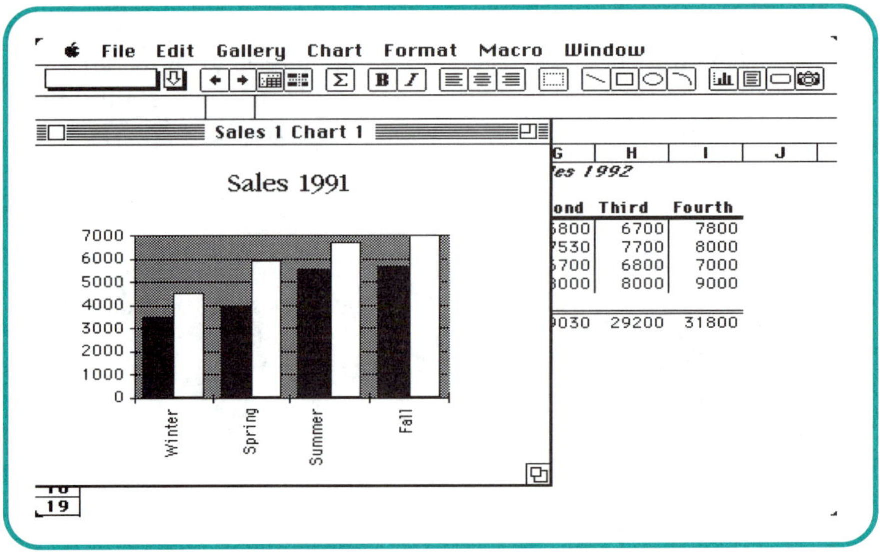

Figure 9.9 Pasting the new category labels into an existing chart using Edit-Paste Special.

Adding Text Labels

You can add all kinds of titles, subtitles, and labels to your chart. Highlight a chart element and select the Chart-Attach Text command. Following are the Quick Steps for this procedure.

Attaching Text to a Chart

1. Highlight the desired chart element using the ↑ and → keys or the mouse. The ↑ key highlights a different element each time you press it. When you have more than one of a particular type of element (for example, there are two axes), use the → key to move among them.
2. Select the Chart-Attach Text command. Make any required changes and then press Return.

   The Attach Text dialog box appears. It shows which element you have highlighted. Use this box to confirm or modify your selection. When you press Return, Excel adds a text box to the chart. This box will contain temporary text as a place holder.
3. Type your new text. Press Return when finished.

   The new text replaces the temporary text. □

The advantage to attaching text using the Attach Text command is that Excel adjusts the chart to make room for the added text. However, you are not limited to adding text to the chart elements listed in the Attach Text dialog box. In fact, you don't have to attach text to any particular element at all. To add descriptive text, just begin typing. Press Return when finished; then the text will appear on the chart. Figure 9.10 shows an example.

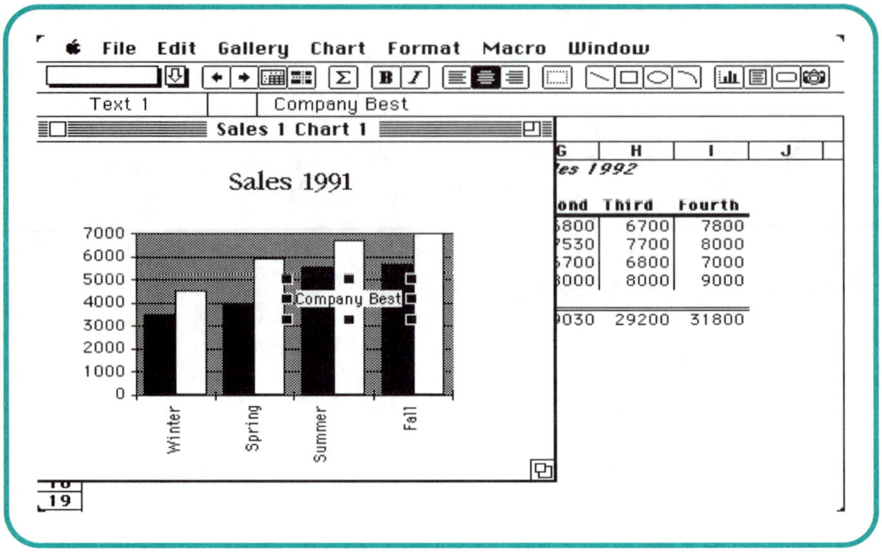

Figure 9.10 Adding descriptive (unattached) text to a chart.

The next step is to move the text to the desired position on the chart. Simply click on the new text and drag it to the desired location.

To remove any added text from the chart, simply highlight the text; then press the Backspace key and Return. The text will be removed.

Aligning Labels

Excel gives you several formatting options for the text that appears in a chart. You can make the text print vertically, horizontally, or stacked. To change the text format, simply highlight the desired text or element to which text is attached and then choose the Format-Text command. The dialog box in Figure 9.11 appears.

Select the desired options in this box and press Return to apply them. Note that some text does not allow all the options shown in this figure.

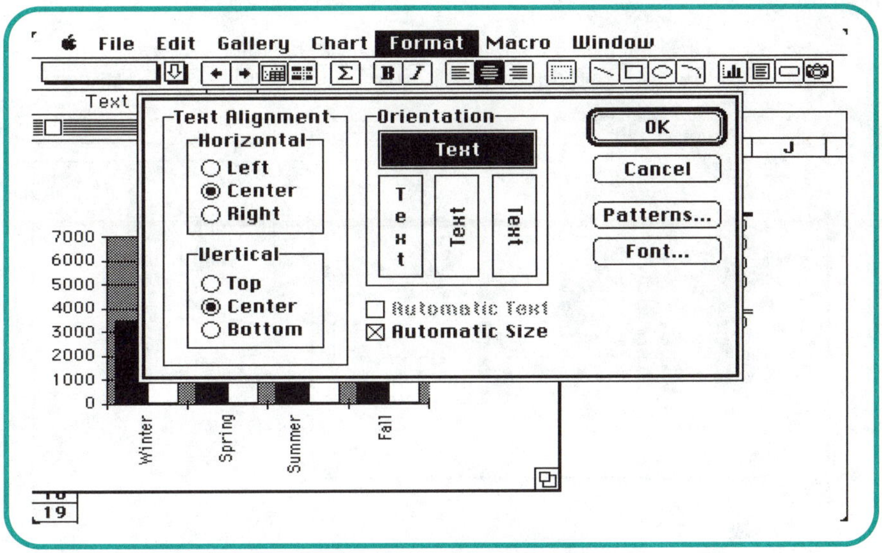

Figure 9.11 The Format-Text dialog box.

Changing Label Fonts

You can change the font of any text showing on the chart. This includes attached text, descriptive text, axis titles, and legend entries. Simply highlight the desired element and select the Format-Font command. Excel's list of fonts appears on-screen. Select the desired font, size, style, and color from the list, and press Return when finished.

Adding a Legend

Adding a chart legend is easy. Excel already knows which chart labels make up the legend—the data series labels in the first column of the chart range. To display these labels in a legend, simply use the Chart-Add Legend command. The chart adjusts to make room for the legend as shown in Figure 9.12.

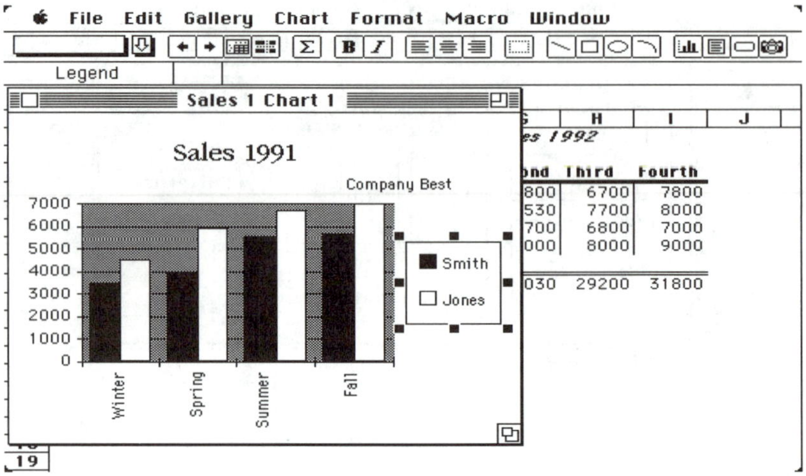

Figure 9.12 Adding a legend.

You can change the placement of the legend by dragging on it with the mouse. If you move the legend to the middle of the chart, Excel will no longer make room for the legend box. This capability can be useful for overlapping the legend with the chart. If you move the chart as far as it will go in any direction, Excel will adjust the chart to make room. The Format-Legend command offers five positions for the legend box: Bottom, Corner, Top, Right, and Left. Experiment for best results. You might also try changing the proportions of the chart to accommodate the legend box.

Adding Gridlines

Another element you can add to a chart is a grid. A grid appears in the plot area of the chart and is useful for emphasizing the vertical scale of the data series. To add gridlines, select the Chart-Gridlines command. Excel presents the four Gridline options. You can add major and minor gridlines for the vertical (value) axis and/or horizontal (category) axis. After adding the gridlines, you can change their colors and patterns as described in the next section.

Changing the Colors and Patterns of Chart Elements

You can change the patterns of many elements. This includes text boxes and interiors, legend boxes and interiors, axis lines, arrows, gridlines, the chart background, the plot area, and data series. As you have probably guessed, first highlight the desired element; then use the Format-Patterns command. Select from pattern options provided and then press Return.

What You've Learned

This chapter has continued the discussion of Excel's charting capabilities. Here you learned how to customize a chart by adding elements, such as text, legends, and gridlines. You also learned how to change the position and style of text and the values on the axes. Following are some things to remember:

- Use the command Format-Scale to change the values along the vertical axis of a chart.
- The Format-Patterns command can change the patterns used for axis lines, series markers, gridlines, and more.
- The Format-Text command changes the positioning of text on the chart.
- Add text labels to a chart using the Chart-Attach Text command by simply typing text onto the chart.
- The Chart-Add Legend command places a legend onto the chart, and the Format-Legend command lets you move the legend. You can also move the legend by dragging it to a new location on the chart.
- Use the Chart-Gridlines command to add gridlines to the graph. You can add these lines vertically, horizontally, or both.

Chapter 10

Managing Data with Excel

In This Chapter

- *The structure of a database*
- *Starting and activating a database in Excel*
- *Inserting records and viewing records*
- *Editing and deleting records*
- *Sorting data*
- *Finding records with the data form*
- *Using wild cards and logical operators in search criteria*
- *Deleting batches of records*
- *Extracting database records*

This chapter explains how to use Excel to store data as a database. The database feature lets you expand on the standard commands and options offered for worksheet data. The only difference between database data and worksheet data is that database data has been "activated" as a database. In this chapter you'll discover reasons for using databases in Excel and the basics for setting them up, adding to them, sorting them, searching them, and extracting records from them.

Database Structure

Using Excel for database operations is really just an extension of the worksheet features. The only difference is in the way you have to access the data. When you have multiple records—such as a list of similar items—and when you have to search those records for particular groups, then you probably need to set up the information as a database. Some examples include customer back orders, sales records, book lists, and address lists, which are shown in Figures 10.1 through 10.4.

Notice in the examples that the information for each item is entered across one row. Each row in a database is called a *record*. Each record is on a different row, and the pieces of information within the records are spread across the row in different cells. The cells within a row, which hold the data for the record, are called *fields*. Notice that each column is labeled with a unique name that describes what's in that column. The column headings above each column are called *field names*.

These are the essential elements of a database in Excel. You'll find that data naturally fits into this pattern and that you hardly have to try to keep database data in the required structure.

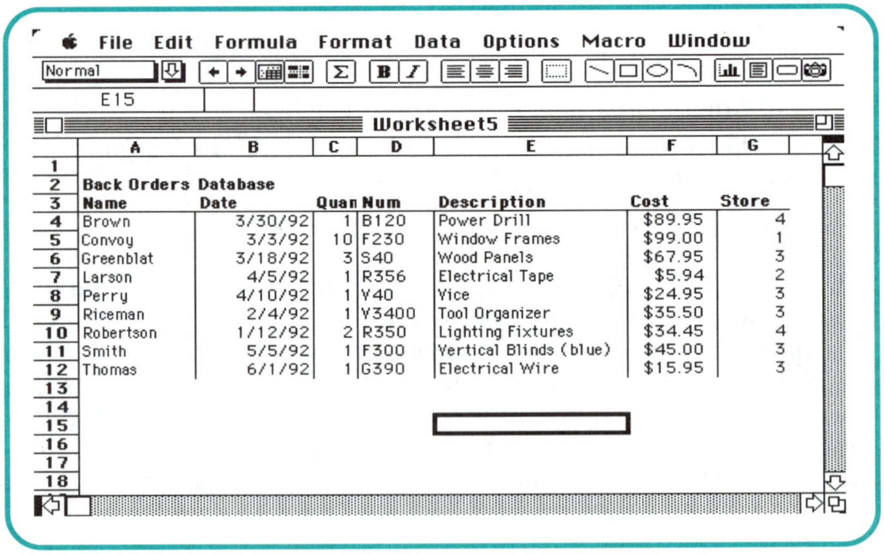

	A	B	C	D	E	F	G
1							
2	**Back Orders Database**						
3	**Name**	**Date**	**Quan**	**Num**	**Description**	**Cost**	**Store**
4	Brown	3/30/92	1	B120	Power Drill	$89.95	4
5	Convoy	3/3/92	10	F230	Window Frames	$99.00	1
6	Greenblat	3/18/92	3	S40	Wood Panels	$67.95	3
7	Larson	4/5/92	1	R356	Electrical Tape	$5.94	2
8	Perry	4/10/92	1	V40	Vice	$24.95	3
9	Riceman	2/4/92	1	V3400	Tool Organizer	$35.50	3
10	Robertson	1/12/92	2	R350	Lighting Fixtures	$34.45	4
11	Smith	5/5/92	1	F300	Vertical Blinds (blue)	$45.00	3
12	Thomas	6/1/92	1	G390	Electrical Wire	$15.95	3
13							
14							
15							
16							
17							
18							

Figure 10.1 A sample database of back ordered merchandise.

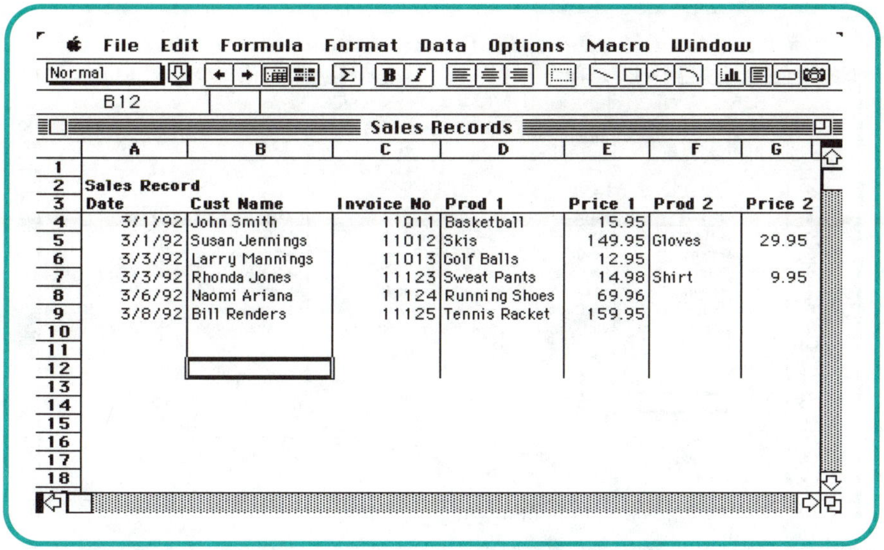

	A	B	C	D	E	F	G
1							
2	Sales Record						
3	Date	Cust Name	Invoice No	Prod 1	Price 1	Prod 2	Price 2
4	3/1/92	John Smith	11011	Basketball	15.95		
5	3/1/92	Susan Jennings	11012	Skis	149.95	Gloves	29.95
6	3/3/92	Larry Mannings	11013	Golf Balls	12.95		
7	3/3/92	Rhonda Jones	11123	Sweat Pants	14.98	Shirt	9.95
8	3/6/92	Naomi Ariana	11124	Running Shoes	69.96		
9	3/8/92	Bill Renders	11125	Tennis Racket	159.95		

Figure 10.2 A sample database of sales records.

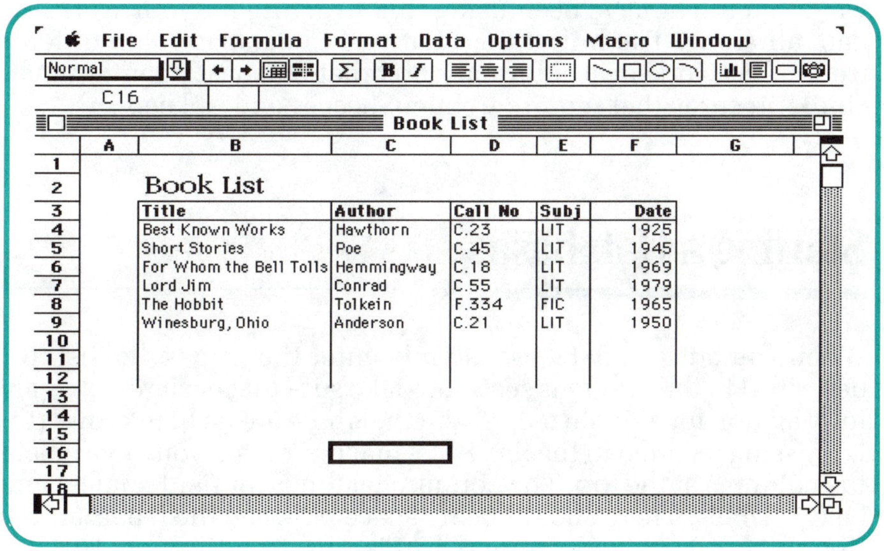

	A	B	C	D	E	F
1						
2		Book List				
3		Title	Author	Call No	Subj	Date
4		Best Known Works	Hawthorn	C.23	LIT	1925
5		Short Stories	Poe	C.45	LIT	1945
6		For Whom the Bell Tolls	Hemmingway	C.18	LIT	1969
7		Lord Jim	Conrad	C.55	LIT	1979
8		The Hobbit	Tolkein	F.334	FIC	1965
9		Winesburg, Ohio	Anderson	C.21	LIT	1950

Figure 10.3 A sample book list.

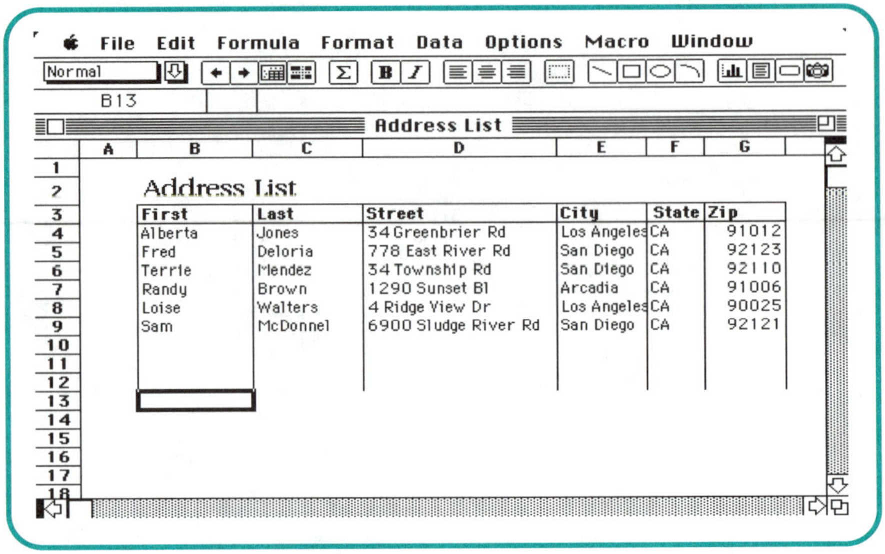

First	Last	Street	City	State	Zip
Alberta	Jones	34 Greenbrier Rd	Los Angeles	CA	91012
Fred	Deloria	778 East River Rd	San Diego	CA	92123
Terrie	Mendez	34 Township Rd	San Diego	CA	92110
Randy	Brown	1290 Sunset Bl	Arcadia	CA	91006
Loise	Walters	4 Ridge View Dr	Los Angeles	CA	90025
Sam	McDonnel	6900 Sludge River Rd	San Diego	CA	92121

Figure 10.4 A sample address list.

Basically, a database is a group of records entered in a specific way. You might have been using this structure for your worksheet data all along. The only thing that makes database data different from other worksheet information is that databases contain many similar records that require frequent access and upkeep.

Starting a Database

When you create a database, simply enter the data in the list form described in the previous section. Make sure that each row contains information for a single record and that there are no blank rows (that is, missing records) in the list. Also, make sure that you have labeled the columns at the top. The column headings (or field names) must be text labels. There should be no space between the labels and the first record. Use the examples in Figures 10.1 through 10.4 as a guide.

Because the nature of a database is to grow, leave enough room at the bottom of the database for added records. You might, in fact, want to give the database its own area of the worksheet, below everything else, to allow nearly unlimited growth. Another idea is to avoid placing a database to the right or left of other worksheet data. Adding or removing database records can affect adjacent areas of the worksheet. The only absolute requirements are that you must include field names (column headings) for the data and that no blank rows should appear below the field names.

After you have established the database area and field names, you can begin entering data. The easiest way to add information is to use the data form, which is described in the next section. Or, you may just begin typing the information under each column heading. Consider highlighting the database range before entering data. Highlighting will cause the pointer to remain in the range as you move from cell to cell with the Tab and Return keys.

You do not have to complete each record in the database. In other words, some fields can remain blank. But remember not to leave an entire record blank. You can use formulas to produce some field values. One column, for example, might be calculated from the values in other columns. The PRICE and QUANTITY fields of each record in a Sales Receipt database might be multiplied to produce a TOTAL field for each record. All normal worksheet operations are available for use with your database data.

Activating the Database Features

So far you have seen how to enter information in a database structure for Excel. But you might be wondering what is so special about this. You might have been using such a structure for all kinds of data. What's special is that you can activate Excel's database features for data that are entered in the correct structure by using the Data-Set Database command.

Highlight all the data you have typed in database format, including all existing records and the column headings at the top. Then select the Data-Set Database command to activate the database. If you don't have records in the database yet, highlight the headings and the blank row beneath them.

By activating the database this way, you have added a number of special features that you can use now with the database you selected. The most important feature is the data form, which is useful for inserting new records into the database, deleting records, and finding specific records.

> **Tip**: You can have more than one database on a worksheet, but only one can be activated at a time. To switch to a different database, highlight the area of the worksheet containing the other database and use the Data-Set Database command. Whichever range you've activated last will be the current database.

Adding Records to the Database

After you activate a database, you can do almost everything with the special data form. For example, you can use the data form to insert new records into the database. You'll find this procedure easier than inserting the records manually at the bottom of the list. And, you can begin using the data form immediately after you create the field names, highlight them and a blank row, and execute the Data-Set Database command. Just use the following Quick Steps.

Adding New Records with the Data Form

1. Select the Data-Form command. — Brings the data form into view. The data form displays the fields you have defined in the database structure. Figure 10.5 shows an example.
2. Click the New button to start a new record. — Clears all data from the form so that you can enter new information.

3. Type the information for each field in the form. Press Tab to move to the next field or Shift-Tab to move back to a previous field. Press Backspace to correct typing errors. All editing commands are available while you are typing in the data form.

4. When finished with the record, press New or Return to add another new record or click Close to exit the data form and return to the worksheet.

Whether you press New or Close, the new record will be added to the bottom of the database.

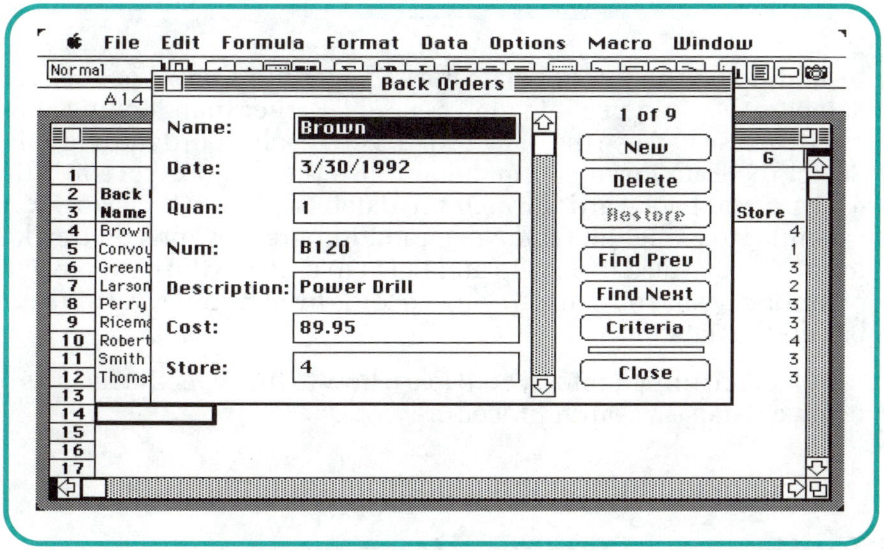

Figure 10.5 The data form.

Data forms are limited to the number of fields that will fit on the screen; on a 9-inch monitor this is about 16 fields. If any of the fields in a database are calculated using formulas, you will be unable to type information for that field in the data form. Instead, Excel assumes that you want to reproduce the formula for all new records and inserts the formula automatically for each new record.

> **Tip**: After you activate the database, adding records by using the data form is best. If you type new records into worksheet rows below the existing data, the new records will not be part of the active database. You'll have to reactivate the database to include the new records. However, you can insert new rows into the middle of the database range and enter new records into those rows. This action does not require that you reactivate the database. The new records will be part of the active database. Still, the data form provides the easiest way to add new records.

Viewing Database Records

In addition to using the data form for adding new records to a database, you can use it to view records. Rather than looking at the full database list, use the data form to view each record individually. Select the Data-Form command and use the ↑ and ↓ keys to "flip" forward and backward through the database. Using the arrow keys is similar to using the Find Next and Find Prev buttons on the data form. You can also use PgUp and PgDn to move to the extreme ends of the database. You can also view records by manipulating the scroll bar on the data form.

Later in this chapter, you'll learn how to find specific records by using a database search procedure.

Editing and Deleting Records

Database information changes frequently. You'll probably find the need to return to a previously entered record and change it. Perhaps a customer has moved, and you need to update an address. Or maybe an order has arrived, and you need to mark it as completed. Whatever the reason, updating records is an important part of database management.

You can update records in two ways. First, you can move the pointer to the row in which the record appears and then select and update the cells that need changing. Use the editing commands described in Chapter 4.

A second way to edit the information in a record is to use the data form. Simply activate the data form and use the ↓ key to locate the desired record. Press the Tab key to move to the field you want to change. As shown in Figure 10.6, pressing the Tab key highlights the fields.

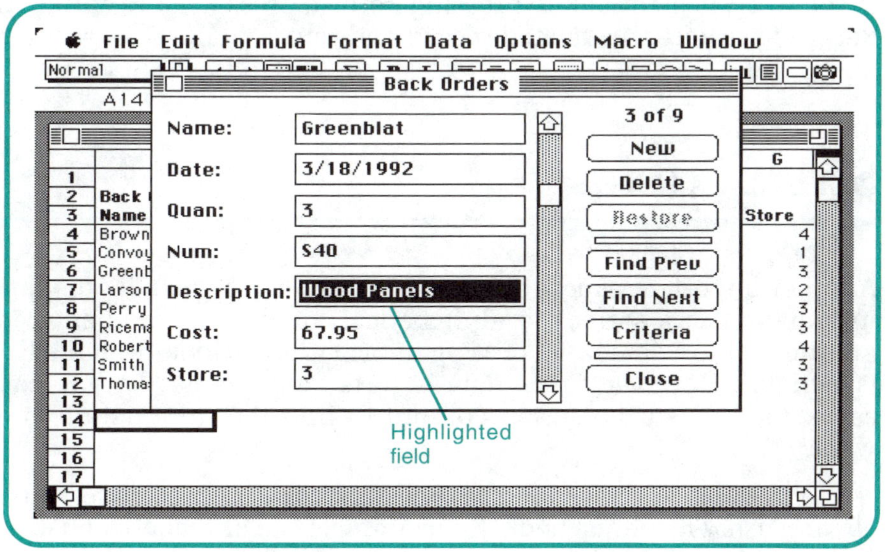

Figure 10.6 Highlighting a field with the Tab key.

With the field highlighted, you can begin typing new data to completely replace the existing data. Or, if you want to change only a part of the existing data, click the mouse inside the box to unhighlight the field. Then use the basic editing commands listed in Chapter 4 to make further changes.

Press Return or Close to accept your changes, or press Esc to reject them and return to the worksheet.

> ▶ **Tip**: As your database grows larger, using the ↓ key to find records with the data form will get less and less practical. Then you should turn to the data searching procedures discussed later in this chapter.

Besides editing a record in the database, you can use the data form to delete a record. As with editing, first locate the desired record so that it is in view in the data form. Then, press the Delete button to delete the record. Press Return to accept the deletion and return to the worksheet, or before pressing Return, press Restore and then Return to restore the deleted record and return to the worksheet.

Sorting Records

Another important aspect of databases is that they usually display information in a sorted (or alphabetical) order. If data is entered randomly into a database, locating information by looking at the list is difficult. However, if the data is sorted alphabetically, you can easily look down the sorted column to find the information you want.

You rely on this type of sorted order in the "databases" you already use. The phone book, for example, is an alphabetical listing of names and phone numbers. The phone book is sorted alphabetically by last names. As a rule, the last name is the best field for sorting because it contains the data you are most likely to know already. Sorting the phone book numerically by telephone numbers would do little good, because that's the information you are probably trying to find.

The same rule applies to the databases you create in Excel. Sorting is for arranging the data on the piece of information (that is, the field) that you are most likely to know already. You can quickly look over the sorted fields to find the record you want, giving you access to the information in the record that you don't know already. The difference between the Excel database and your phone book is that you can re-sort the Excel database over and over again using any piece of information in the database. The phone book is stuck with a last name sort. Re-sorting is particularly useful after you add records to a database.

The final point to note before sorting your data is that Excel uses one of three different sorting methods for the data, based on the field by which you sort the data. If the field contains text, Excel sorts the records alphabetically. If the field contains numeric data, Excel sorts the records numerically. If the field contains dates, then Excel sorts the records chronologically. Finally, you can sort the data in ascending or descending order: that is, from A to Z or from Z to A. An ascending sort is the most common.

The following Quick Steps show you how to sort data.

Sorting the Database

1. Highlight all the records in the database, but do not include the field names at the top.

   Figure 10.7 shows an example.

2. Press the Tab key to position the pointer in the column by which you want the data sorted. For example, if you are sorting by last names, place the pointer in the Last Name column.

   This prepares the sort command for the *key field*, or the field by which you are sorting the data.

3. Select the Data-Sort command.

   The dialog box shown in Figure 10.8 appears, providing choices for the sorting order. Notice that the dialog box contains a reference to the current cell, indicating the column by which you are sorting.

4. Press Return to sort the data in ascending order. Press the Descending button and then Return to sort the data in descending order.

   After pressing Return, the data will be sorted according to the specified key field. Figure 10.9 shows the example database sorted by last names. □

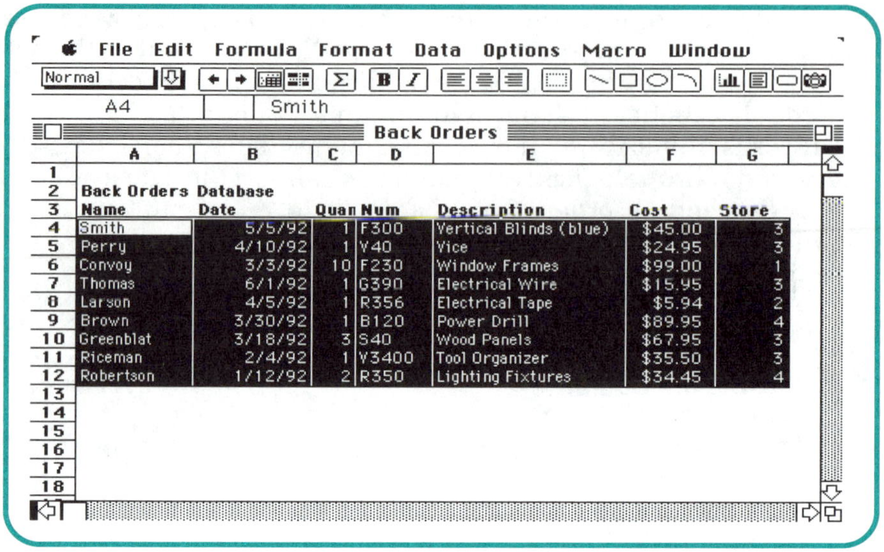

Figure 10.7 Highlighting the database records for sorting.

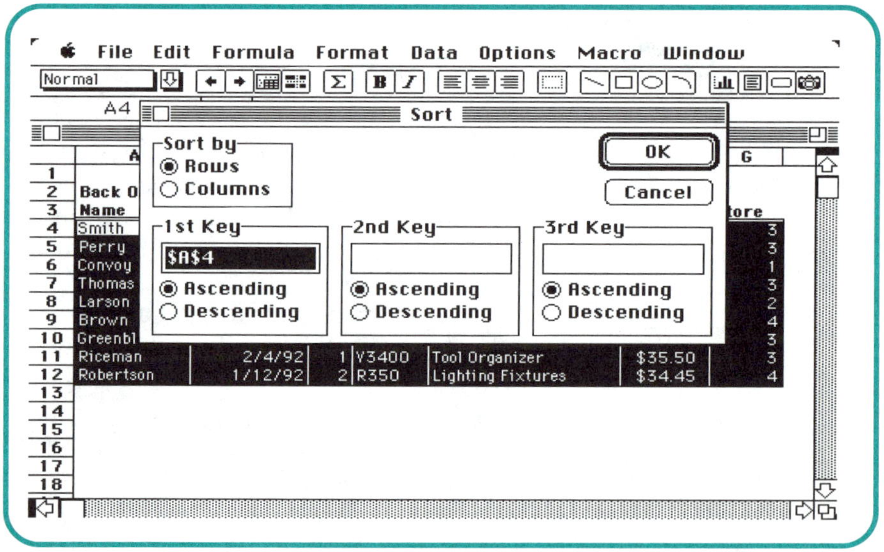

Figure 10.8 The Data-Sort dialog box.

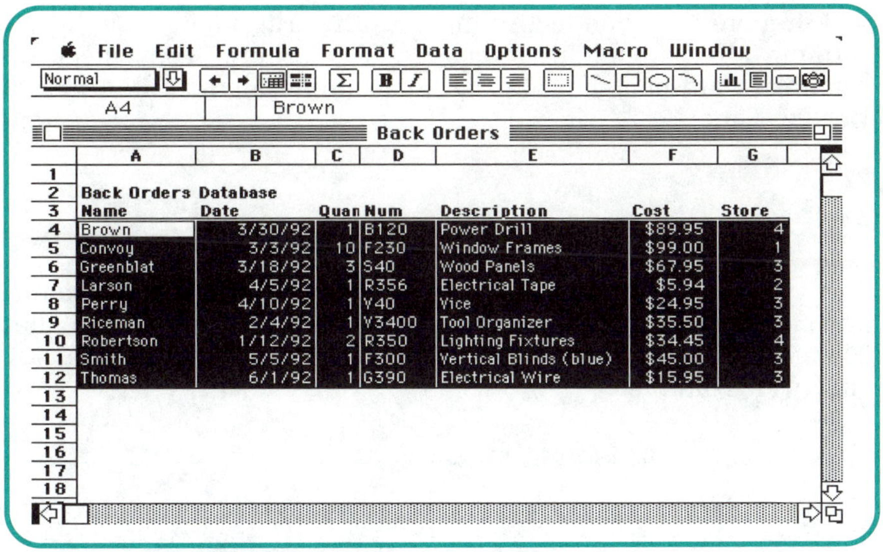

Figure 10.9 Result of sorting the example database by last names.

Remember that you can sort and re-sort the database at any time. When you add records using the data form, you probably will not enter the records in alphabetical order, so you might want to re-sort the database when you have finished.

Finding Records with the Data Form

The easiest way to search for database records is to use the data form. Using the data form, you can locate any record in the database by identifying information in any one of the fields. Finding can be as simple as matching values, such as finding a record that contains "Smith" in the Last Name field. Or you can find records based on more fields, such as all the records with "Smith" in the Last Name field and "NY" in the State field. Using wild cards and logical operators, you can even find records based on special conditions, such as all last names beginning with "S."

If more than one record matches the criteria, you can browse through all the matching records. The criteria you select will establish a subset of the database; for example, all records for Smiths in New York.

Making a Simple Search

To try a simple search, open a worksheet with database information and activate the database range if it has not already been activated. Then view the data form with the Data-Form command. Figure 10.10 shows an example.

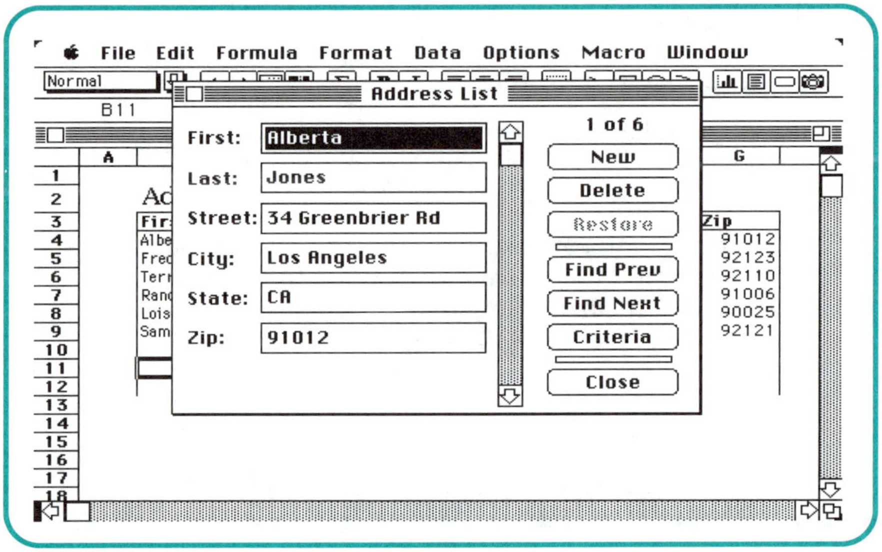

Figure 10.10 The data form for an address database.

Of course, when it first appears, the data form always shows the first record in the database. After the data form is in view, you can begin to find records with three easy steps: Select the Criteria button on the data form; enter the desired criteria into the blank field boxes that are presented; and select the Find Next button. Look at each of these steps in detail.

The first step is selecting the Criteria button to activate the criteria entry form, which is basically a blank version of the data form. Notice that some of the buttons on the form change when you select the Criteria button. For one thing, the Criteria button changes to the Form button so that you can return to the data form whenever you like. Following is a list of the buttons available on the criteria entry form:

Clear — If you have entered criteria information into the fields, this button clears that data so that you can start over.

Restore — If you have used the Clear button, this button restores the criteria you had on the form.

Find Previous — This button finds the previous record that matches your criteria.

Find Next — This button finds the next record in the database that matches your criteria.

Form — This button returns to the data form without searching for the criteria you've set.

Close — The Close button returns you to the worksheet.

The next step is to enter the desired criteria into the fields of the criteria entry form. First, use the Tab key to move to that field. Then enter the data that you are trying to match. For example, to find all records for people in San Diego in an address database, enter `San Diego` into the City field as shown in Figure 10.11.

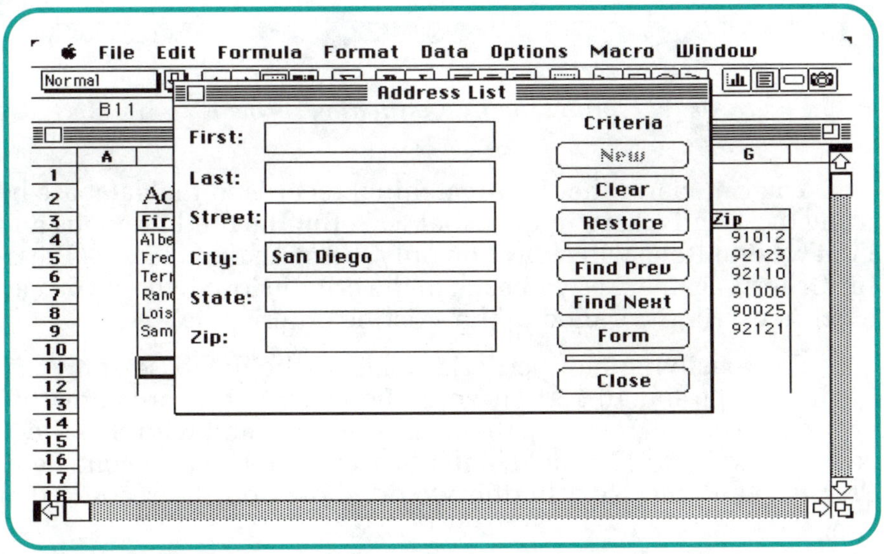

Figure 10.11 Entering criteria for searching.

The last step is to press the Find Next button. Starting from the first record in the database, the Find Next button locates the *next* record that matches the criteria you selected, such as the criteria shown in Figure 10.12. The Find Next button compares the second and subsequent records with the criteria. Press Find Next again to find the next matching record and again for the next. You are viewing a subset of the database, skipping all records that do not match the criteria. Of course, using the Find Previous button flips through the records backward. When you reach the last matching record, Excel beeps to indicate that no more exist.

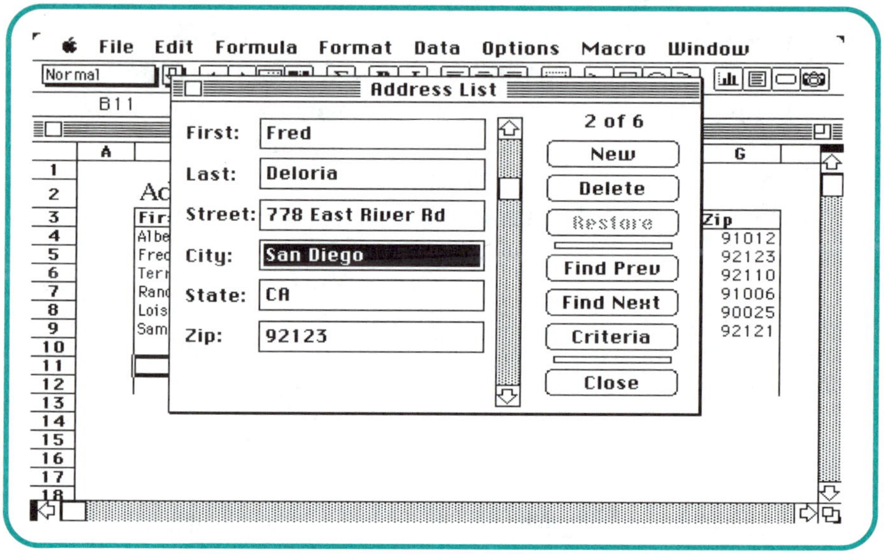

Figure 10.12 Finding the first matching record.

You can view other (nonmatching) records in the database by using the ↑ and ↓ keys in the usual way. But the Find Previous and Find Next buttons will show you only the matching records. Pressing Criteria again takes you back to the criteria form where you can enter new criteria or modify the existing criteria.

Try specifying more criteria fields in the database shown in Figures 10.11 and 10.12 to narrow the matching records down to only one. You can return to the Criteria screen, and with San Diego still entered in the City field, enter `McDonnel` in the Last Name field. Pressing the Find Next button would show you the records that match both criteria: people who have the last name of McDonnel and who live in San Diego.

Note that when you begin searching with Find Next, Excel begins searching from the current record displayed in the data form. If you are currently at the first record in the database, Excel doesn't "look at" the current (first) record but finds the next (second) record in the database that matches. If you are not at the beginning of the database, Excel selects the *next* record that matches rather than the *first* record in the database that matches. For example, imagine that you have a database where records 4, 6, and 10 have "Smith" in the Last Name field. If record 6 is the current record and you search for "Smith," record number 10 will be the first record Excel finds. Therefore, jumping to the first record of the database before starting your search is a good practice. When you first open the data form, you will be at the beginning of the database.

Making a More Complex Match

So far you've seen how to locate records using direct matching of criteria. But direct matches can limit your ability to find information. For example, what if you want to find all people in the database whose last name *begins with* a B? You can search using more complex search criteria—criteria that include a *wild card*.

A wild card is a special symbol that takes the place of unknown information in the search criteria. By using the wild-card symbol in different ways, you can get all kinds of powerful searches. The wild-card symbol is simply the * (asterisk). The following list shows some examples of the wild-card symbol when entered as part of the search criteria in the Last Name field of an address database:

M*	Searches for last names that begin with M.
***m**	Searches for last names that end with m.
m	Searches for last names that contain an m in them, but which do not begin or end with m.
M*m	Searches for last names that begin with M and end with m.

Simply enter the wild card in one of the ways shown. You can use the wild card with numeric entries as well as text.

You might need to find records based on special conditions, such as all records that *do not contain* a particular criteria. Using numeric fields, you can find all values *less than* or *greater than* a particular criteria. To accomplish these matches, you must include one of the following logical operators with your criteria:

<>	Does not equal
>	Is greater than
<	Is less than
>=	Is greater than or equal to
<=	Is less than or equal to

> **Note**: With the exception of the <> operator, these logical operators are meant for numeric information and dates. For example, entering `>10000` finds all records with values greater than 10000. But the > operator (as well as < >= and <=) has no purpose for fields containing text.

For example, suppose you want to find everyone in an address database whose first name is not Fred. Your criteria would look like Figure 10.13.

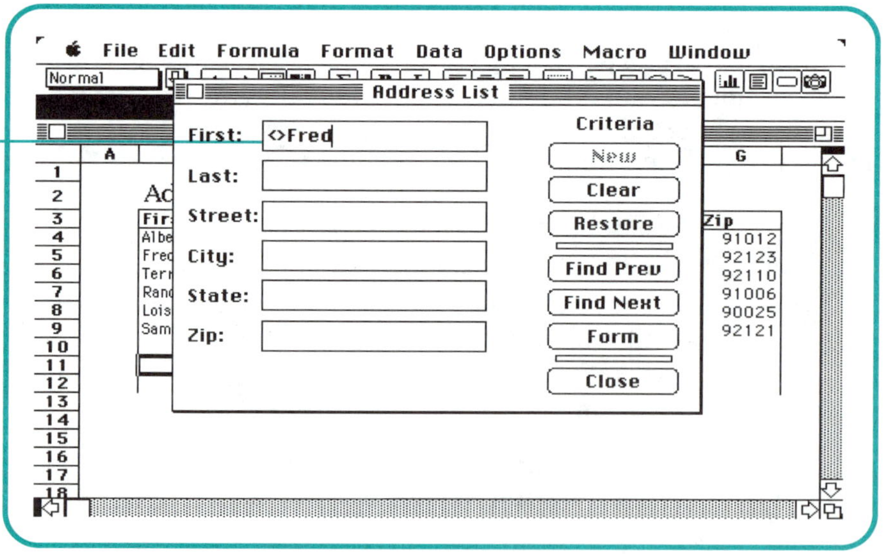

Figure 10.13 Entering logical operators in criteria.

Now the Find Next and Find Previous buttons will ignore all records with Fred in the First Names field. Experimenting with these operators can help you get familiar with their results. Remember that Excel begins searching at the record currently displayed in the data form. To search from the beginning of the database, move to the first record before entering the criteria, or close and then reopen the data form to start at the beginning.

Using a Criteria Range

So far you've seen how to find records in the database by using the data form to establish search criteria. When searching with the data form, you can flip through all matching records. The more search criteria you include, the fewer records you will have to search through to find the specific data you need.

Another way to search for database records is to use a *criteria range* on the worksheet. A criteria range is a range of cells that contains the field names and criteria entries you want to use. The procedure is like duplicating the data form on the worksheet. Figure 10.14 shows a typical criteria range.

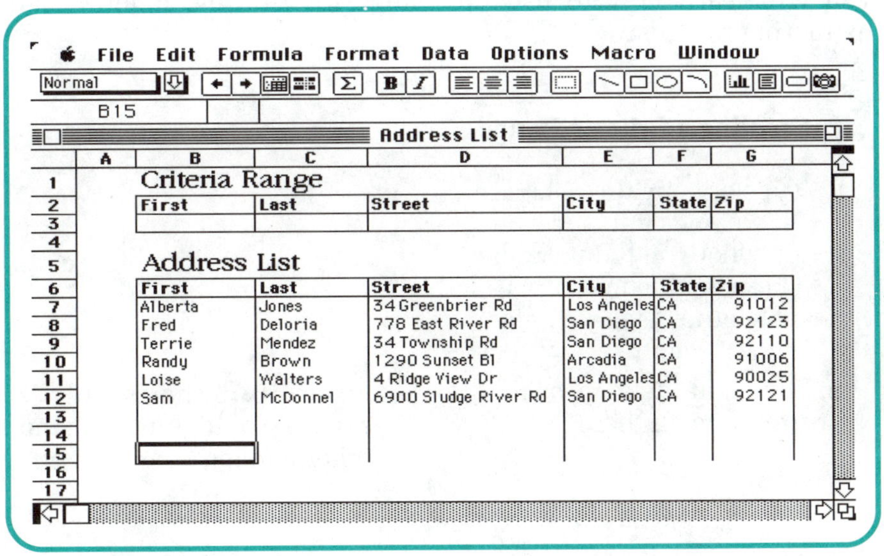

Figure 10.14 A criteria range for the address list.

Notice that the criteria range includes all the field names plus a blank row beneath these names. You enter the criteria into the blank row just as you would enter it into the data form. You may be wondering why you would use a criteria range when you can use the data form in much the same way. Following are the advantages to using a criteria range:

- You can delete a batch of records at one time using criteria entered into the criteria range. Using the data form, you can delete only one record at a time.
- You can extract records from the database and place them in a worksheet range. The extracted data matches the criteria in the criteria range. You cannot extract records using the data form.
- You can establish more complex criteria than available with the data form. Besides matching data with direct entries, wild cards, and logical operators, you can also use OR logic in the criteria range. For example, you can find all people in your database whose first name is Fred OR Sam. The data form allows AND conditions only.

The only disadvantage to using a criteria range is that it's not as simple as the data form. But you might trade some of the data form's simplicity for the additional features offered by the criteria range. The following Quick Steps show how to create a criteria range. Then you will learn how to use this range for finding, deleting, and extracting records.

Creating a Criteria Range

1. Type or copy the database field names into a row anywhere on the worksheet. These field names must match the database field names exactly.
2. Highlight the names and the row beneath them.

   Figure 10.15 shows an example of highlighting the criteria range.

3. Select the Data-Set Criteria option.

Sets the highlighted range as the criteria range and makes it available for use. You only need to create the criteria range once. □

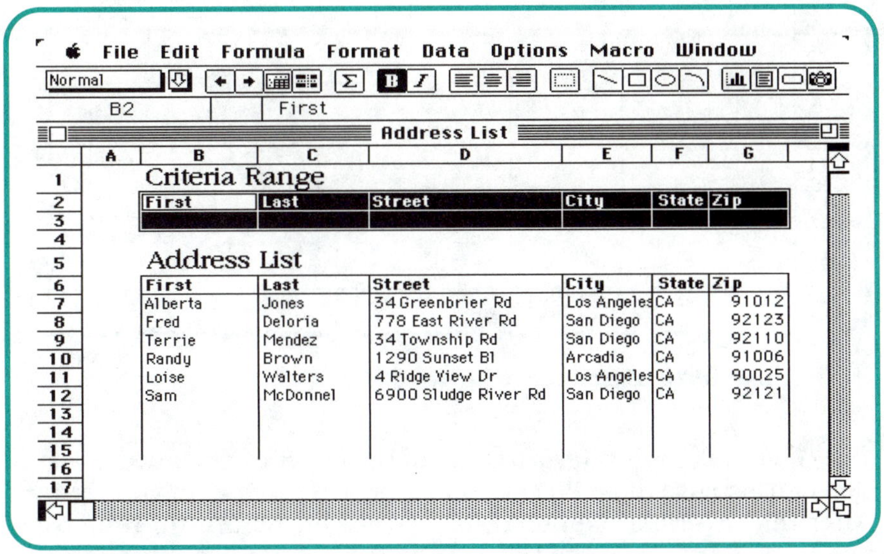

Figure 10.15 Highlighting the criteria range.

Finding Records with the Criteria Range

You are now ready to use the criteria range to find database records. Simply enter the data you want to match in the row below the field names. For example, to find all people who live in San Diego, enter `San Diego` under the City heading as shown in Figure 10.16.

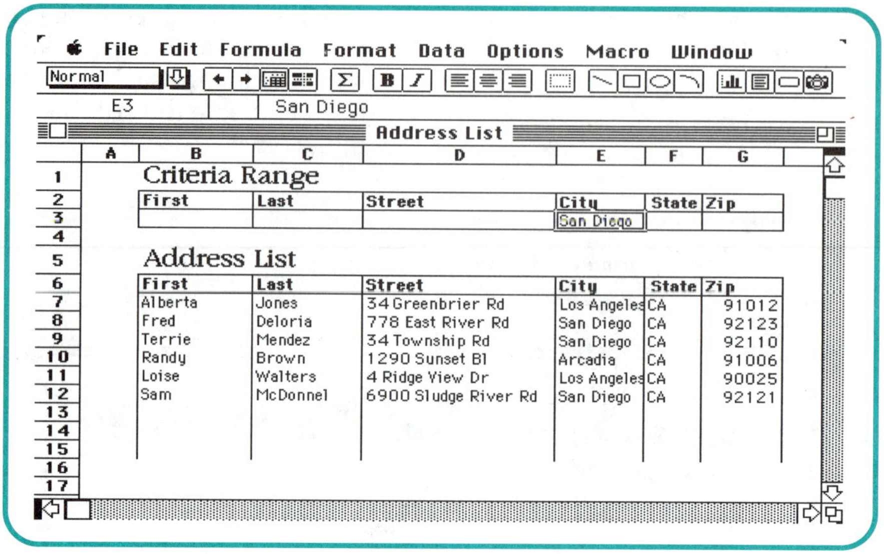

Figure 10.16 Enter the criteria under the headings.

You can enter criteria for any of the fields to narrow the search. You can also use the wild card and logical operators in your criteria. After the criteria are entered, leave the cell pointer in the criteria range and then select the Data-Find command. Excel highlights the first matching record in the database. Figure 10.17 shows an example.

You can now use the ↑ and ↓ keys to view other matching records. Press Esc to return to normal worksheet operation.

Extending Matching Criteria

When you add more criteria to the criteria range, you effectively narrow the possible matching records. For example, you can enter `San Diego` in the City field and `Brown` in the Last Name field. Rather than finding those records that have San Diego in the City field, Excel must find records with San Diego in the City field *AND* Brown in the Last Name field. Fewer records will match both criteria. By making entries in multiple fields of the criteria range, you can create this kind of AND condition for the criteria.

But suppose you want to find records that have San Diego in the City Field *OR* Brown in the Last Name field? In other words, a record will match if it meets *either* condition. OR conditions actually extend the number of possible matching records. To enter an OR condition for criteria, enter the different pieces of data on different rows under the criteria headings. An example would look like Figure 10.18.

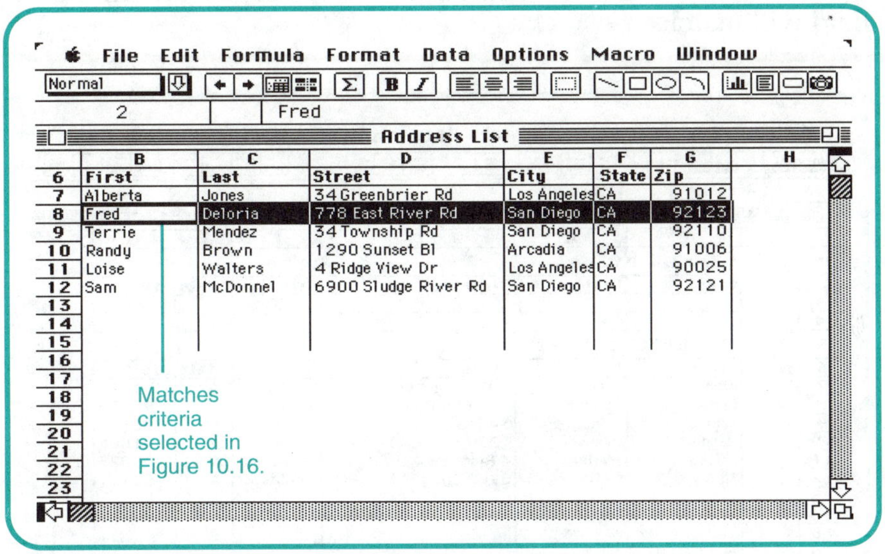

Figure 10.17 Excel finds the first matching record.

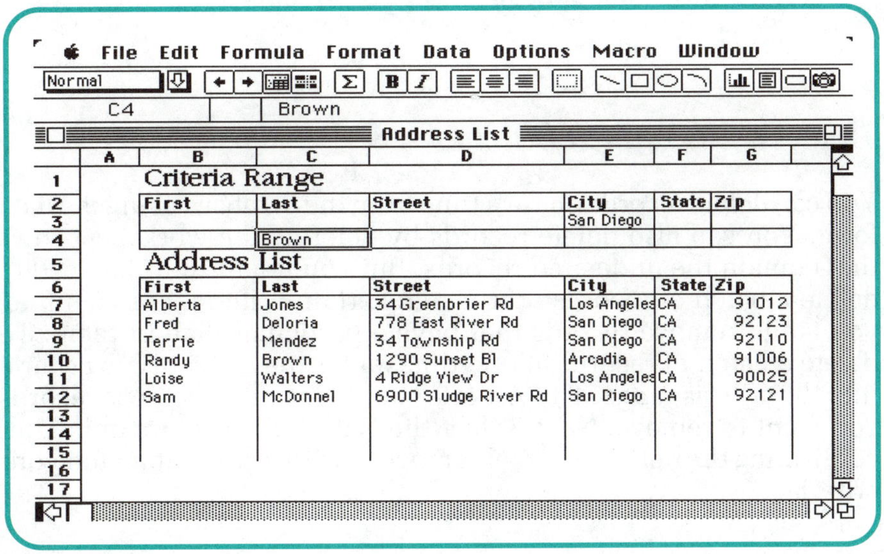

Figure 10.18 Entering OR conditions in the extract range.

Notice that the two criteria entries appear on different rows beneath the criteria headings. Also, the criteria range has been extended to include an extra row of values. You must highlight all rows and use the Data-Set Criteria command to include all rows in the criteria range. Figure 10.19 shows another example. In Figure 10.19's example, all records with San Diego or Arcadia in the City field will match.

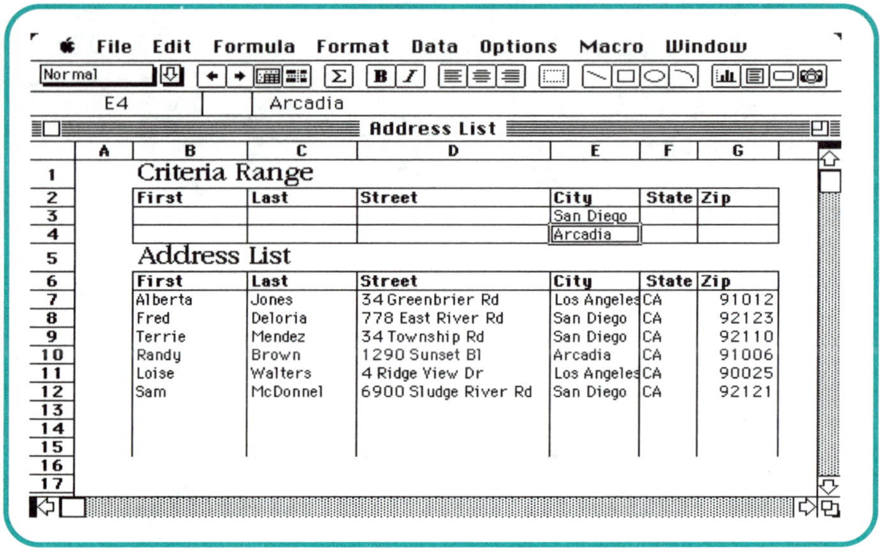

Figure 10.19 Matching San Diego or Arcadia in the City field.

Deleting Records in Batches

You can delete records one at a time from the database using the data form. You can also delete records by deleting the worksheet rows that contain the undesired records. But you might find the need to delete a batch of records that match certain criteria. For example, you could remove records that have a particular date in them. To delete a batch of records at one time, enter the appropriate criteria into the criteria range. This criteria should locate only those records you want to remove. Next, select the Data-Delete command. After confirming the deletion, Excel removes the records that match your criteria.

Caution: Unless you use the Edit-Undo command immediately after deleting, the deleted record will be removed permanently. Saving the worksheet prior to deleting can provide a "safety net."

Extracting Records

Extracting records from a database is an extension of finding records using a criteria range. But instead of highlighting records, Excel duplicates the matching records and places them in a list. You need to prepare three elements to extract records from a database:

- The active database range.
- The criteria range to match the database range.
- The extract range.

The *extract range* is the area of the worksheet where you would like to place the duplicated records. You should place the extract range below the database records on the worksheet, and the range should begin with a row of headings as shown in Figure 10.20. The headings you enter in the extract range must match the field names in the database exactly for the extract to work properly. You can simply copy the headings from the database range.

The next step is to enter the desired criteria into the criteria range. This will determine which records are extracted. For example, use San Diego in the City field to extract all records with this data. Now, highlight the headings of the extract range as shown in Figure 10.21 and select the Data-Extract command. Excel will ask if you want to extract `Unique Records Only`. Press Return at this message to select all matching records. Or, if the database may contain duplicates of some records and you do not want to extract every duplicate, press U to check the Unique Records Only option. Next, Excel will place the records that match the search criteria into the extract range below the highlighted headings. Figure 10.22 shows a completed extract procedure.

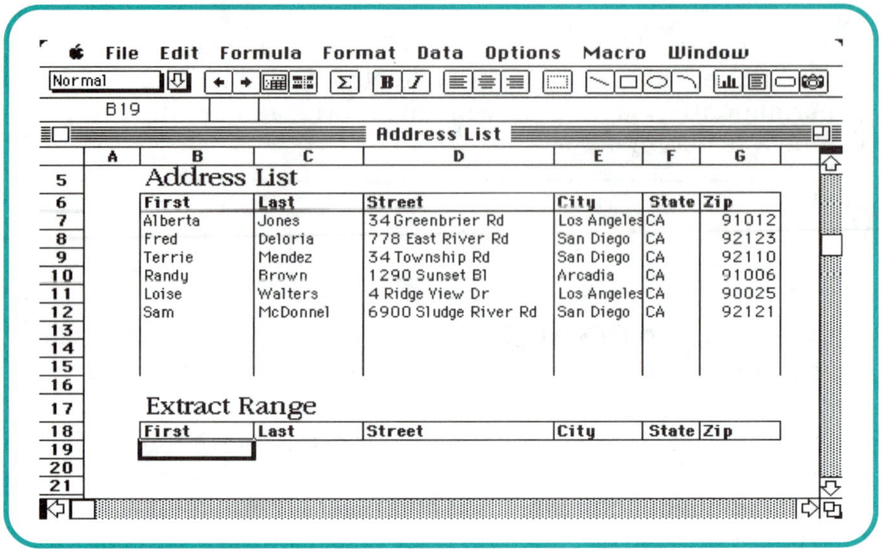

Figure 10.20 An example extract range below the database range.

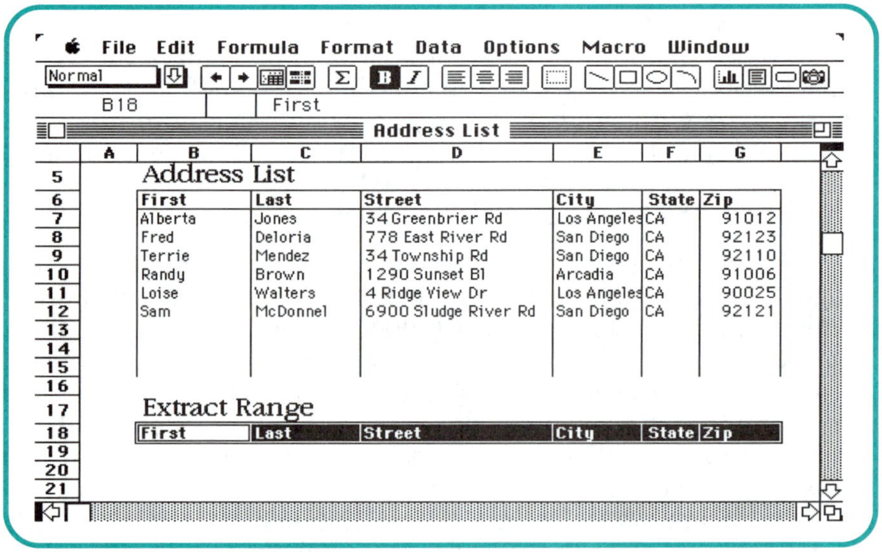

Figure 10.21 Highlighting the extract range before extracting.

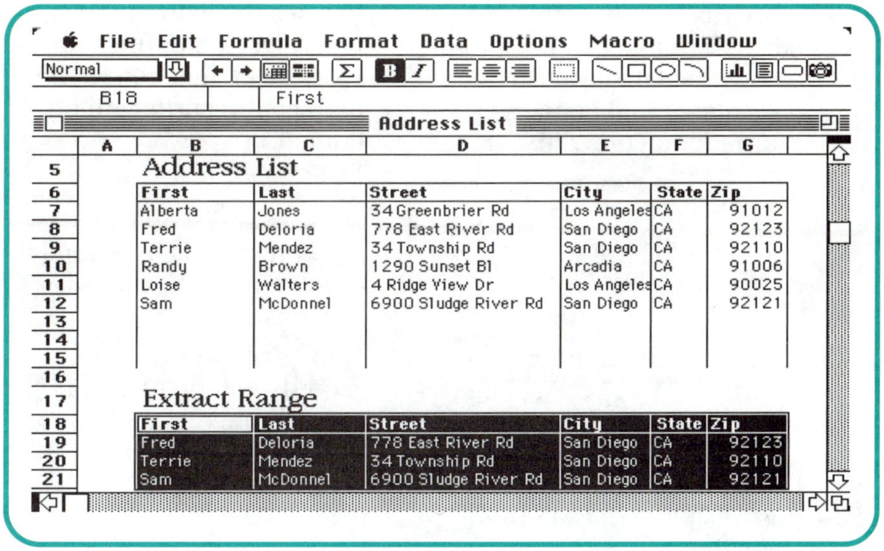

Figure 10.22 The completed extract procedure.

> **Caution**: Make sure that no worksheet data appears below the extract range. When Excel extracts the records and places them into this range, it erases all data below the range.

The procedure for extracting database records is summarized in the following Quick Steps.

Q Extracting Database Records

1. Create the database and criteria ranges as described earlier. Be sure that the criteria range has been activated with the Data-Set Criteria command.
2. Enter all search criteria into the criteria range. — Designates the records that will be selected.

3. Copy the headings from the database range to a new area below the database. Do not use an area that contains information below it. — Creates the extract range headings and defines the worksheet area where the extracted records will be copied.
4. Highlight the copied extract range headings.
5. Select the Data-Extract command. — Excel responds by asking if you want to select `Unique Records Only`.
6. To extract all matching records, press Return. To extract only one copy of each matching record, press U to check the Unique Records Only option; then press Return. — Copies of the extracted records will be placed in the extract range.

□

When you extract records from the database, you don't have to duplicate every field in each record. In other words, you can extract portions of the matching records. In the example in Figure 10.20, you might want to extract only the First Name and Last Name fields for the San Diego records. This capability lets you create specific lists of information by extracting from a database. To select specific fields for the extract procedure, simply list in the extract range only those fields you want extracted. Figure 10.23 shows an example.

> ▶ **Tip**: You can permanently set the extract range by highlighting it and using the Data-Set Extract command. Performing this sequence eliminates the need to highlight the range each time you extract.

Notice that in Figure 10.23 the two extract fields are also in a different order than their appearance in the database range. This change is perfectly okay. Excel will extract the fields you specify, in the order you specify. Figure 10.24 shows the extracted records using the two extract fields.

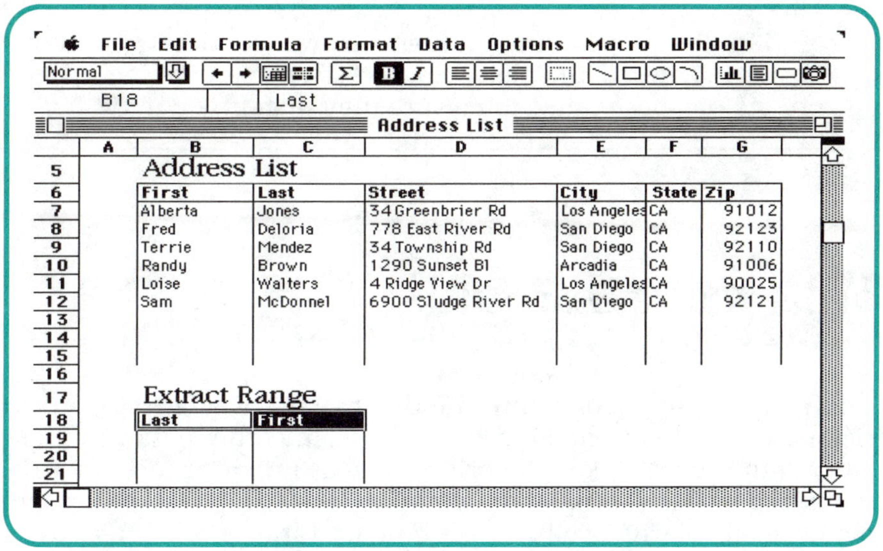

Figure 10.23 Extracting a limited number of fields from the matching records.

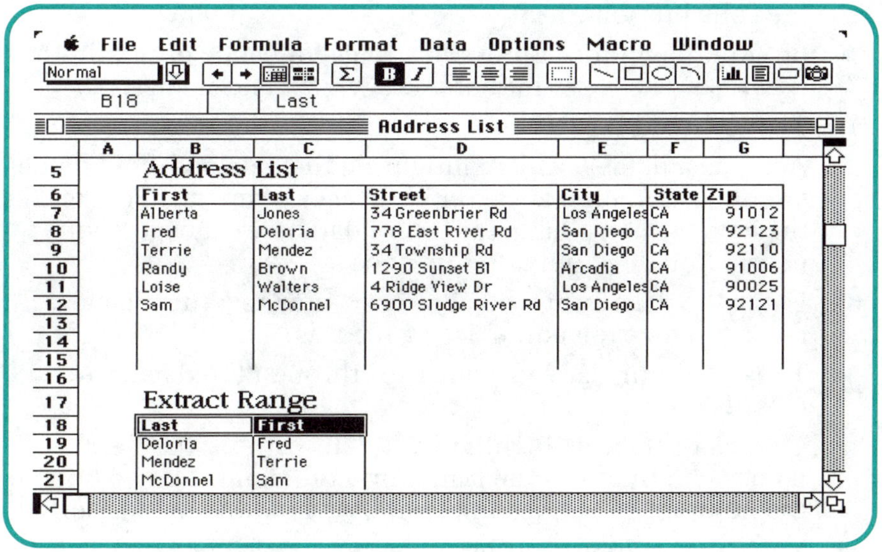

Figure 10.24 The extracted records.

> **Tip**: If you have any problems extracting data, you may have entered the fields incorrectly. Try copying them from the database range to be sure they match.

What You've Learned

This chapter provided an introduction to Excel's database features. Database data is not much different from any other data you might enter into a worksheet. However, database data usually requires more frequent updating, more complex analyzing, and other such management needs. The use of the data form is a key feature in Excel's database capabilities. Following are some points to remember:

- Database data consists of records, which are entered in rows of the worksheet. Within each record are fields, which are the cells in each row.
- Be sure to include column headings for each column in the database. These are formally known as field names.
- There should be no blank records in the database.
- Activate a database by highlighting the data and field names and then using the Data-Set Database command. This makes the data form available for future database management needs. You need only do this once.
- Using the data form, you can insert new records, delete records, and even edit existing records.
- The data form also lets you "flip" through the database records one at a time.
- To sort a database, highlight the data without the field names and then use the Data-Sort command. The position of the pointer determines the field by which the data is sorted.
- You can sort in ascending or descending order.
- Use the Criteria button on the data form to enter search criteria for locating records in the database.

- You can use wild cards and logical operators in the search criteria to increase the power of your searches.
- A criteria range consists of the field names, plus one or more blank rows beneath them. You must set the criteria range with the Data-Set Criteria command.
- Specify the criteria under each heading in the criteria range. Data on the same row narrows the possible matching records by establishing AND conditions. Data on different rows extends possible matching records by establishing OR conditions.
- To extract records, duplicate the desired fields under the database range. This is called the extract range. Highlight these fields and use the Data-Extract command to extract records that match your criteria.

Chapter 11

Excel Macros

In This Chapter

- *Understanding macros*
- *Creating a macro*
- *Using the macro recorder*
- *Saving and running macros*
- *Adding more macros to the worksheet*
- *Running macros from a menu*

This chapter shows you how to tap into Excel's macro powers. Macros are useful for automating tasks in worksheets. You can create macros that operate on any worksheet you like, or you can create macros that work only on specific worksheets. First, the chapter shows you how to create a macro using the macro recording feature in Excel. Then, viewing and editing the macro is covered. Finally, the chapter teaches you how to save the macro for future use so that you can run the macro at any time.

Understanding Macros

A macro is a small program that controls Excel. The macro performs commands, selects data, and generally does anything you would do within Excel—but without your help. Using a macro is like having "autopilot" for Excel. Anything you can do within Excel, a macro can do automatically. You can rest your fingers and let the macro take over. Often, macros are used to perform repetitious tasks, such as formatting data or entering commonly-used labels like month names.

But if macros merely repeat things that you can do yourself, what good are they? For one thing, macros perform tasks much faster than you do. A macro can issue five or six different formatting commands in the blink of an eye. In fact, you probably cannot distinguish between the various commands being issued. Another advantage to a macro is that it repeats the same task over and over without error. If you were to repeat a series of commands over and over, chances are you'd make mistakes occasionally. As you experiment with macros, you'll discover other advantages they offer.

Just because macros are similar to programs, don't let the idea of creating a macro scare you off. Macros are very simple to create and use. While they offer powerful advantages for your worksheets, Excel makes them very easy to create. You don't need to know anything about programming. In fact, Excel does most of the work for you.

Creating a Macro

Excel lets you create macros by recording commands like a tape recorder. Simply turn the recorder on, perform the commands you want the macro to duplicate, and then turn the recorder off. After the "recording" is made, you can play it over and over again by typing a simple command. Everything you do while the recorder is on will be repeated by the macro when you "play" it.

Of course, Excel does not record the macro using an actual tape recorder. Instead, Excel records a series of macro commands that "describe" the tasks you request. For every action you take, Excel enters an equivalent command into the macro recording. You can then save this recording for future use. Following are the Quick Steps used to record a macro.

Q Recording a Macro

1. With the desired worksheet in view, select the Macro Record command.

   This brings up the dialog box shown in Figure 11.1. Excel suggests a name and shortcut key for the macro, but you can replace these as described in the next two steps.

2. Enter a descriptive name for the macro to replace the default name `Record1`. The name should not contain spaces. Press Tab when finished.

3. Enter a one-character shortcut key for the macro. Later, you'll use this character with the Command and Option keys to play back the macro. It's a good idea to use a shortcut key that reminds you of the macro's purpose. Press Return or click OK when finished.

4. Perform any commands you want to record in the macro. When finished, select the command Macro-Stop Recorder.

   Your actions have been translated into macro commands and recorded onto a blank macro worksheet. □

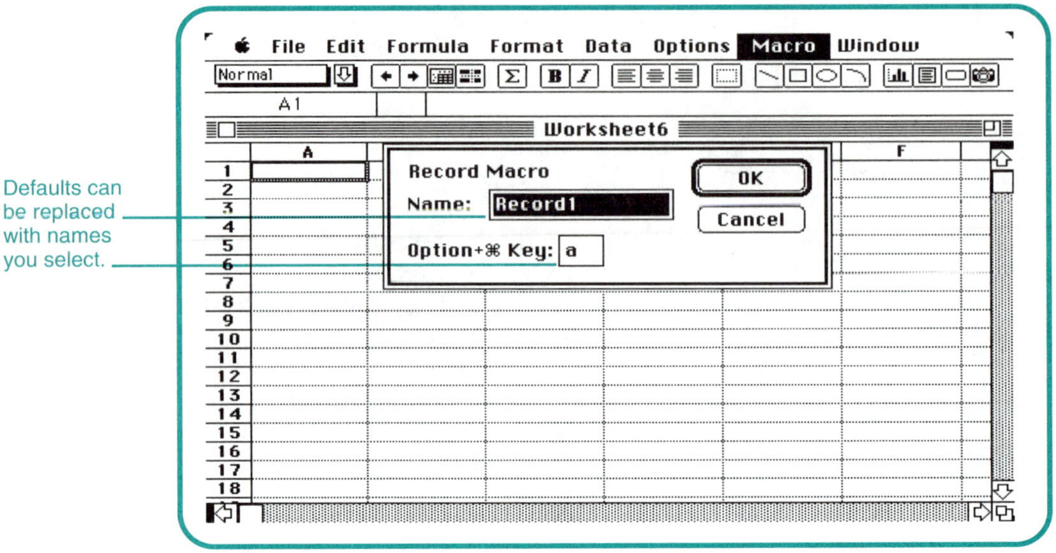

Figure 11.1 Excel asks you to name the macro before recording.

> ▶ **Note**: When you enter shortcut keys, remember that Excel distinguishes between upper- and lowercase letters. For instance, you can use the key **R** for one macro and **r** for another.

Try creating a sample macro to enter the month names at the top of your worksheet. Use the File-New command to open a new worksheet. Select the Macro-Record command. Enter the macro name `MONTHS` into the dialog box. Press Tab and enter `m` as the shortcut key. Press Return when finished.

You are now recording the macro. Move the pointer to cell A4 and begin typing the month names in this row, pressing Tab after each one. Select the Macro-Stop Recorder command when you have finished typing the names to complete the macro.

Viewing the Macro

Now that you have finished a test macro, take a look at the recording. While you were entering the information for the macro, Excel opened a macro worksheet and recorded all your macro commands onto this worksheet. The macro worksheet appears behind your worksheet. To look at the macro worksheet, select its name (`Macro1`) from the Window menu. If you followed the previous steps for creating a sample macro, the macro worksheet should look like Figure 11.2.

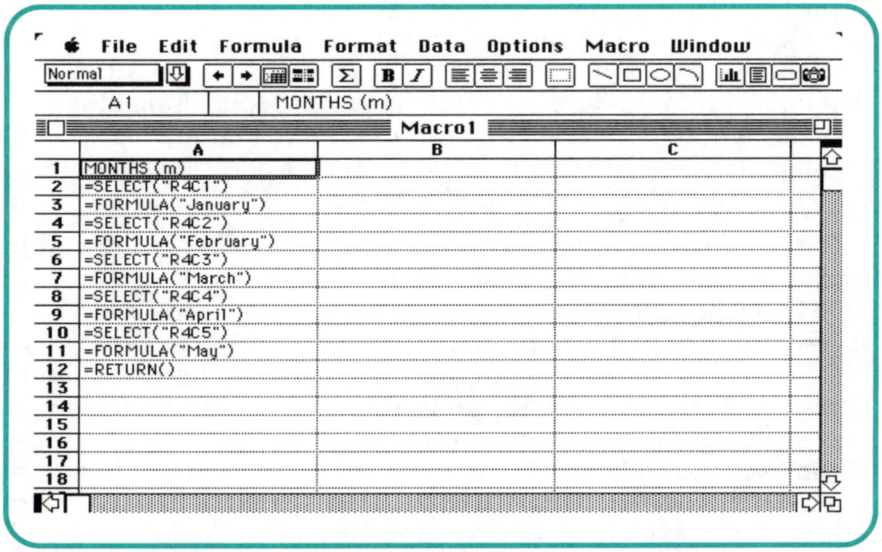

Figure 11.2 The sample macro.

First of all, notice that the macro worksheet looks very much like a regular worksheet. The macro commands that duplicate your actions are listed in column A. The macro begins with the name you specified, and then the commands appear under the name. If you examine these commands, you'll probably find that they are fairly easy to understand because they are similar to the actions you recorded. Another thing to notice is that the macro ends with the RETURN( ) command. All macros begin with a name and end with the RETURN( ) command. (There are a few exceptions, but they are fairly advanced.)

Finally, notice that each macro command, except for the name, begins with an = sign. Because Excel's macro commands are considered to be formulas on a macro worksheet, Excel automatically enters the macro commands as formulas by including the = sign. You'll see why this syntax is important later in this chapter.

Editing the Macro

With the macro worksheet in view on-screen, you can make changes to the macro using Excel's editing commands, which were discussed in Chapter 4. You can remove macro commands, edit the specific contents of a cell in the macro worksheet, or even insert new commands into the middle of the macro. Of course, making some changes will require knowledge of the macro commands. Specific commands that relate to actions you want are described in the *Excel Functions and Macros* manual that came with the software.

Most likely, you'll occasionally want to "clean up" a recorded macro by removing stray commands. For example, if you make mistakes while recording a macro, those mistakes will appear in the macro and will be repeated each time you run the macro. Or, you might make an incorrect entry and then add another command to correct it. The macro will repeat the incorrect entry and the correction each time. The result will be fine, but there is no need to repeat a mistake over and over. In either case, you might want to edit the mistake out of the macro by removing the cells containing the incorrect macro commands. You probably will need to examine the commands to determine where the mistake occurs. Remember to save the macro when you have finished editing.

Saving the Macro

To save a macro, you must save the macro worksheet. Because macro worksheets are similar to standard worksheets, simply use the File-Save command as described in Chapter 3.

After you save the macro, you can close the macro worksheet without losing the macro. Open the macro worksheet again to use the macro in the future. The File-Open command will open a macro worksheet.

Playing (Running) the Macro

After you have recorded a macro, you can run it at any time. Make sure a worksheet and the macro worksheet are open. Then simply press Command-Option along with the shortcut key you specified for the macro. The steps you recorded will be repeated automatically by Excel.

Keep in mind, however, that the same conditions should exist when you run a macro as existed when you created the macro. For example, if you created the macro that enters month names at the top of a worksheet, which you would normally do when you open a new worksheet, you should run the macro when opening a new worksheet or when a worksheet has no information at the top. The macro commands *could* produce errors if the wrong worksheet is open. If you were to run the macro on a worksheet that contains information at the top, some information might be replaced. If you try to run the macro when no worksheet is present, the macro simply would not work.

To run the sample macro you created to enter the months at the top of a worksheet, open the macro worksheet and a new worksheet. The worksheet should be in view. Press Command-Option-m to run the macro on the worksheet. The month names will appear in the same cells where you entered them when you created the macro. You can use this macro on any worksheet you like. Just make sure that the macro worksheet and the desired worksheet are open.

> **Tip**: Macros cannot run without the macro worksheet open. Because you might not want the macro worksheet to be viewed or changed, Excel provides a way to "hide" the worksheet while still leaving it open. This feature can be handy when someone other than yourself uses the worksheets. To hide an Excel worksheet, select the Window-Hide command with the desired worksheet active. The Window-Unhide or File-Unhide command will return the window to normal.

Macro Cell References

If you ran the sample macro on a sample worksheet, you saw that it repeated your recorded keystrokes and actions exactly. The same information was entered into the same cells. Each time you run the macro, it will enter the month names into row 4.

But what if you wanted the macro to enter the month names in any row you specify, rather than row 4 all the time? When you record the macro, you could tell the macro to enter the month names beginning at the current cell position. The entries would be made relative to the cell pointer.

The ability to specify where a macro should place information each time it's run is known as *relative referencing*. Using relative referencing, all movement commands are recorded relative to the pointer's position at the time you begin recording. For example, with normal recording on, if the pointer is in cell A1 when you begin recording the macro and you move the pointer down to cell A2 and enter `January`, the macro will translate your action as "enter January in cell A2." Each time you run the macro, Excel will enter `January` in cell A2. If you use relative referencing, however, the macro will record the same action as "move down one cell and type January." When you run the macro another time, Excel will "move down one cell" from the location of the pointer, wherever it happens to be when you run the macro.

Using relative referencing is easy. Just use the Macro-Relative Record command immediately after turning the recorder on and naming the macro. Try relative referencing by creating a macro similar to the sample macro you made earlier to enter the month names into a worksheet. After you turn the macro recorder on, enter a name and a shortcut key, and then select the Macro-Relative Record command. Place the pointer in cell A4; then type each month name followed by the Tab key. Select the Macro-Stop Recorder command. The new macro will look like Figure 11.3.

If you compare this macro to the first one you created, you'll notice that the cell references are entered quite differently. The new entries are relative references in the macro. When you run this macro on a new worksheet, the month names will begin at the pointer location and continue across the row. You can try to run your new sample macro, placing the pointer at various locations in a worksheet and pressing Command-Option plus the shortcut key you selected.

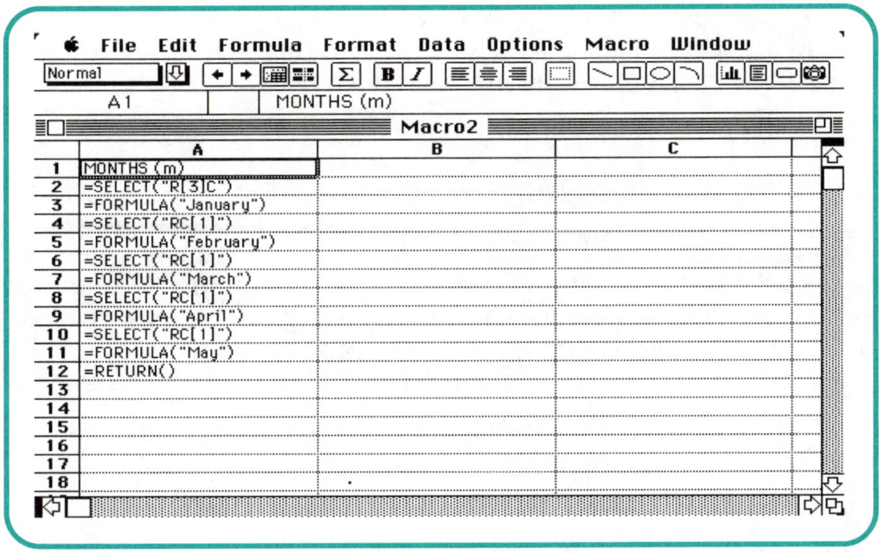

Figure 11.3 The sample macro after recording with Macro-Relative Record.

Adding a Second Macro

You now have the complete procedure for creating, saving, and using macros in your worksheets. You can continue to create macro after macro using the techniques presented. Each macro you create will be recorded in its own macro worksheet. You might find yourself accumulating more macro worksheets than you care to. And since a macro cannot be run unless its macro worksheet is open, this could mean opening several macro worksheets just to have your most useful macros active at the same time.

To avoid macro worksheet overload, Excel lets you place more than one macro on a single macro worksheet. Placing two macros in a single worksheet is especially useful when you plan to use the macros at the same time. For example, two macros may relate to the same worksheet, or a set of general macros might be handy to have available to work on any worksheet. Adding a second macro to an existing macro worksheet is slightly different than creating the first macro. There are, in fact, two ways to create additional macros. The following sections discuss creating additional macros by hand and by using a variation of the macro recorder.

Entering a Second Macro by Hand

One way to create a second macro is to enter the macro commands by hand onto the macro worksheet. This technique is convenient when the macros are very simple (requiring only one or two commands) or very complex (requiring special macro constructs). This book only examines how to enter a very simple macro by hand.

The components of the macro are the name, the commands, and the RETURN function at the end. Following are the Quick Steps.

Q Hand-Entering a Simple Macro

1. Bring the worksheet for the first macro into view on-screen by selecting its name from the Window menu.
2. Position the cell pointer in the cell that will begin the new macro. Use a cell under the existing macro so that if you need to insert or delete rows from the first macro, you won't disturb the second macro. Enter the name of the macro in this cell.

   Figure 11.4 shows an example.
3. Press the ↓ key and enter the macro commands in order down the column. Remember to enter the commands with = signs at the beginning. Conclude the macro with the RETURN( ) command.

   If you enter the commands in lowercase letters, Excel converts them to uppercase when you press ↓ or Return. An improperly entered command will not be converted to uppercase letters. Figure 11.5 shows an example of this stage.

4. Save the macro worksheet to keep the macro you've added. □

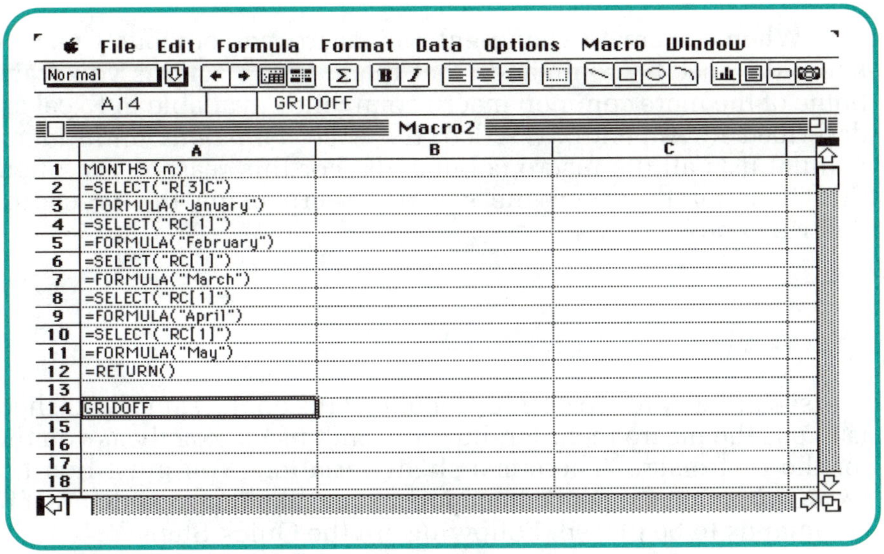

Figure 11.4 Selecting the first cell of a second macro.

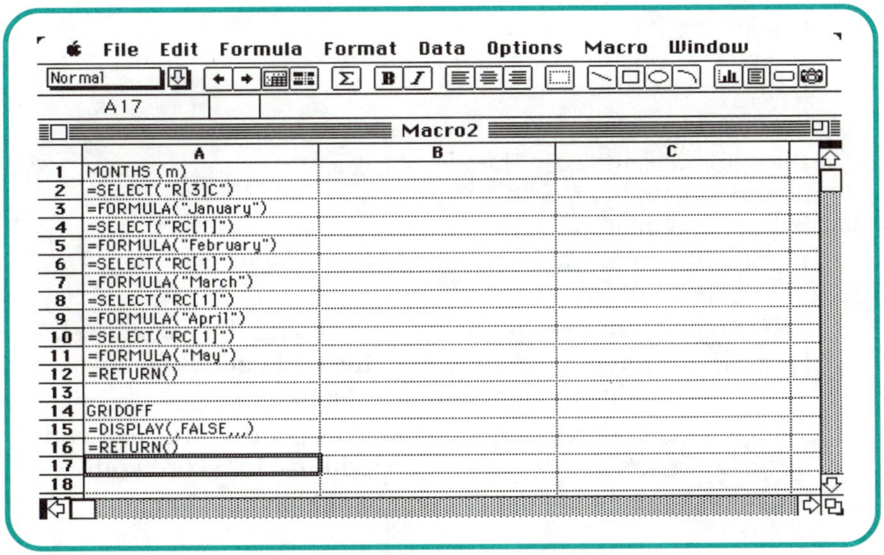

Figure 11.5 Entering the macro commands.

You have now entered the macro, but it's not ready to use yet. Before you can use the macro, you must activate it as described under the heading "Activating the Macro" later in this chapter. But first, examine another way to add a second macro to the macro worksheet.

When you create a hand-entered macro, you obviously need to know the specific commands that relate to the actions you want. Some of the more common macro commands available in Excel are described in Appendix C. Also, the *Excel Functions and Macros* manual lists all the macro commands. For this reason, you might find it easier to record the second macro using the procedure described next.

Recording a Second Macro

The second way to create additional macros on the same worksheet is to use the macro recorder, but you can't use it exactly as you did for the first macro. There is a slight variation. You must first tell Excel where on the worksheet you would like the recorded macro commands to be placed. Following are the Quick Steps.

Q Recording a Second Macro

1. Bring the worksheet for the first macro into view on-screen by selecting its name from the Window menu.
2. Position the cell pointer in the cell that will begin the macro, preferably a cell below other macros in the worksheet. Enter the name of the macro in this cell.
3. Select the Macro-Set Recorder command. — Activates the current cell as the first cell of the new macro.
4. Bring the desired worksheet into view using the Window menu, or open a new worksheet. — This is the worksheet you will use to record your actions.

5. Select the Macro-Start Recorder command. (This is not the Macro-Record command used to create the first macro.)

   Begins the recorder and places all subsequent macro commands into the macro worksheet at the location you specified. Remember that you can also use the Macro-Relative Record command to record relative references.

6. Perform any actions you want to record; then select the Macro-Stop Recorder command when finished. □

After recording a second macro on an existing macro worksheet, you can view the macro worksheet again to see the new commands. They appear in the column at the location you specified. Save the changes to the macro worksheet. As with a hand-entered macro, the recorded macro is not yet ready to use. You must activate it first.

Activating the Macro

After you have entered or recorded an additional macro on a macro worksheet, you must activate the additional macro before you can use it. Activating the macro consists of naming the macro (usually with the same name you entered in the first cell of the macro) and specifying a shortcut key. Remember that each of the macros should have a different name and shortcut key when they appear on the same worksheet and are going to be used at the same time. Use the following Quick Steps for activating a macro.

Q Activating the Macro

1. Bring the macro worksheet into view on-screen and then place the pointer in the first cell of the macro you want to activate. This cell contains the macro's name.

2. Select the Formula-Define Name command.

   The Formula-Define Name dialog box appears on-screen. The name of the macro (as entered in the current cell) is already displayed in the dialog box. Figure 11.6 shows an example.

3. Verify that the name is correct and then select the Command option.

   Tells Excel that you are naming a macro.

4. Press Tab and enter the desired shortcut key for the macro. Use any single character. Press Return or click OK when finished.

   The macro is now active, and you can save the macro worksheet again.

□

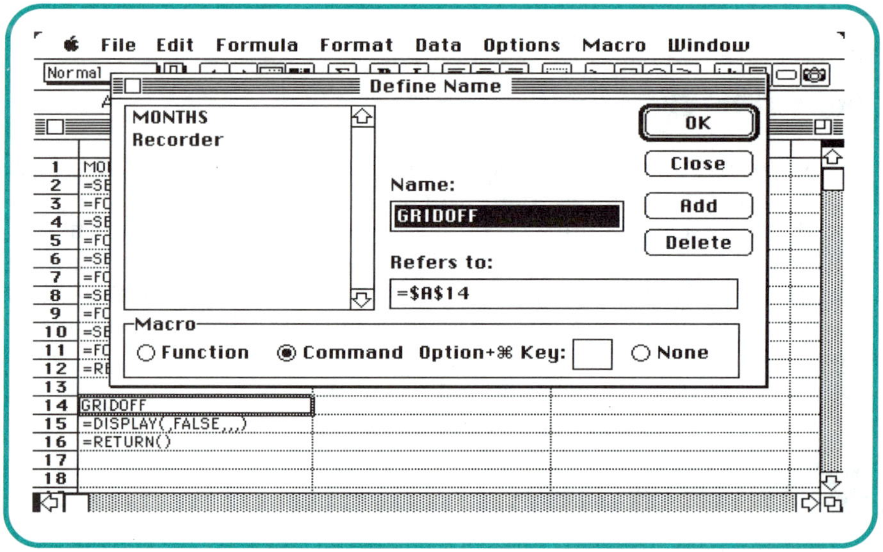

Figure 11.6 Naming the macro.

After you have activated the macro, you can use it any time the macro worksheet is open. Filling up a macro worksheet this way helps you avoid creating too many macro worksheets for your needs.

Using Macro Buttons

You learned in Chapter 6 that Excel lets you draw several types of objects onto the worksheet. Here you'll explore a special type of object: a macro button. A macro button is very much like a text box. It is rectangular and contains text. But it has a special property: it can be used to invoke a macro. When you click on a button object, Excel runs the macro attached to it. You can attach any macro to a button.

Use the button tool (to the right of the text box tool) in the Toolbar to draw buttons on the worksheet. Draw them as you would draw a rectangle (described in Chapter 6). Figure 11.7 shows a button drawn on the worksheet.

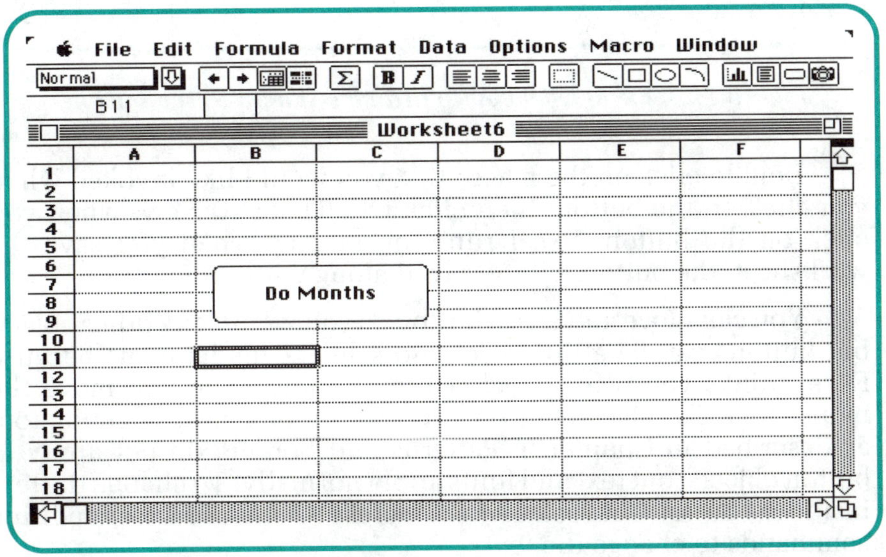

Figure 11.7 A macro button object.

When you finish drawing a button, Excel asks you to attach a macro to it and presents the list of available macros. (Adding buttons after you create macros for a worksheet is best because all your macros will be available at the time you create the button.) Figure 11.8 shows this dialog box.

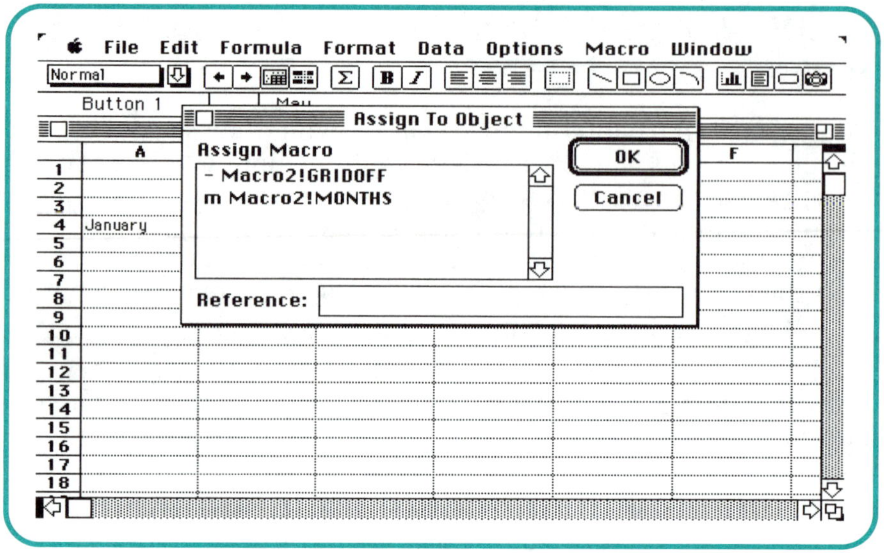

Figure 11.8 Excel asks you to attach a macro to the button.

Double-click on the macro that you would like invoked when you click on the button; then click OK. That's it. Now, when you click on the button, Excel runs the macro. When you save the worksheet, the button will be saved along with it.

You can move and size a button as you would any other object, but buttons can be a little tricky to select. This happens because Excel thinks you want to "click" the button when you move the mouse to it. To select a button, always use the object selection tool as described in Chapter 6. Patterns and borders do not apply to button objects, but text and fonts apply normally. To change the text inside the button, first select it; then press F2 and use Excel's editing commands to change the text.

You can turn any graphic object into a macro button by simply attaching a macro to it using the Macro-Attach to Object command. (First select the desired object.) After selecting the desired macro, Excel attaches it to the object and turns it into a button.

What You've Learned

Macros are a powerful and timesaving tool when using worksheets. You can use macros to automate lengthy tasks that require several commands, including changing fonts, setting print areas, setting up printer specifications, formatting data, and more. Appendix C lists some of the more common macro commands. Following are some points to remember from this chapter:

- Macros are useful for automating repetitious tasks or for combining a series of actions into a single macro command.
- You can create a macro by recording your own actions. Do this with the Macro-Record command.
- When you record a macro, Excel adds a macro worksheet to the screen and translates your actions into macro commands. You can save the macro worksheet for future use.
- You can run a macro by pressing Command-Option with the shortcut key you specify for the macro.
- To run a macro, the macro worksheet must be open. However, it can be behind the desired worksheet.
- You can change a macro by altering the entries in the macro worksheet with basic worksheet editing commands.
- You can add a second macro to the macro worksheet by using the Macro-Set Recorder and Macro-Start Recorder commands.
- After adding a second macro, use the Formula-Define name command to activate it. Activating a macro makes it available for use and lets you specify the shortcut key that will run it.
- After drawing a button with the button tool, assign a macro to it. When you click on the button, the macro runs.
- Add a macro to any object by selecting the object and choosing the Macro-Attach to Object command. Choose one of the active macros to attach to the object. You can then click on the object to run the macro.

Chapter 12

Using the Solver

In This Chapter

- *What Is the Solver*
- *Using the Solver*
- *Solver Options*
- *Examples*

This chapter describes Excel's new Solver tool. This tool is useful for analyzing business needs by solving formulas in reverse. That is, instead of calculating a value from various inputs and variables, the Solver calculates the inputs needed to reach a particular result. This chapter explains how you might use this tool and provides instructions for using it. You'll also see an actual example and how it is accomplished because examples and scenarios are the best way to understand what the Solver achieves.

What Is the Solver?

You may be using worksheets to perform "what if" analysis. After setting up a series of calculations, you can change the values of certain cells to view different scenarios. "What if I sold 10% more widgets this year? What if I reduced inventory? How would these changes affect my total income?" And so on. This capability is what makes a spreadsheet so valuable.

But you also may want to find the values that calculate a particular result. For example, "How many more widgets do I need to sell to increase total income by 30%?" In this case, the result of your calculation, total income, is set to a particular value, and the goal is to find the inputs needed to reach that value. This is, in a way, the reverse of normal "what if" analysis.

Certainly, you could enter various sales figures until you increase total income by 30%. However, this may require several guesses. The Solver can do this calculation for you in minutes. And when your scenarios (or models) are more complex, guessing can become tiresome. For example, suppose you want to purchase inventory for your music store. You have five types of instruments you need to buy and $60,000 to spend. Given that each item has its own quantity discounts and cost, you want to know what kinds of combinations you can purchase without exceeding your $60,000. This is a job for the Solver. In this example, the goal is to calculate a price of $60,000 by adjusting the inventory inputs. When there is more than one right answer—as in this case—the Solver can show all the answers or just the ones that meet certain conditions (called *constraints*).

Now, extend this example to include some constraints. Suppose you want to purchase $60,000 of inventory, but you want 30% more guitars than the other products (because you sell so many of them) and you want to purchase at least $1000 of each product. The constraints can be expressed as

Guitars = 130% * Drums
Guitars = 130% * Trumpets
Guitars = 130% * Keyboards
Guitars = 130% * Saxophones
Drums >= 1000
Trumpets >= 1000
Keyboards >= 1000
Saxophones >= 1000

Excel will find the various combinations that meet these constraints and keep your budget at $60,000.

But the Solver can do even more than this. You can use it to calculate the maximum result from a combination of values that has certain restraints. For example, suppose you want to know how many of each instrument you should purchase to maximize your net sales. This number is accounting for each instrument's markup value and cost. To the previous example you would add markup figures for each item, and your budget would become a constraint rather than the goal:

Total Cost <= Budget

The goal would now be the total net sales amount from selling these items. This figure is based on the quantity of each item and its particular markup amount. The Solver can tell you how many of each item to purchase (within the given constraints) to maximize your income.

Later in this chapter, you'll see how each of these examples can be accomplished. First, take a look at the steps for activating the Solver.

Activating the Solver

The Solver is a special utility, called an "add-in." To activate an add-in utility, you must open it with the File-Open command. In this case, use the File-Open command and search for the file called Solver in the Macro Library folder. Double-click on this file to open it.

After you open the Solver add-in file, the Formula menu contains the new command Solver.

> **Note:** You may have installed the Solver when you installed Excel, as described in Appendix A. In this case, the Solver option will already be in the Formula menu, and you will not need to open the Solver File.

Using the Solver

After you open the Solver file, you are ready to use the utility. You do this by setting up a worksheet model and using the Formula-Solver command. Following are the steps:

Q Using the Solver

1. Create your worksheet model using any values and variables.

   This model can be an existing model or one created specifically for the Solver.

2. Select the Formula-Solver command.

   The Solver dialog box appears. This contains the initial Solver options.

3. Highlight the Set Cell box and enter the cell that will contain the goal you want to reach.

   You can click on the worksheet to select this cell and enter its address into the dialog box.

4. Click one of the Equal To options.

   If you select the Value Of option, then enter the desired value into the space provided. This is the goal to be reached in the cell indicated.

5. Highlight the By Changing Cells box, and type in the cells or click on the worksheet cells that contain the variables to be adjusted until you reach the goal. Insert a comma between each cell if you require more than one.

6. To enter constraints, click the Add button and enter constraint formulas using the dialog boxes.

   The Constraints dialog box appears. When finished entering formulas, select OK to return to the Solver dialog box.

7. Select the Solve button to begin solving the problem.

□

Constraints should be expressed as formulas that can be evaluated to TRUE or FALSE. Thus, you should enter a cell reference in the Cell Reference box, select an operator from the list, and then enter a value, cell reference, or expression in the Constraint box. An example would be

```
C10 > 1000
```

If you require several constraint formulas, use the Add button after entering each one so that you don't return to the Solver dialog box each time. If the Solver comes up with a solution, it will enter the results into the appropriate cells and inform you of its success. You can then keep the results it has found or return the original results.

If you want to view other solutions to the same problem (assuming there is more than one solution), then accept the first solution and repeat the Solver process using the new cell values as the starting values. (The Solver begins its calculations using the current cell values. Changing these values can result in different solutions.)

Examples

Now, construct the example used earlier in this chapter. It begins with a simple table showing the ordering quantities of five musical instruments. The table includes the quantity ordered, description, unit cost, and extended total cost for each item. Plus, a grand total (total of purchase) is calculated at the bottom. Figure 12.1 shows this worksheet.

The first Solver task is to come up with scenarios for the various quantities, while maintaining a total cost of $60,000. In this case, you would open the Solver dialog box and enter the following data:

```
Set Cell: E11
Equal to Value of: 60000
By Changing Cells: B5,B6,B7,B8,B9
```

That's it. Now click on the Solve button and Excel finds the first solution. Note that the starting values in the cells determine the first result when more than one result is possible. The result from Figure 12.1 is shown in Figure 12.2.

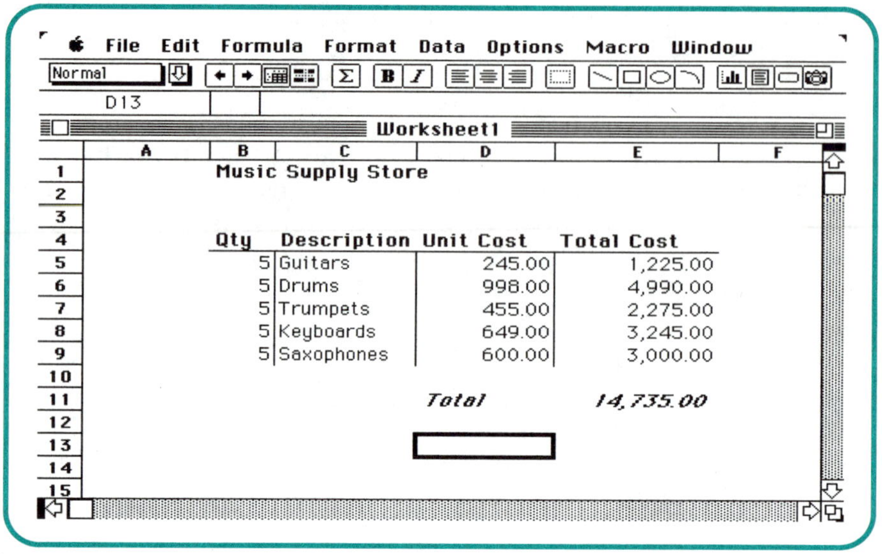

Figure 12.1 The example worksheet.

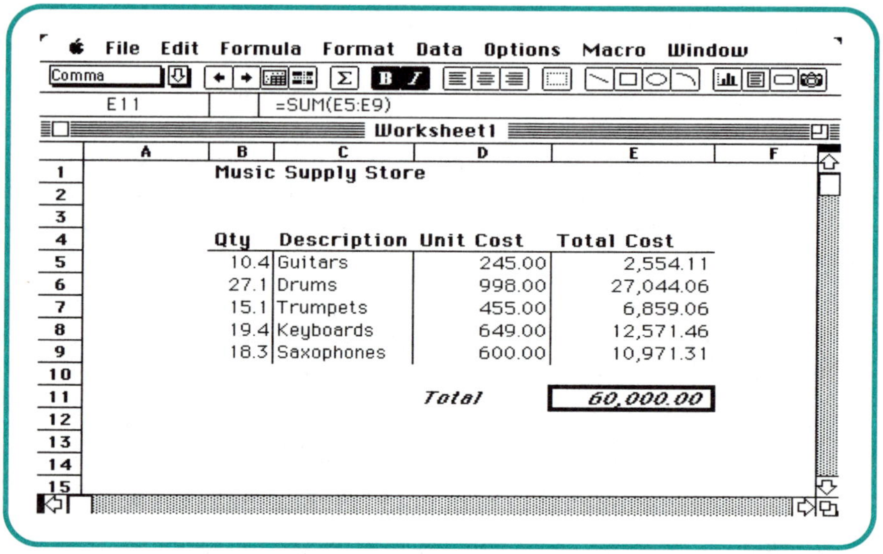

Figure 12.2 The result of the first Solver model.

The next step is to add some constraints. In this case, you want to spend at least $1000 on each item and purchase 30% more guitars than other items. Therefore, you should enter the following constraints (refer to the "Using the Solver" Quick Steps for steps to enter constraints):

```
B5 = 130% * B6
B5 = 130% * B7
B5 = 130% * B8
B5 = 130% * B9
E6 >= 1000
E7 >= 1000
E8 >= 1000
E9 >= 1000
```

Notice that constraints can control any cells used in the worksheet—not just the ones containing the input variables. There will be fewer solutions to this model than the first.

The final example is for the Solver to suggest ordering quantities for each item to provide maximum income from the sales of those items. For this, you'll need to add some data to the model. Figure 12.3 shows the same model with the markup figures and total income added for each product. Also, the grand total of income is calculated in cell H11. Note that the total income column is calculated with the following formula:

=B5*G5

Finally, you enter the budget amount in cell E12, under the total purchase. In this case, you want to maximize the value of cell H11 while adhering to the established constraints. Hence, you'll need to add the following constraint:

```
E11 = E12
```

This constraint keeps the total of the purchase equal to the budget. Following are your Solver settings to accomplish this goal:

```
Set Cell: H11
Equal to Max
By Changing Cells: B5,B6,B7,B8,B9
```

The result will be the number of each item you should purchase under these conditions to maximize your income.

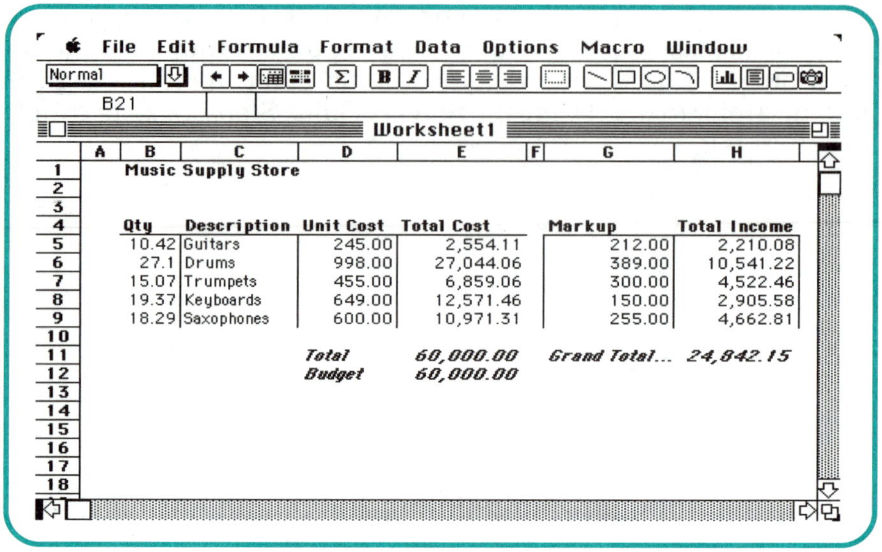

Music Supply Store

Qty	Description	Unit Cost	Total Cost	Markup	Total Income
10.42	Guitars	245.00	2,554.11	212.00	2,210.08
27.1	Drums	998.00	27,044.06	389.00	10,541.22
15.07	Trumpets	455.00	6,859.06	300.00	4,522.46
19.37	Keyboards	649.00	12,571.46	150.00	2,905.58
18.29	Saxophones	600.00	10,971.31	255.00	4,662.81
		Total	*60,000.00*	*Grand Total...*	*24,842.15*
		Budget	*60,000.00*		

Figure 12.3 Maximizing income by calculating quantities with the Solver.

What You've Learned

The Solver is a powerful tool for business analysis. You can use it on existing worksheets or build worksheets specifically to exploit its powers. Experiment for best results. Remember, the Solver can get complex; double-check the solutions to be sure you have set up the Solver model properly. Following are some things to remember about the Solver:

- The Solver is useful for calculating the values required to reach a particular goal or result.
- The Solver also can find the maximum value under certain conditions.
- You must open the Solver file before you can access it from the Formula menu.
- Establish constraints as formulas that can be evaluated to TRUE or FALSE. Stack as many constraints as desired.
- The starting values used in the variable cells affect the results of the Solver if there are multiple results possible.

Appendix A

Installing Excel

Excel's installation process is easy. Most of the work is done for you, so you just have to watch the screen for specific questions and answer them as best you can. You should have at least 3M of disk space available for the new program.

The first step is to insert your Excel Setup disk into the floppy drive. This disk contains the Setup program icon, as shown in Figure A.1.

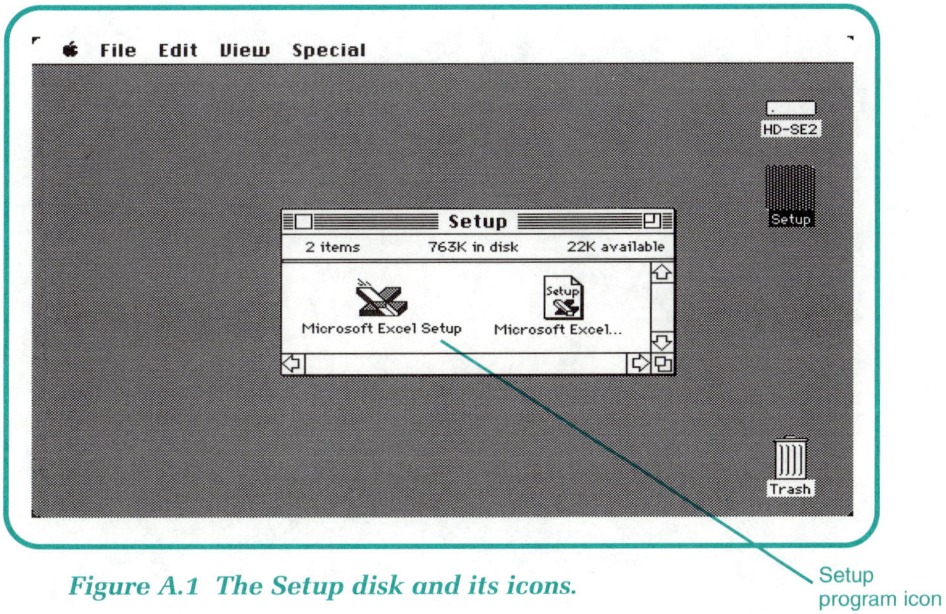

Figure A.1 The Setup disk and its icons.

Double-click on the Setup icon and follow the instructions presented on the screen. You will be asked to personalize your copy of Excel and then to choose which Excel features you want to install. If you have enough disk space, install them all. Otherwise, you can forgo any element except the Excel program itself.

When Excel has finished installing, it will return you to the Macintosh desktop.

Appendix B

Worksheet Functions

Chapter 3 explained the uses of worksheet functions and showed examples of some functions in action. If you've read Chapter 3, you have a basic understanding of the purposes of functions and how they work. This appendix provides a listing of several more Excel functions and simple examples of each. Check Chapter 3 for more details about some of these functions.

Each function is listed along with an indication of where arguments should be included.

Mathematical Functions

Mathematical functions perform general mathematical operations, such as finding the absolute value of a number or rounding a number. Excel also can perform some logarithmic functions. Following are the mathematical functions provided in Excel.

ABS(value)

The ABS function calculates the absolute value of a number. That is, this function gives you a number without indicating whether it's positive or negative. For example, the absolute value of –52 is 52. Enter any number, formula, or cell reference for the *value* argument.

Examples of the ABS function and its results are

=ABS(–25)	25
=ABS(A5), where A5 contains –25	25

INT(value)

The INT function rounds a number *down* to the nearest integer, resulting in a positive or negative number without decimal values. For example, the INT value of 24.87 is 24. Enter a number, formula, or cell reference as the argument.

Examples of the INT function and its results are

=INT(24.55)	24
=INT(A5), where A5 contains 24.55	24

MOD(dividend,divisor)

The MOD function calculates the *modulus* of a divisor and a dividend. The modulus is the remainder after a divisor is divided by the dividend. For example, 26 divided by 5 equals 5, with a remainder of 1. Therefore, the modulus of 26 and 5 is 1.

The *dividend* and *divisor* can be any number or expression resulting in a number. The divisor cannot be zero.

Examples of the MOD function and its results are

=MOD(16,4)	0
=MOD(A5,A6), where A5 contains 26 and A6 contains 5	1

PI( )

This function can be used in place of the value *pi*. Excel calculates *pi* to 14 decimal places. Be sure to include the empty parentheses, even though there is no argument for this function.

An example of the PI function and its result is

=PI( )*A5 ^ 2, where A5 contains 3	28.27433

PRODUCT(value,value,value...)

The PRODUCT function calculates the product of the specified values. The PRODUCT function multiplies the values to arrive at a total using the following formula: value * value * value * ....

References to blank cells or cells containing text are ignored by the PRODUCT function. Enter any value, cell reference, or formula as each of the values, or enter a range to specify the entire list of values. You may enter as many values as needed.

Examples of the PRODUCT function and its results are

=PRODUCT(3,5,2)	30
=PRODUCT(A1:A3), where A1:A3 contain the values 3, 5, and 2	30
=PRODUCT(SALES), where SALES is the name of the range A1:A3	30

ROUND(value,precision)

The ROUND function rounds a value to a specified number of places. Although you can use the Format-Number command and Excel's number formats to round a number, the number rounded is only *displayed* as a rounded number. In this case, any calculations that use the number are made with the entire, unrounded value. On the other hand, the ROUND function permanently changes the value of a number to a rounded value. Enter the number to be rounded as the *value* and the desired number of places as the *precision*.

Examples of the ROUND function and its results are

=ROUND(24.55,1)	24.6
=ROUND(A5,2), where A5 contains 24.5589	24.56

Statistical Functions

Statistical functions work on groups of numbers. Common statistical functions include calculating the average of a group, finding the minimum and maximum value from a group, and adding the numbers in a group. Statistical functions can get much more advanced than this, such as standard deviation and sample statistics calculations.

AVERAGE(range)

AVERAGE calculates the mean average of a group of numbers. Enter the *range* containing the numbers you want to average. This function interprets text as values of zero and skips blank cells.

An example of the AVERAGE function and its result is

=AVERAGE(A1:A5), where A1:A5 contains the values 3, 4, 25, 30, and 5	13.4

COUNT(range) and COUNTA(range)

These two functions count the number of cells in a range. The COUNT function counts only numeric values, and the COUNTA function counts all cells that are not blank. Enter any *range* as the argument.

For example, suppose that the range A1:A5 contains the following values:

A1:	3
A2:	Text
A3:	25
A4:	(Blank)
A5:	0

Using the above values, results of using the COUNT and COUNTA functions are

=COUNT(A1:A5)	3
=COUNTA(A1:A5)	4

MAX(range) and MIN(range)

The MAX and MIN functions return the maximum and minimum values in a range of cells. The argument can be a range of cells, random cell references, formulas, constant values, or some combination of these values.

Examples of these functions and the results are

MAX(A1:A5), where A1:A5 contains 3, 4, 20, 25, and 10	25
MIN(A1:A5), where A1:A5 contains 3, 4, 20, 25, and 10	3
MAX(A1,25,C23*3,"green"), where A1 contains 5 and C23 contains 3	25

SUM(range)

The SUM function calculates the total of a group of cells, which can consist of a range reference or a list of individual cells or values. A *range* can be in a row, column, or block. If you want to add values that are not in a row or a column, enter them individually as a list.

Examples of the SUM function and its results are

=SUM(A1:A5), where A1:A5 contains 3, 6, 2, 5, and 9	25
=SUM(3,6,A3,A4+12,9), where A3 contains 2 and A4 contains 5	27

Financial Functions

Financial functions are used for various financial calculations involving interest rates, loan terms, present values, and future values. Financial functions are essential for performing in-depth financial analysis of purchases, investments, and cash flow.

DDB(cost,salvage,life,period,factor)

The DDB function calculates depreciation using the double declining balance method, which accelerates the rate of depreciation early in the life of an asset. When the asset's book value depreciates to the salvage value, depreciation stops.

Enter values (cell references or constant values) for the initial *cost*, the *salvage* value, the *life* of the asset, and the *period* for which depreciation is being calculated. The life and period should both be in the same time measurement, such as years, months, or days. Optionally, you can enter a *factor* for the rate of depreciation. If you do not enter a factor, the function assumes a factor of 2 (that is, double declining).

For example, suppose you are depreciating an asset over a 10-year life and want to calculate the depreciation in year 10. The cost (10,000) is in cell A5 and the salvage value (500) is in cell A6. The formula with the DDB function and the result of the calculation would be as follows:

=DDB(A5,A6,10,10) 268.44

FV(interest rate,periods,payment amount,present value,type)

FV calculates the future value of an investment after payments have been made at a particular rate over a particular amount of time. The function finds the total dollar value of an investment after the investment has matured. Enter the *interest rate* as the periodic rate (usually a monthly or yearly rate). The *periods* argument contains the number of periods that the investment is active. You should use the same type of period for this argument and the interest rate (in months, years, etc.). The *payment amount* is the amount of each payment to the investment and represents a regular amount. The *present value* is the starting value of the investment. The *type* indicates whether payments are made at the beginning or end of the period. Entering `1` indicates the beginning and `0` indicates the end. Of course, any of these arguments can be cell references.

Remember that cash paid out must be shown as a negative number, and interest or cash received is a positive number. Therefore, if you are calculating the future value of a savings account, the present value (amount deposited) and the payment amount (monthly deposits) will be negative numbers because they are "paid out" to the investment.

Consider the following example of a formula with the FV function and its result:

=FV(12%/12,120,–125,0,1) 29042.38

Notice that the annual interest rate is converted to a monthly (periodic) rate using the formula 12%/12, and that the term and payment values reflect the same type of period (months). The result shows that you will have $29,042.38 after ten years (120 months) of depositing $125 monthly at a 12% annual interest rate.

IPMT(rate,period,periods,present value,future value,type)

This function calculates the interest paid for a particular payment given the interest *rate*, the number of *periods* in the term, and the *present value*. Specify the *period* for which you want to determine the interest being paid. The *type* determines whether payments are made at the beginning (1) of the period or at the end (0).

NPV(rate,range)

This function calculates the present value of a series of cash flow transactions. The *rate* is the periodic interest rate of an investment of equivalent risk, and the *range* is the range of cells containing the cash incomes or outflows. If you are the investor or lender, remember that the loan paid out will be negative and the payments in are positive. If the result is a positive number, the investment can be considered a good one.

PPMT(rate,period,periods,present value,future value,type)

This function calculates the amount of principal being paid during any of the payment periods, given the periodic interest rate and number of periods. A complete example of using this function to view the principal amount of each payment appears later in this section.

SLN(cost,salvage,life)

The SLN function calculates depreciation using the straight line method. This method accelerates depreciation at a constant rate for the entire life of the asset. Enter the initial *cost*, the *salvage value*, and the *life* of the asset (in years).

An example of the SLN function and its result is

=SLN(A5,A6,10), where A5 contains 10,000 and A6 contains 500	950.00

SYD(cost,salvage,life,period)

This is a third depreciation method called the sum of the years' digits method. Enter the initial *cost*, the *salvage value*, the *life* of the asset, and the *period* for which depreciation is calculated.

You can use the SYD function to calculate depreciation in year 10 when the asset has a 10-year life, cell A5 contains 10,000, and cell A6 contains 500. The formula and its result are as follows:

=SYD(A5,A6,10,10) 172.73

Example Loan Calculations

Excel provides a number of functions for calculating loan amounts. There are four parts of a loan: the *principal amount*, *periodic interest rate*, *periodic payment*, and *number of payments* (or term). These might be entered into a worksheet as shown in Figure B.1.

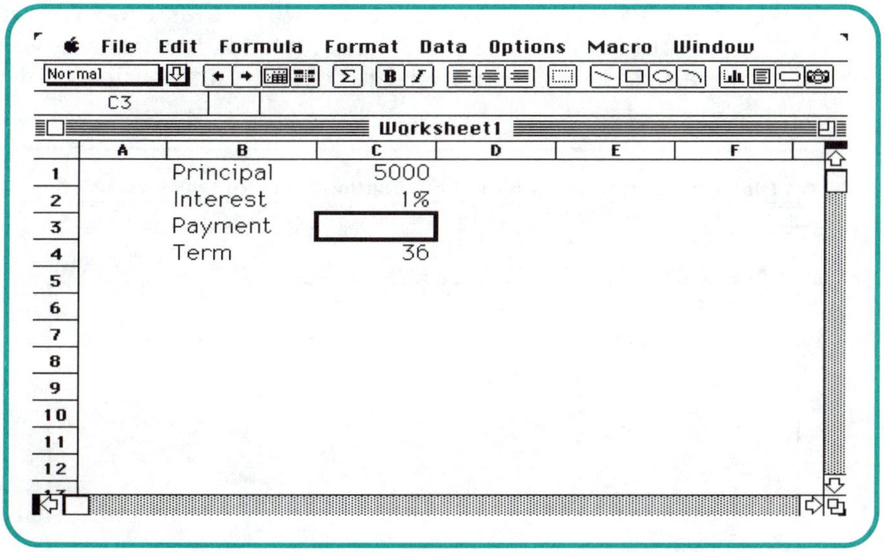

Figure B.1 The beginning of a loan calculation worksheet.

The purpose of the worksheet is to calculate any one of these amounts when you know the other three. For example, you can calculate the monthly payment amount when you know the principal, interest rate, and term. Following are the Excel functions for calculating the interest, payment, or term of a loan (or number of periods):

PMT(rate,periods,principal) Calculates the periodic payment when you enter the *interest rate*, *periods*, and *principal* as arguments.

NPER(rate,payment,principal) Calculates the periods when you enter the *interest rate*, *periodic payment*, and *principal* amounts as arguments.

RATE(term,payment,principal) Calculates the interest rate when you enter the *periods*, *payment*, and *principal* as arguments.

Suppose you want to calculate the monthly payment amount using the worksheet from Figure B.1. Simply enter the formula `=PMT(C2,C4,C1)` into cell C3 as shown in Figure B.2. In this case, you would enter values for the principal, interest rate, and periods only.

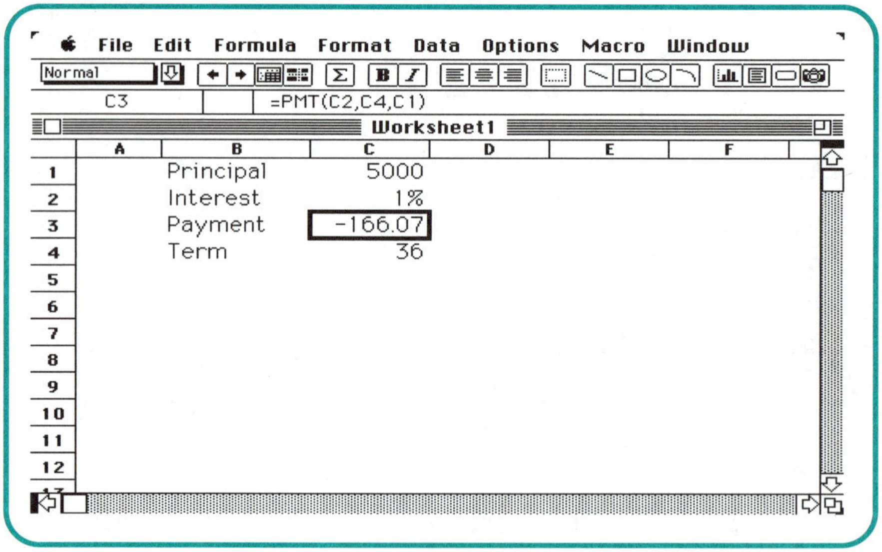

Figure B.2 Example of calculating the principal of a loan.

Note that the interest rate is entered as the periodic rate. This periodic rate should be for the same time periods entered in the periods argument. In the example, the term is 36 months (36 periods), so you should enter the monthly interest rate. If you know only the annual interest rate, simply divide the annual rate by 12 to get the monthly rate. Or you can enter the formula `=12% / 12` to calculate the periodic rate from the annual rate.

Another thing to notice is that the payment amount appears as a negative because it represents cash out. When using sums you have borrowed, the principal is positive (cash in) and the payment is negative (cash out). For sums loaned, the principal is negative and the payment is positive.

The next step of this worksheet example is to calculate the amount of interest and principal paid at each payment. As you might already know, you pay more interest at the beginning of a loan than at the end. The proportion of interest to principal is different for each payment. Using the PPMT function, you can determine how much principal is paid with each payment. This function uses the following arguments:

=PPMT(rate,payment number,periods,principal)

Given the rate, term, and principal, PPMT calculates the principal payment for any given payment number. First, enter the payment numbers from 1 to 36 (or whatever the term requires) down column B as shown in Figure B.3. Figure B.3 also shows some basic formatting applied to the worksheet, including the border around the table of values and some number formats.

The next step is to create the first formula. This will calculate the interest paid at the first payment. Enter the formula in cell C9 as follows:

```
=PPMT($C$2,B9,$C$4,$C$1)
```

Notice that all the references are absolute except the payment number, which will be copied down column C to produce each payment. But first, enter the formula for the interest amount in cell D9 as follows:

```
=$C$3-C9
```

This simply takes the payment amount and subtracts the PPMT amount for each payment number. You can see that the first payment consists of $116.07 of principal and $50.00 of interest. To view the remaining payments, highlight the range C9:D44 and then select the Edit-Fill Down command. The result should look something like Figure B.4.

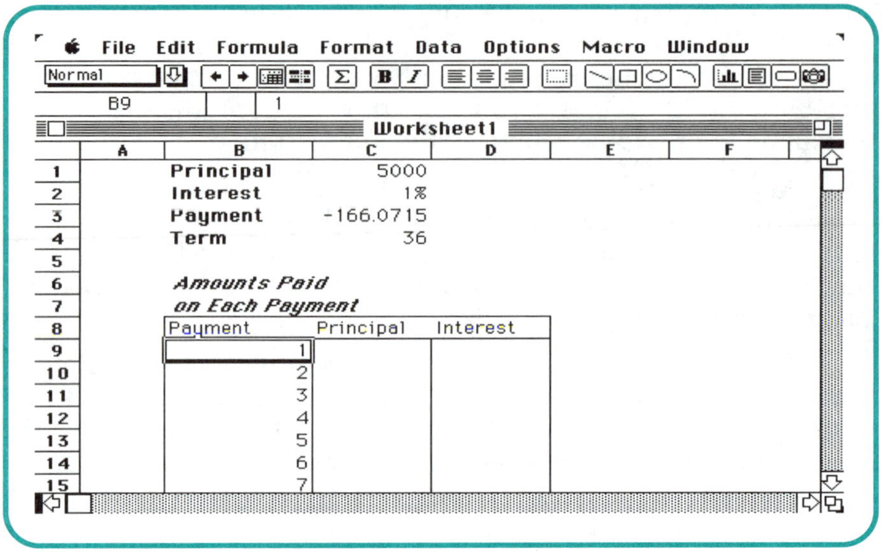

Figure B.3 Enter the payment numbers on the worksheet.

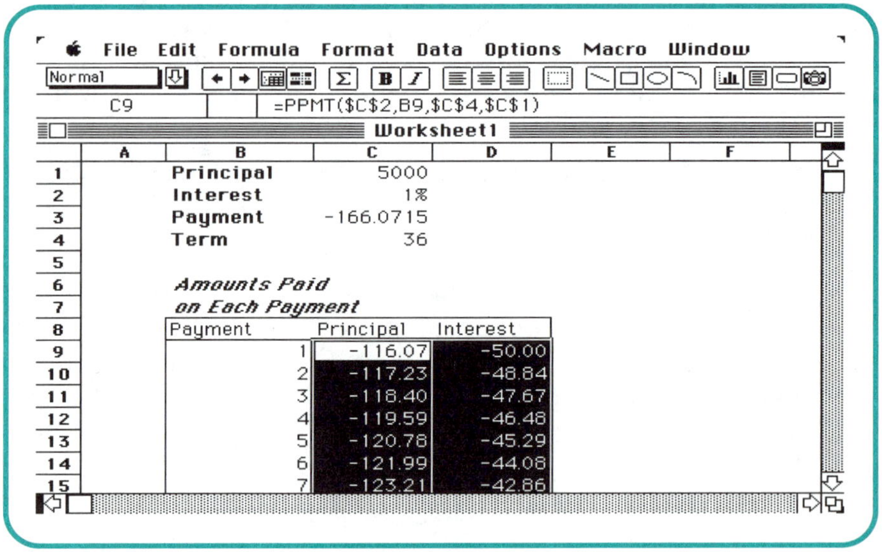

Figure B.4 Completing the payment formulas.

The final step is to use the SUM function to total each column at the bottom. Then, add the two totals for the entire amount of the loan, including principal and interest. The totals are shown in Figure B.5.

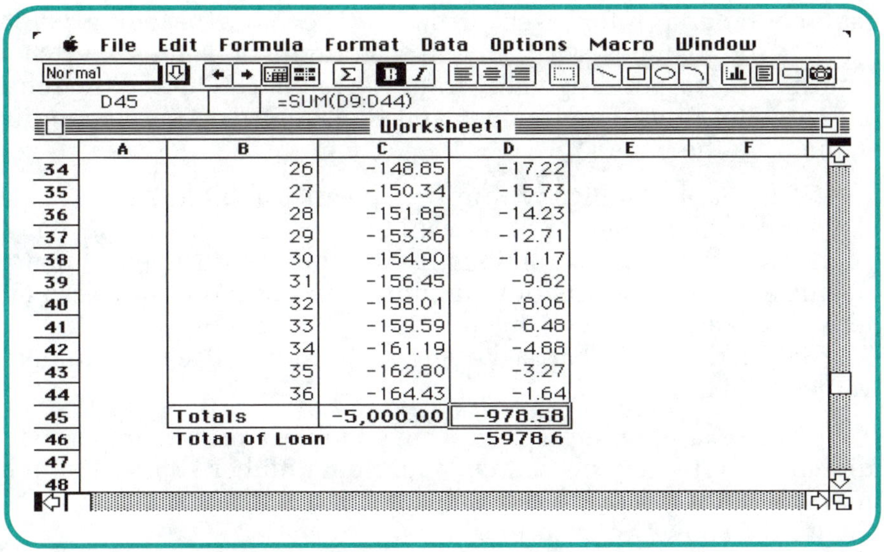

Figure B.5 Adding totals.

Lookup Functions

Lookup functions search for values within tables or lists. Each lookup function uses a different method for searching and returning values. You'll find each method suited for a particular task. Any time your worksheet uses tables to hold values, such as tax tables or price tables, you can employ a lookup function for added power in the application.

HLOOKUP(value,range,row offset)
VLOOKUP(value,range,column offset)

These two lookup functions search for values in tables based on a *lookup value*, the value you are trying to match. For example, a tax table contains tax rates based on income. Income is the lookup value. VLOOKUP searches vertically in a column of values and then returns a corresponding value from the table. HLOOKUP searches horizontally in a row of values and then returns a corresponding value from the table.

If the lookup range within the specified table range contains text strings, then the search variable must also be a text string. In such cases, the lookup function must be able to find an exact match for the specified information, including upper- and lowercase letters. If no match is found, the function will return the error: #VALUE! The data in the table (that is, the value to be returned) can be numeric values or text.

As an example, suppose you have a table of prices for merchandise and want to search that table for item number 125. When item number 125 is located in the table, the price of the item is returned. Figure B.6 shows an example.

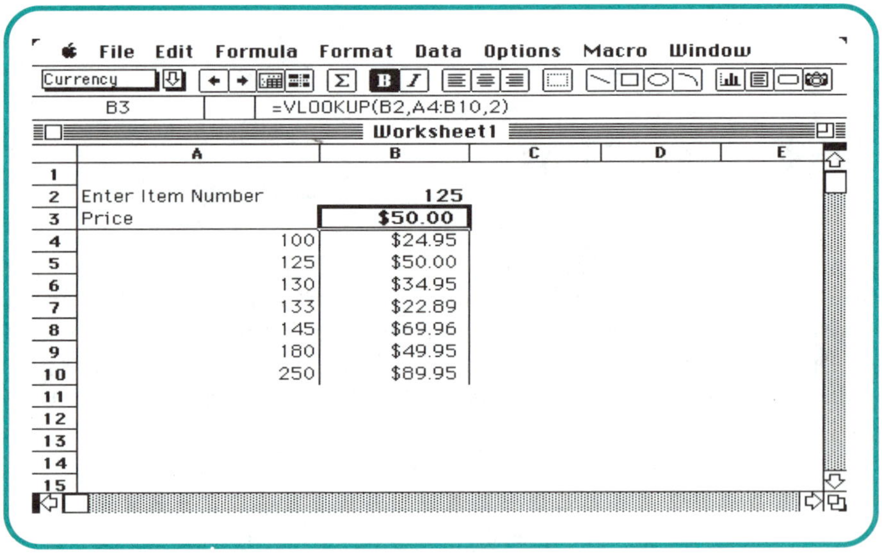

Figure B.6 A simple lookup table.

The VLOOKUP function searches vertically in a column of values and then returns a corresponding value from another table column. The function works like this:

=VLOOKUP(value,table range,offset)

The lookup function in Figure B.6 appears in cell B3 as follows:

```
=VLOOKUP(B2,A4:B10,2)
```

The value is the number or text in the first column of the table that you are trying to match with corresponding information. This can be any number, text, cell reference, or formula. For the example in Figure B.6, the value was entered as the cell reference B2 so that any number entered into cell B2 becomes the value for the lookup. The *table range* is the worksheet range containing the table. The first column of this range, called the *lookup column*, should include the list of values for which you will be searching. The table can then include as many more columns as necessary to contain all information. Additional columns are called *offset* columns, and they contain the cells with information you want to return when you select a value from the lookup column. When entering the VLOOKUP formula, the lookup column is referred to as offset 1, the next column is offset 2, and so on. The example in Figure B.6 shows only one offset column.

When the function finds the lookup value in the lookup column, it remembers the row position of the lookup value. Then the function searches across the table to return information from the column specified by the offset value listed in the formula. Figure B.7 shows how Figure B.6 looks with more offset columns. The lookup formulas in cells B3, C3, and D3 return information from each of the columns of the table, using the following functions:

=VLOOKUP(B2,A4:D10,2)
=VLOOKUP(B2,A4:D10,3)
=VLOOKUP(B2,A4:D10,4)

Notice that the formulas are identical, except that they contain different offset values, selecting values from different columns along one row of the table.

When you create lookup tables and the lookup formulas that use them, keep some basic rules in mind. First, the values in the lookup column must be in ascending order (sorted), as they are in Figure B.7. If the values are text, they must be in alphabetical order.

If the lookup column is not in ascending order, the function may return incorrect values. Excel searches the lookup column until it finds a direct match. If a direct match cannot be found, the closest value smaller than the search variable is used. Therefore, if a lookup value is greater than all values in the table, then the last value in the table is used because it's the largest. If the lookup value is smaller than all values in the table, then the function returns the error: #VALUE!

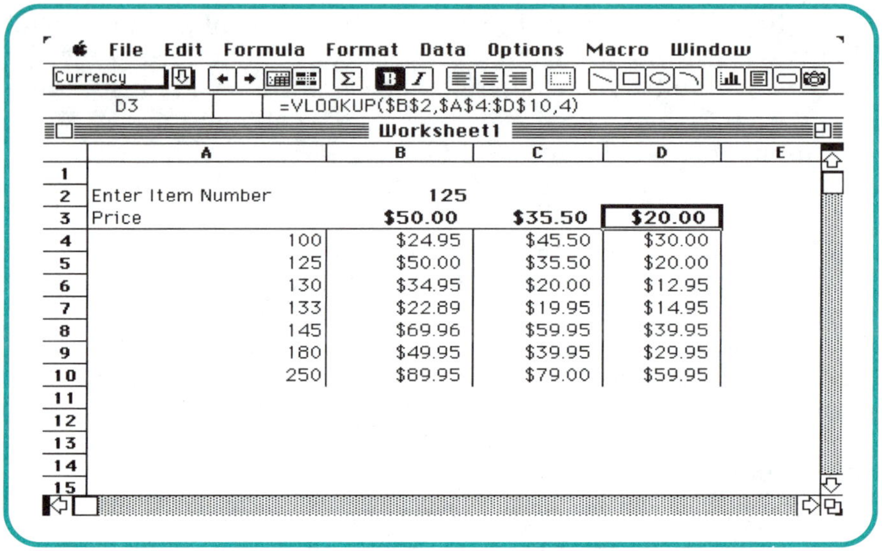

Figure B.7 An extended table with three offset columns.

If the lookup column contains text, then the lookup function must be able to match the lookup value exactly, including upper- and lowercase letters. When no match is found, the function will return the error: #VALUE! Even if the lookup column contains text, the offset columns can contain numeric values or text.

Logical Functions

Logical functions are used to create logical tests. A test enables a formula to make a decision based on particular data. A test may determine if a value is greater than 25, and the formula making the test can perform one function if true and another if false. The most common and useful logical function is the IF function, which allows you to develop several kinds of tests based on the operators used in the test statement. IF is often combined with other logical functions to create more specific tests.

IF(condition,value if true,value if false)

The IF function tests that a condition is true or false. If the condition proves true, one value is returned. If the condition proves false, another value is returned. To prove a condition true or false requires a relational operator. Excel offers several:

>	is greater than
<	is less than
=	is equal to
>=	is greater than or equal to
<=	is less than or equal to
<>	is not equal to

In the following example, you can substitute any of these operators for the one given:

IF(A1=A2,"Right","Wrong")

If the value of A1 is equal to that of A2, then the formula will return `Right`. Otherwise, the formula will return `Wrong`. The *value if true* and the *value if false* can be any constant value, cell reference, or formula.

ISBLANK(cell)

This function tests whether a cell is blank. If the specified cell is blank, a value of `TRUE` is returned; otherwise, `FALSE` is returned. The referenced *cell* can be any valid cell in the worksheet. The ISBLANK function is commonly used along with the IF function to test for a blank cell and then perform some action based on the outcome. For example, you can use ISBLANK along with IF to print a message next to cells that need to be filled in and then remove the message once the data is entered. Following is that formula:

=IF(ISBLANK(B5) = FALSE, "", "Please enter the amount in cell B5")

ISERR(cell)

This function tests whether a specified *cell* contains an error. If so, then a value of `TRUE` is returned. Otherwise, `FALSE` is returned. The ISERR function is commonly used along with the IF function to "trap" errors in the worksheet and allow control over the result of the error. Normally, any calculation that references a cell containing an error will cause `#VALUE!` or some other error message to be returned. But, using the ISERR function, you can pinpoint the error. For example:

=IF(ISERR(B5) = TRUE,"Invalid entry in cell B5", B5*B6)

This formula tests if the value of B5 is an error. If so, the phrase `Invalid entry in cell B5` is returned. Otherwise, the desired calculation is performed.

Date/Time Functions

Date and time functions are used specifically for date and time math calculations and conversions. *Date math* and *time math* have the capability to calculate elapsed time, add time to a given date or time, or calculate the difference between two dates or times. The following functions are used for these calculations. For more information about date math, see Chapter 3.

DATEVALUE(text)

This function converts a text string into a valid date (in other words, a date serial number). The text string must contain data that is recognizable as a date. The function recognizes *text* entered in any of the date formats shown in the Format-Numbers command. You can specify any date from January 1, 1904 to February 6, 2040.

An example of the DATEVALUE function and its result is

= DATEVALUE (B5), where B5 contains 1/25/91	31801

The result, 31801, is the number of days between 1/1/04 and 1/25/91. You can format this date value using any of the date formats in the Format-Number command.

DAY(date)
MONTH(date)
YEAR(date)

These functions return the day, month, or year corresponding to a specified date. The *date* variable can be any valid date entered as the number of days elapsed since January 1, 1904. The value also can be a reference to a cell containing a valid date, or it can be any date expression resulting in a valid date. These functions break a date into its various portions. For example, suppose cell B2 contains the date 2/24/91. Following are some examples of these functions and their results:

DAY(B2)	24
MONTH(B2)	2
YEAR(B2)	1991

NOW( )

The NOW function pulls the current date and time from the DOS startup date and time. The value is returned as a number with a decimal value, as in 2245.2025. The integer part of this number represents the date (in "days elapsed" format) and the fractional part represents the time (in "time elapsed" format).

There is no argument for the function. You can simply format the value into a date using any of the date formats in the Format-Number menu, or you can format the value into a time using the time formats in the Format-Number menu. You can also use the TRUNC function to separate the two portions, as in =TRUNC(NOW( )). This formula strips off the decimal portion of the date/time serial number, turning it into a date only. You can then format this date or use the DAY, MONTH, and YEAR functions to split the value even further.

TIMEVALUE(text)

The TIMEVALUE function converts a text string into a valid time. The text string must be recognizable as a time entry. It should resemble any of the time formats in the Format-Number command. The result will be displayed in the "time elapsed" format, but it can be formatted with the Format-Number command. Enter times as text strings by typing them in two or three parts (for example, 12:30 or 12:30:15) or by including the AM/PM (for example, 12:30:00 AM).

Following is an example of the function and its result:

=TIMEVALUE(B4), where B4 contains 11:35:15 PM	0.9828125

The numerical result can be formatted as the valid time 11:35:15 PM.

WEEKDAY(date)

This function returns the weekday name of any valid date as a value from 1 to 7. The value 1 equals Sunday, 2 equals Monday, and so on. To format this value as the appropriate day name, use the Format-Number command and specify the custom date format "dddd."

An example of this function and its result is

WEEKDAY(1/1/91)	6

The 6 can be formatted as the weekday name Thursday using the "dddd" format.

Appendix C

Macro Command Listing

This appendix provides information about some of the more common macro commands available in Excel. Some of these commands are automatically used by Excel when you record a macro and perform equivalent actions. Others, however, can only be used when you type a macro by hand. Some of these commands duplicate the menu options with which you have become familiar. Others are the equivalent of mouse or keyboard actions you can perform. There are many more commands available in Excel's macros. For a complete listing, see the *Functions and Macros* manual that comes with Excel.

Macro Cell and Range References

When you use the macro recorder, Excel takes care of entering cell and range references for you. However, if you attempt to type a macro by hand, you should know some basics about these references. Some of the macro commands listed in this appendix require that you enter a cell or range reference. One way to enter a cell reference is as a standard cell or range address, as in C5 or the range C5:G9. When used in a macro, these references refer to cells in the macro worksheet itself, not in the worksheet that might be active when you run the macro. For this reason, these references are used only for a macro's internal needs.

The most common need is to refer to the worksheet that is active when you run the macro. Because some macros can be useful for many different worksheets, you'll want to allow any worksheet to be active for the macro. To tell the macro to look for cell references in the currently active worksheet, simply enter an *exclamation point* in front of the reference, as in the following examples:

```
!C5
!C5:G9
!Sales
```

Another way to enter a reference is to use the *"RC"-style* address. This is a reference that applies to the current location of the pointer. You use this type of reference when you select the Macro-Relative Record command when recording macros. However, when programming a macro by hand, you must enter these relative references yourself. Some examples include


```
"RC"
"R[1]C"
"R[4]C[-1]"
```

When you use this type of reference, you should include the quotation marks, making it a text string. The "RC" example refers to the current cell. The numbers in brackets move the reference either forward (positive) or backward (negative) by the indicated number of cells. Hence, the reference *R[1]C[1]* moves the pointer to the right and down one cell from the current position.

Remember that you can use any of these types of cell or range references whenever the macro command requests a reference. In the next section you will find some useful macro commands.

Duplicating Menu Options

Excel includes many macro commands that emulate standard menu commands. In fact, when you use a menu command while the macro recorder is on, Excel converts your actions to macro commands. Each menu command you select while recording becomes a command equivalent on the macro worksheet. Following are some of the more commonly used macro command equivalents for menu commands. These will be helpful when you want to edit a macro or type a macro by hand.

ALIGNMENT(type)

The ALIGNMENT command aligns information in the current cell, like the Formula-Alignment menu command. Enter a value from 1 to 5 as the *type* argument: `1` is General alignment, `2` is Left, `3` is Center, `4` is Right, and `5` is Fill.

BORDER(outline,left,right,top,bottom,shade,outline_color, left_color,right_color,top_color,bottom_color)

This command is equivalent to the Format-Border command. It creates a border line at the top, left side, right side, or bottom of the active cell or range. It can also outline the range or fill it with a shade. Enter a number from 0 to 7 for any of the first six arguments. Add one of the eight line styles (entering `0` removes the line). Use a number from 1 to 16 for the color parameters. Omit an argument to leave it as is. For example, entering `=BORDER(1,...,)` outlines the selected range. Entering `=BORDER(,2,2,2,2,,)` removes the top and bottom outline and adds the left and right.

CLEAR(value)

This command clears data like the Edit-Clear command. First, select the cell or range that you want to clear (you can do this in the macro also) and then use this command to clear the selected data. Or you can enter the type of information you want to clear in place of the *value*: entering `1` clears everything, `2` clears formats, `3` clears formulas, and `4` clears notes.

CLOSE(logical)

This command is equivalent to the File-Close command. CLOSE removes the active window from the screen. Enter either `TRUE` or `FALSE` as the *logical* value. Entering `TRUE` saves the worksheet and closes it. Entering `FALSE` closes the worksheet without saving. Entering no value (using empty parentheses) brings up a dialog box asking if you want to save changes made.

COLUMN.WIDTH(width,reference)

This command sets the column width for any column like the Format-Column Width command. Enter the desired column width as the *width* argument and the column number as the *reference* argument. You'll have to convert the column letter into a value. The Options-Workspace-R1C1 command can be helpful for this. For example, entering `=COLUMN.WIDTH(15,2)` increases column B to 15 characters. It can be useful to stack several of these commands in a macro to adjust many columns at once.

COMBINATION(number)

This command sets a combination chart for the currently active chart. Enter the desired combination chart *number* (as shown in the options produced by the Gallery-Combination command).

COPY( )
CANCEL.COPY( )

The COPY command copies information in the currently selected cell or range. This is useful in preparation for pasting the information with the PASTE command. The CANCEL.COPY command removes the marquee after copying.

CUT( )

Equivalent to the Edit-Cut command, CUT is useful for moving data from one location to another. The macro should select the data, issue the CUT command, and then move to the new location and paste.

DATA.DELETE( )

This command is equivalent to the Data-Delete menu command. Use it to delete records according to the current criteria range.

DATA.FIND(logical)

This command finds a record in the database, or exits the find procedure. Enter TRUE to find records or FALSE to exit the find procedure.

DATA.FORM( )

This command brings up the database data form for the currently set database. Use it after defining the database and criteria ranges.

DISPLAY(formula,gridline,heading,zero,color)

This command displays or hides various elements on the worksheet. Enter TRUE in any argument that you want displayed or FALSE if you don't want it displayed. Enter a value from 1 to 8 for the *color* option to select a color for the worksheet. These arguments correspond to the check boxes on the Options-Display dialog box.

EXTRACT(logical)

The EXTRACT command extracts data from the active database according to the active criteria settings. Enter TRUE to extract unique records only or FALSE to extract all matching records.

FORMAT.FONT(name,size,bold,italic,underline,strike)
FORMAT.FONT(color,background,apply,name,size,bold,italic,underline,strike)

This command is equivalent to using the Format-Font menu command. It applies a font, size, and style to the currently selected cell or range. There are two versions of this command. Use the first version on normal worksheets and macro sheets. You should use the second version to manipulate the fonts on a chart.

Enter the name of the font in the *name* argument. Be sure to enter it with quotation marks. Enter TRUE or FALSE for any of the remaining arguments to turn them on or off. In the chart version, the *color* argument should be a value from 0 to 8 representing the color you want for the font. The value 0 tells Excel to select the color automatically. Background values can be any of the following:

1	Automatic
2	Transparent
3	White Out

The *apply* argument applies the font selection to all like elements in the chart. Enter TRUE or FALSE as the value of this argument.

FORMAT.NUMBER(format)

This command chooses a numeric format for the currently selected cell or range. Enter the number *format* as a text string, as in =FORMAT.NUMBER("#,##0.00"). Use any format from the list provided in the Format-Number command.

FORMULA.GOTO(reference, corner)

This command performs the same function as the Formula-Goto menu option. Enter an address for the cell or range that you want to locate. You also can enter a range name, provided the name is already defined for a range. If *corner* is TRUE, Excel places the referenced cell in the upper-left corner of the screen when moving to it.

GALLERY.AREA(number)
GALLERY.3D.AREA(number)
GALLERY.BAR(number)
GALLERY.COLUMN(number)
GALLERY.3D.COLUMN(number)
GALLERY.LINE(number)

GALLERY.3D.LINE(number)
GALLERY.PIE(number)
GALLERY.3D.PIE(number)
GALLERY.SCATTER(number)
PREFERRED( )

These commands are equivalent to the various Gallery options. They set the type of chart for the active chart. Enter the respective chart type number as the *number*. To see these numbers, use the corresponding menu command.

NEW(type)
NEW?( )

This command is equivalent to the File-New command. The *type* argument represents the type of worksheet to open. Enter 1 to create a worksheet, 2 to create a chart, or 3 to create a macro sheet. If you use the ? (question mark) after the command, Excel brings up the standard File-New dialog box where you can choose one of the three types of windows to create.

OPEN(name text)
OPEN?( )

This command is equivalent to the File-Open menu command. Enter the name of the file that you want to open in place of the *name text* argument. Make sure that you enter the name with quotation marks, as in OPEN("myfile").

PASTE( )

The PASTE command pastes information from the clipboard into the worksheet at the pointer location. PASTE is useful after you use the COPY or CUT command.

PRINT?( )

This command is equivalent to the File-Print command. When this command is encountered in a macro, Excel brings up the Print dialog box and waits for you to make your selections. This can be useful as the final command in a macro that performs many of the print setup operations for you and then prints the worksheet.

ROW.HEIGHT(height)

This command is equivalent to the Format-Row Height command. It sets the height of the active row in the worksheet. Enter the desired *height* in points (a point is 1/72 of an inch) as the height argument. Be sure to select the desired row first by simply moving the pointer to that row.

SET.CRITERIA
SET.DATABASE

These commands set the current criteria range and database range, like the Data-Set Criteria and Data-Set Database menu commands. Be sure to select the desired range before using these commands.

SET.PREFERRED( )

This is equivalent to the Gallery-Set Preferred command, which sets the Preferred chart type to match the currently selected chart. Then, when you use the PREFERRED command (listed above), Excel duplicates the chart you set.

SET.PRINT.AREA( )

This command activates the currently selected range as the current print area. It is equivalent to the Options-Set Print Area command. If only one cell is selected, the command removes the print area.

SET.PRINT.TITLES( )

This command activates the currently selected range as the titles range for printouts. First, select the desired range of cells; then use this command as you would use the Options-Set Print Titles menu command.

WORKSPACE(fixed,decimals,r1c1,scroll,status,formula, menukey,remote,entermove,underlines,tools,notes, interface,menu key action)

This function is equivalent to using the Options-Workspace dialog box and changing its settings. You can easily match the arguments in this function to the dialog box settings. Options relating to check boxes should get the value TRUE (checked) or FALSE (unchecked). Other options should get values. You should enter the menu key option as text by using the quotation marks.

Duplicating Keyboard and Mouse Actions

Excel provides a number of macro commands that duplicate actions you can take with the mouse or keyboard. This includes entering information into cells, selecting cells, and so on. Following are explanations of the common commands and their arguments.

FORMULA(formula text,reference)

The FORMULA function enters data into a cell of the worksheet as if you had typed it yourself. This data can be a text string, a number, or a formula. The *formula text* is the data you would like entered. Be sure to surround this data with quotation marks. Excel deciphers whether your entry is a number, formula, or text string. Excel uses the same criteria for making this decision as it does when you type data from the keyboard. Anything beginning with an = sign is a formula; anything beginning with an alphabetic character (except a range name) is a text string, and so on. The *reference* is the cell into which you want to enter the data. If the reference is omitted, Excel uses the current cell. If the cell receiving this data already contains information, Excel will replace the old data with your new entry.

MOVE(x position,y position,window)

This command moves a window to another screen location, as when you drag on its title bar. The *x position* and *y position* represent the horizontal and vertical positions of the upper-left corner of the window. The x and y positions are measured in points from the upper-left corner of the screen. The *window* is the name of the window you want to move. Enter the name in quotation marks.

SELECT(selection)

The SELECT command is equivalent to selecting a cell or range. Simply enter the desired cell or range in the *selection* argument. You can specify the selection as a cell or range on the current worksheet, using the form !A5 or !A5:B6. You can also refer to a named range, as in !Sales.

Alternatively, you can make the selection relative to the currently active cell by making the argument an R1C1-style reference entered as a text string. For example, entering `=SELECT("RC[3]")` moves the pointer three columns to the right. Entering `=SELECT("R[-3]C[2]")` moves the pointer three rows up and two columns to the right.

SIZE(width,height)

This command is equivalent to changing the size of a window with the mouse or command menu. Enter the desired *width* and *height* in points. Excel changes the lower-right corner of the active window to match your specifications.

Controlling Macro Operation

Excel includes a group of commands that control how macros operate. You'll find these commands useful for many of your macros.

ALERT(message,type)

This command brings up an alert box containing a message that you design. Enter any message for the box as the *message* argument. Specify the type of alert box by entering its numeric value as the *type* argument. Entering 1 creates a "caution" box, 2 creates a "note" box, and 3 creates a "stop" box. These are simply three different styles of messages.

BEEP(value)

This command causes a beep to sound. Enter any number for the *value* argument to control the length of time the beep sounds.

RETURN( )

This command is used at the end of a macro to return operation to the macro's starting point.

Sample Macros

Enter the following macro to add an outline to the currently selected range:

```
OUTLINE
=BORDER(TRUE,FALSE,FALSE,FALSE,FALSE,FALSE)
=RETURN()
```

The following macro removes the gridlines and the scroll bars from the worksheet:

```
GRIDS
=DISPLAY(FALSE,FALSE,TRUE,TRUE,0)
=WORKSPACE(FALSE,,FALSE,FALSE,TRUE,TRUE,"/
",FALSE,TRUE,3)
=RETURN()
```

As a good alternative to using the mouse to widen columns, you can enter the following macro that widens the current column by two characters each time you press the macro command.

```
WIDEN
=COLUMN.WIDTH(GET.CELL(16)+12)
=RETURN()
```


To shrink the current window and move it to the bottom-right side of the screen, enter the following macro:

```
SHRINK
=SIZE(240,240)
=MOVE(250,80)
=RETURN()
```

Index

C

D

F

G

H

I

K

L

M

N

X–Z

Sams—Covering The Latest In Computer And Technical Topics!

Audio

- Audio Production Techniques for Video $29.95
- Audio Systems Design and Installation $59.95
- Audio Technology Fundamentals $24.95
- Compact Disc Troubleshooting and Repair $24.95
- Handbook for Sound Engineers: The New Audio Cyclopedia $79.95
- Introduction to Professional Recording Techniques $29.95
- Modern Recording Techniques, 3rd Ed. $29.95
- Principles of Digital Audio, 2nd Ed. $29.95
- Sound Recording Handbook $49.95
- Sound System Engineering, 2nd Ed. $49.95

Electricity/Electronics

- Basic AC Circuits $29.95
- Electricity 1, Revised 2nd Ed. $14.95
- Electricity 1-7, Revised 2nd Ed. $49.95
- Electricity 2, Revised 2nd Ed. $14.95
- Electricity 3, Revised 2nd Ed. $14.95
- Electricity 4, Revised 2nd Ed. $14.95
- Electricity 5, Revised 2nd Ed. $14.95
- Electricity 6, Revised 2nd Ed. $14.95
- Electricity 7, Revised 2nd Ed. $14.95
- Electronics 1-7, Revised 2nd Ed. $49.95

Electronics Technical

- Active-Filter Cookbook $19.95
- Camcorder Survival Guide $ 9.95
- CMOS Cookbook, 2nd Ed. $24.95
- Design of OP-AMP Circuits with Experiments $19.95
- Design of Phase-Locked Loop Circuits with Experiments $19.95
- Electrical Test Equipment $19.95
- Electrical Wiring $19.95
- How to Read Schematics, 4th Ed. $19.95
- IC Op-Amp Cookbook, 3rd Ed. $24.95
- IC Timer Cookbook, 2nd Ed. $19.95
- IC User's Casebook $19.95
- Radio Handbook, 23rd Ed. $39.95
- Radio Operator's License Q&A Manual, 11th Ed. $24.95
- RF Circuit Design $24.95
- Transformers and Motors $24.95
- TTL Cookbook $19.95
- Undergrounding Electric Lines $14.95
- Understanding Telephone Electronics, 2nd Ed. $19.95
- VCR Troubleshooting & Repair Guide $19.95
- Video Scrambling & Descrambling for Satellite & Cable TV $19.95

Games

- Beyond the Nintendo Masters $ 9.95
- Mastering Nintendo Video Games II $ 9.95
- Tricks of the Nintendo Masters $ 9.95
- VideoGames & Computer Entertainment Complete Guide to Nintendo Video Games $ 9.50
- Winner's Guide to Nintendo Game Boy $ 9.95
- Winner's Guide to Sega Genesis $ 9.95

Hardware/Technical

- Hard Disk Power with the Jamsa Disk Utilities $39.95
- IBM PC Advanced Troubleshooting & Repair $24.95
- IBM Personal Computer Troubleshooting & Repair $24.95
- IBM Personal Computer Upgrade Guide $24.95
- Microcomputer Troubleshooting & Repair $24.95
- Understanding Communications Systems, 2nd Ed. $19.95
- Understanding Data Communications, 2nd Ed. $19.95
- Understanding FAX and Electronic Mail $19.95
- Understanding Fiber Optics $19.95

IBM: Business

- Best Book of Microsoft Works for the PC, 2nd Ed. $24.95
- Best Book of PFS: First Choice $24.95
- Best Book of Professional Write and File $22.95
- First Book of Fastback Plus $16.95
- First Book of Norton Utilities $16.95
- First Book of Personal Computing $16.95
- First Book of PROCOMM PLUS $16.95

IBM: Database

- Best Book of Paradox 3 $27.95
- dBASE III Plus Programmer's Reference Guide $24.95
- dBASE IV Programmer's Reference Guide $24.95
- First Book of Paradox 3 $16.95
- Mastering ORACLE Featuring ORACLE's SQL Standard $24.95

IBM: Graphics/Desktop Publishing

- Best Book of Autodesk Animator $29.95
- Best Book of Harvard Graphics $24.95
- First Book of DrawPerfect $16.95
- First Book of Harvard Graphics $16.95
- First Book of PC Paintbrush $16.95
- First Book of PFS: First Publisher $16.95

IBM: Spreadsheets/Financial

- Best Book of Lotus 1-2-3 Release 3.1 $27.95
- Best Book of Lotus 1-2-3, Release 2.2, 3rd Ed. $26.95
- Best Book of Peachtree Complete III $24.95
- First Book of Lotus 1-2-3, Release 2.2 $16.95
- First Book of Lotus 1-2-3/G $16.95
- First Book of Microsoft Excel for the PC $16.95
- Lotus 1-2-3: Step-by-Step $24.95

IBM: Word Processing

- Best Book of Microsoft Word 5 $24.95
- Best Book of Microsoft Word for Windows $24.95
- Best Book of WordPerfect 5.1 $26.95
- Best Book of WordPerfect Version 5.0 $24.95
- First Book of PC Write $16.95
- First Book of WordPerfect 5.1 $16.95
- WordPerfect 5.1: Step-by-Step $24.95

Macintosh/Apple

- Best Book of AppleWorks $24.95
- Best Book of MacWrite II $24.95
- Best Book of Microsoft Word for the Macintosh $24.95
- Macintosh Printer Secrets $34.95
- Macintosh Repair & Upgrade Secrets $34.95
- Macintosh Revealed, Expanding the Toolbox, Vol. 4 $29.95
- Macintosh Revealed, Mastering the Toolbox, Vol. 3 $29.95
- Macintosh Revealed, Programming with the Toolbox, Vol. 2, 2nd Ed. $29.95
- Macintosh Revealed, Unlocking the Toolbox, Vol. 1, 2nd Ed. $29.95
- Using ORACLE with HyperCard $24.95

Operating Systems/Networking

- Best Book of DESQview $24.95
- Best Book of DOS $24.95
- Best Book of Microsoft Windows 3 $24.95
- Business Guide to Local Area Networks $24.95
- Exploring the UNIX System, 2nd Ed. $29.95
- First Book of DeskMate $16.95
- First Book of Microsoft QuickPascal $16.95
- First Book of MS-DOS $16.95
- First Book of UNIX $16.95
- Interfacing to the IBM Personal Computer, 2nd Ed. $24.95
- Mastering NetWare $29.95
- The Waite Group's Discovering MS-DOS $19.95
- The Waite Group's Inside XENIX $29.95
- The Waite Group's MS-DOS Bible, 3rd Ed. $24.95
- The Waite Group's MS-DOS Developer's Guide, 2nd Ed. $29.95
- The Waite Group's Tricks of the MS-DOS Masters, 2nd Ed. $29.95
- The Waite Group's Tricks of the UNIX Masters $29.95
- The Waite Group's Understanding MS-DOS, 2nd Ed. $19.95
- The Waite Group's UNIX Primer Plus, 2nd Ed. $29.95
- The Waite Group's UNIX System V Bible $29.95
- The Waite Group's UNIX System V Primer, Revised Ed. $29.95
- Understanding Local Area Networks, 2nd Ed. $24.95
- Understanding NetWare $24.95
- UNIX Applications Programming: Mastering the Shell $29.95
- UNIX Networking $29.95
- UNIX Shell Programming, Revised Ed. $29.95
- UNIX System Administration $29.95
- UNIX System Security $34.95
- UNIX Text Processing $29.95
- UNIX: Step-by-Step $29.95

Professional/Reference

- Data Communications, Networks, and Systems $39.95
- Gallium Arsenide Technology, Volume II $69.95
- Handbook of Computer-Communications Standards, Vol. 1, 2nd Ed. $39.95
- Handbook of Computer-Communications Standards, Vol. 2, 2nd Ed. $39.95
- Handbook of Computer-Communications Standards, Vol. 3, 2nd Ed. $39.95
- Handbook of Electronics Tables and Formulas, 6th Ed. $24.95
- ISDN, DECnet, and SNA Communications $44.95
- Modern Dictionary of Electronics, 6th Ed. $39.95
- Programmable Logic Designer's Guide $29.95
- Reference Data for Engineers: Radio, Electronics, Computer, and Communications, 7th Ed. $99.95
- Surface-Mount Technology for PC Board Design $49.95
- World Satellite Almanac, 2nd Ed. $39.95

Programming

- Advanced C: Tips and Techniques $29.95
- C Programmer's Guide to NetBIOS $29.95
- C Programmer's Guide to Serial Communications $29.95
- Commodore 64 Programmer's Reference Guide $19.95
- DOS Batch File Power $39.95
- First Book of GW-BASIC $16.95
- How to Write Macintosh Software, 2nd Ed. $29.95
- Mastering Turbo Assembler $29.95
- Mastering Turbo Debugger $29.95
- Mastering Turbo Pascal 5.5, 3rd Ed. $29.95
- Microsoft QuickBASIC Programmer's Reference $29.95
- Programming in ANSI C $29.95
- Programming in C, Revised Ed. $29.95
- QuickC Programming $29.95
- The Waite Group's BASIC Programming Primer, 2nd Ed. $24.95
- The Waite Group's C Programming Using Turbo C++ $29.95
- The Waite Group's C++ Programming $24.95
- The Waite Group's C: Step-by-Step $29.95
- The Waite Group's GW-BASIC Primer Plus $24.95
- The Waite Group's Microsoft C Bible, 2nd Ed. $29.95
- The Waite Group's Microsoft C Programming for the PC, 2nd Ed. $29.95
- The Waite Group's Microsoft Macro Assembler Bible $29.95
- The Waite Group's New C Primer Plus $29.95
- The Waite Group's QuickC Bible $29.95
- The Waite Group's Turbo Assembler Bible $29.95
- The Waite Group's Turbo C Bible $29.95
- The Waite Group's Turbo C Programming for the PC, Revised Ed. $29.95
- The Waite Group's TWG Turbo C++Bible $29.95
- X Window System Programming $29.95

For More Information, Call Toll Free

1-800-257-5755

All prices are subject to change without notice. Non-U.S. prices may be higher. Printed in the U.S.A.

Reader Feedback Card

Thank you for purchasing this book from SAMS FIRST BOOK series. Our intent with this series is to bring you timely, authoritative information that you can reference quickly and easily. You can help us by taking a minute to complete and return this card. We appreciate your comments and will use the information to better serve your needs.

1. Where did you purchase this book?

- ☐ Chain bookstore (Walden, B. Dalton)
- ☐ Independent bookstore
- ☐ Computer/Software store
- ☐ Direct mail
- ☐ Book club
- ☐ School bookstore
- ☐ Other ______________________________

____

2. Why did you choose this book? (Check as many as apply.)

- ☐ Price
- ☐ Author's reputation
- ☐ Quick and easy treatment of subject
- ☐ Appearance of book
- ☐ SAMS' reputation
- ☐ Only book available on subject

3. How do you use this book? (Check as many as apply.)

- ☐ As a supplement to the product manual
- ☐ In place of the product manual
- ☐ For self-instruction
- ☐ As a reference
- ☐ At home
- ☐ At work

4. Please rate this book in the categories below. G = Good; N = Needs improvement; U = Category is unimportant.

- ☐ Price
- ☐ Amount of information
- ☐ Examples
- ☐ Inside cover reference
- ☐ Table of contents
- ☐ Tips and cautions
- ☐ Length of book
- ☐ How can we improve this book? ______________________________
- ☐ ______________________________
- ☐ Appearance
- ☐ Accuracy
- ☐ Quick Steps
- ☐ Second color
- ☐ Index
- ☐ Illustrations

5. How many computer books do you normally buy in a year?

- ☐ 1–5
- ☐ 5–10
- ☐ More than 10
- ☐ I rarely purchase more than one book on a subject.
- ☐ I may purchase a beginning and an advanced book on the same subject.
- ☐ I may purchase several books on particular subjects.
- ☐ (such as ______________________________)

6. Have your purchased other SAMS or Hayden books in the past year? ____________

If yes, how many ______________________________

7. Would you purchase another book in the FIRST BOOK series? ______

8. What are your primary areas of interest in business software? ______

- ☐ Word processing (particularly ______)
- ☐ Spreadsheet (particularly ______)
- ☐ Database (particularly ______)
- ☐ Graphics (particularly ______)
- ☐ Personal finance/accounting (particularly ______)
- ☐ Other (please specify ______)

Other comments on this book or the SAMS' book line: ______

Name ______
Company ______
Address ______
City ______ State ______ Zip ______
Daytime telephone number ______
Title of this book ______

Fold here

NO POSTAGE NECESSARY IF MAILED IN THE UNITED STATES

BUSINESS REPLY MAIL
FIRST CLASS PERMIT NO. 336 CARMEL, IN

POSTAGE WILL BE PAID BY ADDRESSEE

SAMS

11711 N. College Ave.
Suite 141
Carmel, IN 46032–9839